Irony in the Work of Philosophy

Irony

IN THE WORK OF PHILOSOPHY // CLAIRE COLEBROOK

UNIVERSITY OF NEBRASKA PRESS LINCOLN AND LONDON

© 2002 by the University of Nebraska Press

All rights reserved

Design and composition by Jeff Clark and Megan Geer

at Wilsted & Taylor Publishing Services

Manufactured in the United States of America

Library of Congress Cataloging-in-Publication Data

Colebrook, Claire.

Irony in the work of philosophy / Claire Colebrook.

p.   cm.

Includes bibliographical references and index.

ISBN 0-8032-1517-7 (cl.: alk. paper)

ISBN 978-0-8032-2230-4 (pa.: alk. paper)

1. Irony. I. Title.

B11301.17C65 202

190—dc21

2002017962

For Jane

CONTENTS

El(ev)ation

Aristotle opens his *Metaphysics*—which will insist on the knowledge of first principles—with the specific capacity and desire of human vision.[1] There is a desire to see, for its own sake, regardless of any use or end. At the same time, this desire to see or wonder of seeing also allows the human soul to think beyond sensible knowledge to those principles that are not given to the senses. The human eye is at one and the same time captured by this world and prompted to think beyond it. It is this capacity to see beyond one's point of view that opens the possibility not only of philosophy and speculation but also of dissimulation, deception, and error. Seeing this present and evident world is bound up with a view toward what is not given. The human eye is ironic, capable of viewing this world from an unworldly perspective. The tradition of irony is a tradition that interrogates the essentially bifurcated

possibility of the human point of view, at once within and beyond its
own world.

According to Lactantius, man's divine destiny is displayed in his
specular physiognomy. He, of all the animals, has a neck that allows
him to gaze up toward the heavens and thereby transcend his worldly
being.[2] His body possesses a mode of vision that takes him beyond the
body. Immanuel Kant also regarded the human soul as auspiciously
endowed with a heavenward gaze (even though this "wonder and respect" for the heavens was liable to fall into a merely human vision):
"The observation of the world began from the noblest spectacle that
was ever placed before the human senses and that our understanding
can undertake to follow in its vast expanse, and it ended in—astrol-
ogy."[3] Kant was explicit in defining himself against those premoderns
who believed the supersensible could be viewed directly.[4] It is the look
itself—our capacity to avert our eyes from what is empirically given
—that allows us to think of ourselves as beings with a moral destiny;
but we should not believe that this gaze of the soul encounters any in-
tuitable object. Indeed, it is our capacity to gaze upward that indicates
our ability to think beyond what is already seen. Attacking those who
felt that the task of philosophy was so much empty speculation, Kant
argued for the legitimacy of the pure regard of reason, a regard that
thinks the supersensible not by looking ever more intently at the given
but by delimiting the given: "Such illusory wisdom imagines it can
see further and more clearly with its mole-like gaze fixed on experience than with the eyes which were bestowed on a being designed to
stand upright and to scan the heavens."[5] Eventually, this upward gaze
is directed to a higher version of ourselves, to an image of humanity
that must have come down from the heavens:

> Now it is our universal human duty to *elevate* ourselves to this ideal of
> moral perfection, i.e. to the prototype of moral disposition in its entire

purity, and for this the very idea, which is presented to us by reason for emulation, can give us force. But precisely because we are not its authors but the idea has rather established itself in the human being without our comprehending how human nature could have ever been receptive of it, it is better to say that that *prototype* has *come down* to us from heaven, that it has taken up humanity (for it is not just as possible to conceive how the *human being, evil* by nature, would renounce evil on his own and *raise* himself up to the ideal of holiness, as it is that the latter take up humanity—which is not evil in itself—by descending to it).⁶

Some centuries later, when Sigmund Freud and Jacques Lacan wanted to explain humans as moral animals, they did so by deriving conscience from a gaze toward the ideal other, who was also an elevated projection of one's self. Indeed, the self does not preexist this production of the narcissistically invested and elevated other.⁷ This other or double is not just the ideal self that one imagines one once was,⁸ and it is not just the internalization of the social and parental authority that will allow one to attain cultural recognition.⁹ The moral nature of this ideal other, who is both one's own lost self and the self that might be regarded by others, lies in the look toward the future. Free will, according to Freud, emerges from this fantasy of that self I will become:

A special faculty is slowly formed there, able to oppose the rest of the ego, with the function of observing and criticising the self and exercising a censorship within the mind, and this we become aware of as our "conscience." . . . The fact that an agency of this kind exists, which is able to treat the rest of an ego like an object—the fact, that is, that man is capable of self-observation—renders it possible to invest the old idea of a "double" with a new meaning and to ascribe a number of things to it—above all, those things which seem to self-criticism to belong to the old surmounted narcissism of earlier times.

But it is not only this latter material, offensive as it is to the criticism

of the ego, which may be incorporated in the idea of the double. There
are also all those unfulfilled but possible futures to which we still like to
cling in phantasy, all the strivings of the ego which adverse external
circumstances have crushed, and all our suppressed acts of volition
which nourish in us the illusion of free will.[10]

Both Freud and Lacan also argue that paranoia has a structural tie
with this production of conscience. One becomes self-critical only in
imagining and projecting this voice of an elevated other, an other
whom we must see not as another thing within the world but as a subject. The paranoid projection of voices and the voice of conscience
both emerge from this look that is directed back to the self from the
fantasized ideal self. The voice of law and the look of the high and
ideal self of the future can, Freud suggests, explain the somewhat
paranoid nature of speculative philosophy: "The complaints made by
paranoics also show that at bottom the self-criticism of conscience coincides with the self-observation on which it is based. Thus the activity of the mind which has taken over the function of conscience has
also placed itself at the service of internal research, which furnishes
philosophy with the material for its intellectual operations. This may
have some bearing on the characteristic tendency of paranoics to con-
struct speculative systems."[11]

It is our physiological dependence at birth that requires us to look
to an other for the needs of life. But it is also through this very look
that we go beyond life itself, for the other to whom I address my demands must be *addressed as other*, not just as an object to be taken in
but one whose will or desire mediates any object that I may require.
My demand for life must pass through the look and desire of the other;
and what the other may want from me is the enigma to which all my
demands will be subjected.[12] The look I direct to the outside world is
structured by the higher point of view that the other presents to me:

what is the *sense* of this world, what does this world demand of me? The child's apprehension of the mother is not the look of subject to object but a look directed toward what cannot be perceived: the mother's desire. The other, *as other*, is therefore necessarily *ideal* and other than mere life, for my demand must be addressed to her will—and what the other wants can only be the object of speculation. It is the ideal or image of the other that opens the relation of speech and recognition. I can speak to another only if I recognize that other as one who can hear: the other who hears me must be a subject, endowed with the law of sense and speech. Between the I who speaks and the other who hears there must be this originally fictive ideal Other to whom all demands are addressed and who will make sense of what I say. Conscience is this otherness or look within me, such that the vigilance I exercise over my being is at one and the same time an act of self-love (loving the ideal self that constitutes me as a subject) and the outcome of a speculation that is extrinsic to any natural self (hearing an address from an other who is necessarily absent).

For Freud and Lacan, this look toward the other that is internalized as the look of self-regard constitutes the very opening of philosophy and ontology. How else could we explain our desire to grasp what is not present? The question of being, of that presence that lies above and beyond any intuited particular, would not be possible without that first fantasized absence, an absence that allows me to address the other not as a thing but as a desiring subject.[13] It is the other *as subject* who enables me to think beyond "my" world to a world in general. In order to think *being* or what lies beyond this or that particular gaze, I have to think of what lies beyond my subjectivity, what might be there for a subject in general. This other *as subject* is only given in the relation of speech, for it is through signification or the message that the other's look is more than what can be perceived. I must presuppose the other's *soul* in order for signification to have any meaning, in order that there might be a sense to be recognized behind what I say.[14] Lacan, in this and so many other respects, was a faithful Hegelian. As Hegel argued, "It is to this, its soul, that the external points. For an appearance that means something does not present *itself* to our minds, or what it is *as* external, but something else."[15]

The Grammar of the Look

This book is about the "look" and the grammar of Western theory, and the capacity of that look to generate a world that is not given. Over the last decades of the twentieth century much had been written about a peculiarly Western elevation of vision and a specific mode of the Occidental gaze.[16] Feminist theory has long been critical of the objectifying male gaze;[17] phenomenology has challenged the dominance of scientific detached observation by appealing to more involved forms of perception;[18] and there has been an even more general criticism of metaphors of vision and optics being used to explain knowledge and experience.[19] But how could this recent tradition of meditating upon Western *theoria* and its concomitant metaphors of *eidos* and reflection have anything to do with grammar and, in particular, with the trope of irony?

Even the earliest forms of Socratic irony were described and explained through metaphors of height and elevated viewpoint.[20] Today, the everyday usage of the word "ironic" seems to refer to a God's-eye view of the world. We often use the word "irony" to describe a fateful connection we could not have foreseen; it is as though the gods were playing with us, seeing the unfortunate outcome of our finite acts. We describe as "ironic" the situation of a manager who loses his job as a result of the very corporate downsizing he set in motion. Or we use the word "ironically" to describe infelicitous future outcomes: "Ironically, it was only the day after he decided to cancel his thirty-year-old health insurance policy that he discovered he was terminally ill." To use the word "irony" in this sense is to suggest that we are subject to a fate that cannot be foreseen. What ties the linguistic and visual strands of irony together is the notion of point of view, a term that refers as much to perspective and visibility as it does to narrative and sentence forms. *Linguistic* irony is saying one thing and meaning another, and this is enabled by two points of view: the literal speech act is doubled by those who "see" the irony. Cosmic irony, or the sense that life has a logic we cannot see, imagines a higher or God-like viewpoint. Irony in general is only possible through the speculation that posits a point of view higher than the immediately present or visible.

The Western project and "sensibility" of irony has always intertwined these two modalities of point of view, the point of view of the sentence and the point of view of the viewer. Metaphors of "seeing" have done as much to explain meaning and cognition as metaphors of language and grammar have been used to theorize perception. Phenomenology is the crucial moment for the explicit rendering of this connection. From Edmund Husserl to Jacques Derrida, the word "intentional" has been used to explain both perception and conceptuality.[21] Seeing "intends" or aims toward the fulfillment of perceptions in an object; but concepts also "intend" by invoking a sense that lies beyond the tokens of language. It is not surprising that Gilles Deleuze's book on *sense* was also a book about irony, for sense is both the visual/sensible and the ideal/semantic (see *LS*). Those such as Martin Heidegger and Gilles Deleuze who have written about a specifically Western grammar have also written about the narrowness of Western understandings of perception. According to Deleuze, philosophy has been preoccupied with the first-person singular proposition and has also regarded perception as primarily human and cognitive (see *DR*). For Heidegger, the task of a future philosophy would be to free logic

from grammar.[22] Before the logical proposition there is a more general "logos" that gathers the world, not in an objective and detached
viewpoint but through a seeing that is *proximate* and concerned. It is
the proposition form that has governed Western knowledge; and this
subject-predicate structure imposes a certain grammar on the Western look or *logos*. It is no accident, Heidegger argues, that philosophy
culminates in idealism. From *eidos* as the real being or essence of what
appears, philosophy itself becomes a looking that views nothing other
than itself. The history of philosophy that leads to idealism is inaugurated with the notion of substance as *subject*, when what is viewed coincides with the viewer, when all *relation* to Being becomes determined in advance as what is already present. Ontology, for Heidegger,
is determined from a certain grammar and temporality, which is also
a way of regarding the world as so much objective presence. Ontology
relies on positing a primary substance from which any representation
or viewpoint emerges. There is a being (substance or subject) that *then*
bears certain qualities or predicates. The subject of enunciation is one
who judges and represents this substance according to its perceived
qualities. Heidegger did not write about irony, but he did insist that a
philosophical text always says more than it means, and it does so because Being speaks through us. When we speak, it is as though Being
has a history all its own.

   Deleuze, however, was far more explicit about finding a "superior
irony" that might free us from subjectivism, representation, and the
primacy of the proposition. Irony consists in treating things and beings as so many responses to hidden questions, so many cases for problems yet to be resolved" (*DR*, 63). A *superior* irony does not see the
problem as a philosophical question that merely awaits a true proposition that is there to be discovered. Irony should see problems as productive of the propositions they seemingly disclose (*DR*, 182). And

Deleuze recognized that this superior irony was intertwined with a modern "optics" where there is no being *behind* the differential movement of questions, simulations, and problems: "All identities are only simulated, produced as an optical 'effect' by the more profound game of difference and repetition" (*DR*, xix). Following Henri Bergson, Deleuze argued that perception was the very "being" of the world. Each cell "perceives" the world insofar as it acts and responds; human perception is differentiated by its own "speed." It is in the delay or "zone of indetermination" between perceiving and acting or responding that we locate human freedom. Deleuze's appeal to a superior irony occurs within a more general project of considering visibility and point of view beyond the human subject and beyond speech: "To open us up to the inhuman and the superhuman (*durations* which are inferior or superior to our own), to go beyond the human condition: This is the meaning of philosophy."[23]

Deleuze's work is at once sympathetic with and diametrically opposed to a more general postmodern irony. The first part of this book negotiates this broadly postmodern irony through the work of Richard Rorty.[24] Irony in its textualist or contemporary form is, Rorty insists, postmetaphysical. Unlike Socratic irony, postmodern irony plays with the limits of speech but does not do so in order to grasp or intimate some truth beyond speech. Irony remains within its finite human contexts. Fredric Jameson, Linda Hutcheon, Henri Lefebvre, Paul de Man, and Umberto Eco have all drawn attention to the ironic nature of modernity or postmodernity.[25] More generally, notions such as simulacra, parody, pastiche, and play have described forms of speaking and representation that suspend reference or desist from making truth claims. It is in this broad context of "depthlessness" that Rorty and others have described postmodern and postmetaphysical irony: a form of speaking that recognizes the limits of its own point of view while precluding any existence beyond those limits. If there are *liter-ary* devices for signaling our point of view or perspective, and if irony is one of those devices, then this suggests that liberation from West-ern *theoria* might be an aesthetic project. We would become post-metaphysical, not through philosophy itself but through philosophy's other: text. This aesthetic critique of philosophy is not a claim that is new to postmodernism. The German Romantics, well before Nietz-sche and poststructuralism, put forward a theory of irony as a liter-ary sensibility that would overcome the impasse of speculative meta-physics.[26]

Beginning from the work of Richard Rorty, this book explores the possibility of a literary or aesthetic demarcation of the objectifying gaze of philosophy. Chapter 1 explores whether Rorty's claims relate to irony as a literary device or whether irony is a theory of meaning and existence. Chapter 2 looks at the literary tradition of irony and its de-velopment in modernism into free-indirect style. (Free-indirect style is both used and celebrated in contemporary poststructuralism, a philosophical movement that also has its own specific aesthetic com-mitments.) Chapter 3 looks at the ways in which the figure of Socrates has been appropriated by contemporary philosophers in order to mark the limits of the West, for Socrates represents both the opening of phi-losophy and a practice of philosophy that has not yet fallen into mere theory. It is only through certain modes of speech and reflection that the soul can be formed and intuited. Chapter 4 looks at the explicitly modern reformulation of metaphysics in Kant. The history of the soul and the subject reaches self-consciousness with Hegel, whose critique of Kant and German Romanticism was also a critique of irony. Kierke-gaard's existentialism and the passage from existentialism through to structuralism and poststructuralism are the focus of chapter 5. Chap-ter 6 negotiates the possibility of contemporary irony through the poststructuralism of Deleuze, Derrida, and postmodern aesthetics. In conclusion, I argue that if we want to understand and live up to the challenge of what has been written in contemporary theory and literature, we need to consider the intimate link between modes of speaking and modes of seeing that take thought beyond the human eye and mouth. Irony is the question of the possibility and the impossibility of the inhuman.

ACKNOWLEDGMENTS

This book would not have been written if it were not for the helpful advice, encouragement, support, and intelligence of the students and staff at Monash University in Melbourne. I am particularly grateful to Gail Ward (who retrieved this manuscript from a computer when I had left for Scotland), Kevin Hart, Andrew Milner, Chris Worth, and David Neil. Once again, I owe a great debt to Lee Spinks, who worked his way through a draft of the manuscript. As always, Lubica Ucnik was her indispensable, inspired, and ironic self.

Parts of this book have been previously published as "The Meaning of Irony," *Textual Practice* 14.1 (2000), and "Inhuman Irony," in *Deleuze and Literature*, ed. Ian Buchanan and John Marks (Edinburgh: Edinburgh University Press, 2001). I am grateful to the publishers for the permission to use that material in this book.

Irony in the Work of Philosophy

1

The Meaning of Irony

We might be forgiven for having the feeling that philosophy, in the grand sense of the term, has had its day. Since Kant we have learned not to ask the big but unanswerable questions. We have learned to talk about language games, discourses, structures, social construction, and paradigms. Any sense of justification or legitimation that we might have is critical and immanent. A language game might be modified, adjusted from within, critically inhabited, but certainly not founded. It makes a lot of sense, then, to accept Richard Rorty's claim that philosophy has come of age when it is no longer philosophy. Good philosophy is either literary criticism—a sense of our own thorough textualism—or else it is ironic—a recognition that our language games are language *games* and that they are *our* language games.[1] But we might wonder whether this quasi-utopian vision of a postmeta-

physical ironic philosophy is possible or desirable. There are sugges-
tions in Rorty's own writing that perhaps we can never be fully ironic.
Irony might depend upon the residue of some old-fashioned, "Par-
menidean," representational, realist, or metaphysical arguments in
order that we might have claims to feel contingent or ironic about.[2] If
so, irony could never be adopted as a public or general norm. At the
same time, though, Rorty does feel that irony is possible at least at the
level of personal self-definition. Irony, for Rorty, has (at least) two edifying features. Irony is the ability to resist "going transcendental" as
well as being a recognition of the contingency of our position. Such a
description of irony sounds possible and attractive. Epistemologically
and politically, irony may be unworkable, but at the level of self-
definition it sounds feasible and somewhat appealing. Knowledge
practices may always require a posited reality, and public policy might
need a fixed and stable language game. But as a personal attitude we
should realize, ironically, that such conventions *are* conventions and
that no metaphysical grounding is possible or desirable. And it is not
just Rorty who seems to think so. The idea that we are postmetaphysical seems to have a wide currency: we no longer seek ultimate justifications, true descriptions, or universal agreement, nor do we rely on
fictional entities like "ideas," "meanings," or "subjects."[3] The "perspectivism" that follows from Rorty's ironic standpoint is also de ri-
gueur, if not in philosophy, at least in literary theory, cultural studies,
postcolonial theory, and some descriptions of what constitutes postmodernity. Rorty's promotion of irony is symptomatic of a general dis-
comfort that surrounds contemporary antifoundationalism. On the
one hand, there is a general postenlightenment recognition that there
are no universal grounds or laws. On the other hand, it is also recognized that to live according to such an absence of foundations is a
seemingly impossible task. The very idea of irony is oddly defined
around this ambivalence. Irony can be seen as a particular technique

that reflects on our conditions of making meaning of the world. Because we cannot step outside our language games, we can only play ironically within those games. Irony takes those terms that seem to be foundational and opens them up for question.

It is hard to find examples of such irony in Rorty, but they do abound in the tradition of Western philosophy and literature. The word "reason," for example, was originally used in the eighteenth century to interrogate the blindness and tyranny of divine right. But when the word "reason" itself became yet one more tyrannical dogma, a remedy was provided by the irony of authors like Jonathan Swift and William Blake, writers who could repeat the very uses of the concept of reason to show—if not state—its thoroughly irrational workings.[4] New concepts might be forged by philosophers to shake up our language games: just think of the ways in which "discourse," "culture," or "society" questioned the notion of the human individual. Even Hegel employed local irony in order to avoid the wholesale collapse of philosophy. When we use the word "absolute," he argued, we think we know what we mean, but if we look at the way we use the concept, our statements become incoherent. If we really *mean* that something is absolute, then how could we speak of having a relation to it? This was the problem Hegel identified in the German ironists of his own day, writers who used concepts in an unreflective manner.[5] Hegel employed local irony in order to reject the wholesale irony of Romanticism; only if we make some of our concepts strange can we resist losing the meaning of what we say altogether. Local irony of this type plays with certain words within an otherwise stable language and is a way of showing that the concepts we think are mere expressions of the way things are are actually *concepts*. They have a meaning or force that is often at odds with what we take to be natural or unproblematic. So when a philosopher employs irony she can tear a language away from its representational illusions. To a certain extent, this seems to be the form of irony favored by Rorty. We cannot step outside our language and justify it, but we can make incursions into a language by questioning some of its concepts or ways of speaking.

In addition to being local and therapeutic, irony can also be theorized at a metasemantic level. Here, irony is not a device *within language* used to reflect upon meaning but is a certain way of living or existing toward meaning in general. Irony would not just be the local and therapeutic use of a word to show its particular incoherence or linguistic redundancy. Irony might effect a distance from speech in general. The ironist does not utter statements as though they expressed her inner being, nor does she utter propositions as though they were mirrors of the world. Ironists speak with an awareness of the emptiness of what they say; there is no deep human meaning "we" express or some ultimate reality we describe. Such human depths and ultimate realities are effects of speech and not its grounds. Whereas local irony can be used within a language to recall us to certain concepts that have gone awry and lost their meaning, existential irony adopts a point of view toward meaning in general. Irony, in this existential sense, is more than just the inadequacy of this or that concept; irony is the predicament of conceptuality in general. In order to speak, we must use concepts that "we" did not form (and who "we" are is just an effect of those concepts we find ourselves inhabiting). We then apply these concepts to a world that is also only given *as preconceptual* through the concepts we have of it. Rorty's position is typically poised between the use of irony as a trope within a language game (local irony) and the idea of irony as a theory of language in general. On the one hand, Rorty does seem to advocate a local irony. The edifying conversation of philosophy is possible only if we renew our lexicon and prevent certain concepts from becoming natural or unquestioned. "Democracy," for example, can be formed as a concept in order to

function as an ideal of speech and interaction. But if we start to ask
"What *is* democracy?" then we treat the concept as a label (for something that exists) and not a function. We need irony to remind us of
our linguistic contingency. But Rorty also extends irony beyond its use
within the academic enterprise of keeping philosophy alive, and this
suggests a more existential approach to irony. Irony is a way of life. Instead of submitting themselves to the force of concepts (lamenting
that they do not know what justice *is* or that they cannot really seem
to grasp the real), ironists free themselves from the history of Western metaphysics.

In this postrepresentational and ironic landscape the ironist adopts
the point of view of the child, for whom language, while inherited,
also has the quality of strangeness or distance about it. The childlike
ironist plays with words as though language were a game, aware that
the game's rules are not immutable laws but just the way we happen
to be playing at present. Modernity or enlightenment in general may
be characterized as the desire to no longer be governed by an external
or received authority.[6] Rather than a God's-eye view of the world, in
which it is assumed that there can be an absolute knowledge of which
humans have only a partial share, modernity affirms human locatedness, finitude, and autonomy. America itself is a crucial image in
this ideal of the world made new, the site where the radical Puritan
demand for a heaven here and now might be fulfilled.[7] Locke claimed
that "in the beginning all the World was America."[8] And Derrida,
ironically and much later, declared that "America *is* deconstruction."[9]
But this America is not just another landscape to be colonized by Euro-
pean vision; it would be a landscape where the tyranny of vision
would fall away. We would no longer determine the world through a
pregiven system of concepts; our concepts would be renovated by being confronted with a world seen anew.[10] From the very beginnings of

American thought in Emersonian philosophy, there has been an elevation of the virgin or childlike glance. Emerson wrote of the desire to view nature as a "transparent eyeball," as though there might be a pure seeing without the weight of personality or consciousness, a "look" that is not the look *of* some subject.[11] The canonized works of American literature, however ironically, also valorize the child's-eye view. From *Huckleberry Finn* and *What Maisie Knew* to *The Catcher in the Rye*, it is not just that writers speak from the point of view of the child. There is also a far more general idealization of the childlike glance that extends to vision in general. Against the objectifying gaze of a history of Western theory, the New World offers itself as open and unchartered. Such an unencumbered mode of looking would also issue in new modes of writing and speaking. Henry James's famous sentences are attempts to grasp the fluidity and enigma of experience itself. While subsequent writers may have reacted against the excessive inwardness and psychologism of James's style, their response tended to focus even more on freeing vision from the structures of language. There is a strong tradition within American poetry and fiction that seeks to write from the point of view of the object itself,[12] as though language might be freed from its rigid location within the point of view of the speaking subject. This extends from an American modernism that attempts to formulate a "poetry of the object itself" to the minimal and antipsychologizing styles of Ernest Hemingway and Raymond Carver.

Rorty's advocation of irony can be regarded as a peculiarly philosophical move within this tradition of freeing vision from an ossified and inherited language. His great work, *Philosophy and the Mirror of Nature*, is ostensibly a critique of the visual metaphors that have dominated philosophy. What is wrong with the Cartesian model of knowledge as a picture of the world is that it represents mind as an apparatus that mirrors or re-presents an external reality. But it is not vision per se that is Rorty's target so much as a particular construal of vision as separate, disengaged, camera-like, and representationalist. American pragmatism in general was highly critical of the ways in which philosophers had made seeing the world into some sort of epistemological problem, as though seeing had somehow to find or judge an outside world. Against this, the "look" of pragmatism is not that *of* a subject who must come to know a world; subject and world are given through the ongoing process of engagement and action. We "see" the world, they argued, not in the way that a camera takes a picture but in the way that Emerson's eyeball might wander through nature: constituted by what it receives rather than determining its world in advance. This is a look that is freed from inherited conceptual schemas and foundations; it is an open, fluid, and dynamic glance that is not the glance *of* some viewing subject.[13] This is where Rorty's critique of the mirror metaphor for knowledge connects with his approach to language. Central to the American tradition of pragmatism is a critique of linguistic realism, objectivism, and detachment. Our language is a dynamic engagement with the world, formed through action, interaction, and life. When language ossifies we tend to think of it as a mere vehicle through which the world is pictured or represented. But language is originally a mode of action and only subsequently falls into the "logic" of metaphysical schemas. Irony, for Rorty, is a way of reminding us that language is not a means for re-presenting life but is life itself. Language does not capture accurate pictures of a world we view prelinguistically. Language and vision are inextricably intertwined. Both are thoroughly within the world, not set over and above the world. When we adopt an ironic attitude to language we reconfigure both vision and speaking. We speak with a full attention to language as a process of life and action. And we see not with the objective theoretical gaze of the detached philosopher but with the childlike vision of one whose world is as much played out in us as we determine our world. Irony is not a figure we use *within* our language to enliven certain words that impede the play of speech. All speech is irony, not a speaker's detached representation of an objective world but a free and untrammeled commerce of tokens that has no foundation other than the dynamism of life itself.

Existential and Local Irony

On the one hand, then, irony is a therapy within language; on the other, it is a therapy that will free us from language, for we will now regard language neither as a representation nor as a law to which we are bound but as material for play and self-creation. Rorty is by no means the first philosopher to be poised between these two possibilities of irony. Socratic irony has also been interpreted both as a technique within dialogues and as a form of life or existence. This ambivalence that surrounds the status or extent of irony is part of the very character of irony. The use of irony as a local figure or trope within a language can always *and essentially* place a question mark or distance over language in general. There is something both demonic and uncanny about irony. Demonic, because irony can *begin* as an attempt to retrieve a language that has become alien and rigid. But once we revivify our language through a local use of irony it is possible for all language to become strange, other, and insecure. The uncanniness —or unhomeliness—of irony lies in the essential possibility of language. We could have no sense of ownness without a language, but language only works if it is never *fully* our own. (It must be capable of being translated, quoted, and extended—necessarily beyond any private intent.) This raises the question of the *place* or context of irony— a strange nonplace or unhomeliness that has always been both the site and undermining of any relativism. And we can see this ambivalence in Rorty's own work. On the one hand, Rorty insists that if we abandon our great metaphysical strivings, then we will no longer be anxious about relativism; we will realize that we can have no justification beyond the language we speak. We should be at home in our language and not regard it as a lens through which we might grasp some world in itself. Such homeliness would be enabled by local ironic interventions. When our language becomes a rigid paradigm we should recall its provisional and arbitrary nature, reminding ourselves that language is an outcome of speech and interaction and not its foundation. On the other hand, if we accept Rorty's claim that it makes no point to see our language as the representation of some world by a separate subject, our irony might take on an abyssal or demonic dimension. How possible is *speech* and interaction if all we say is provisional, unfounded, and antirepresentational? How would we know just when to read or speak ironically?

If we consider irony as a movement or trope *within meaning*, then we are given the first stage of standard relativist arguments. Irony adopts a "distanced," critical, or contingent attitude toward one's utterances. What is said is quite other than what (if anything) is believed. And so we might arrive at something like Rorty's postmetaphysical ironic philosopher, a philosopher whose arguments are nothing more than literary devices. There is a clear divide, for Rorty, between public claims, norms, assertions, and positions and the ironic or edifying philosopher who is capable of seeing all such claims as literary acts. Here, irony would be a tropic movement contained *within* a world of serious or committed utterances. Philosophy would not have its own object nor even its own style of proposition, nor would philosophy be a metaposition that arbitrated the competing truth claims of the various sciences. Philosophy would have a shifting, immanent, and demystifying role. Its style would simply be dictated by the imperative to be *stylistic*. If our statements start to sound like propositions about objects, then the ironic philosopher should form propositions that problematize references. Philosophy should look like *writing* or the production of text and not like propositions or factual statements that refer to an independent world. The ironist's point of view would not be that of an elevated onlooker but of a skeptical participant. All other discourses could get along with the idea that language has its objects and its rules, while the ironic philosopher would only play the game up to a certain point. If the rules start to seem like laws rather than game rules, then this is precisely when a bit of rule breaking needs to take place.[14]

Our everyday practice may require rules, but we also need a practice of debunking the supposed lawlike nature of these rules. A language game cannot be healthy if we are all ironic, but it cannot be healthy if none of us are. Between rampant and chaotic relativism and a totalitarian submission to the realism of rules, there lies the ironic point of view of the philosopher, injecting local irony when required, but not so much that we all start to rewrite the rules with each move of the game. Being a philosopher would be a private, local, and essentially parasitic affair, requiring the rigidity and banality of everyday belief. The philosopher would certainly not be the elevated philosopher-king of Plato's *Republic*. Far from being the privileged contemplator of eternal ideals, the philosopher would be separated only by sustaining the child's-eye view of the world, for the ironic philosopher lives language as a network of rules within which he tentatively makes his way, keeping the sense of the arbitrariness of these rules alive and disruptive. Rorty's ironist will not look up to the law as some force that governs his play. There is nothing other than the game itself: no voice of reason and no principle other than the continual newness and self-invention of the perennially nascent conversationalist.

Human Modernity

Modernity in general may be characterized as a critique of absolute or inhuman points of view. Kant's "Copernican turn" is avowedly modern, insisting that progress in metaphysics only begins when we abandon claims to know what is real in itself regardless of human vision. But Kant still maintained that while we could not *know* the absolute we could nevertheless form Ideas—of freedom, God, and immortality—that would enable us to act *as if* there were some law that governed our specific and finite points of view. The very Idea of the absolute indicates a capacity of reason to think beyond what it can know, beyond its local concerns. Rorty's irony aims to free us once and for all from such grandiose Kantian aspirations. What we should really be trying to achieve is a sense of the perspectival nature of our being in the world. The only viewpoint capable of recognizing perspectivism in general is a viewpoint always open to revision (as re-vision, seeing again and seeing anew). Despite its efforts to remain thoroughly provisional (or pro-visional, in the sense of always being about to see), Rorty's position raises the question of the viewpoint of irony. And it is here that irony's *place* raises the enduring problem of any attempted perspectivism. For it seems that in *recognizing* all claims as context-dependent viewpoints, irony risks becoming an elevated viewpoint. This would be reflected in the tradition of irony that goes back to Socrates. It is the everyday citizens who live the unquestioned life and accept their world as real, who speak language with a full sense of belief and commitment, and who take what they see as an unproblematic representation of the world. It is the "high urbanity" of the Socratic philosopher who demands that life be examined.[15] While Rorty wants to distance himself from the Western tradition of high justification, his irony is nevertheless a critical position adopted against what he sees as a prevalent and unquestioned dogma. (*Philosophy and the*

Mirror of Nature is a wide-ranging attack not just on one or two philosophical views but on modernity in general.) At the very least, irony
elevates itself above all other position takings with a recognition of position taking as such. Rorty's attempt to do away with the "meta" of
metaphysical philosophy aims at a transformation of philosophy from
being a privileged and elevated arbiter to a game alongside other
games. The problem is, of course, that if Rorty is right about philosophy, then he will be wrong about irony.

Rorty states clearly that irony cannot be a publicly adopted attitude, and so if it were possible to have ironic philosophy, then philosophy would once again be elevated above quotidian literalism. (Philosophy could not be a shared public enterprise.) If philosophy today
could become a form of speaking aware of itself *as speaking*, then philosophy would be set apart from the referentialism of everyday speech
and the positive sciences. If philosophy were to become truly ironic,
freed from making truth claims about an outside world or Real, then
it would once again adopt a position above the naïveté of ordinary
speech acts: "In the ideal liberal society, the intellectuals would still be
ironists, although the nonintellectuals would not."[16]

Not surprisingly, and in contrast with Rorty's insistence on liberation and liberalism, irony has traditionally been explained through
metaphors of height, elevation, and hierarchy. The ironist sees more,
overlooks everyday speech, possesses an expanded point of view or a
"high urbanity." Irony, then, is not just a trope or movement within a
world of meaningful utterances but an attitude toward meaning in
general. Everyday speech operates as though the world could be described in objective propositions, but ironic speech opens a gap between what we say and what is said, aware of the power of language to
exceed private intent. Irony therefore elevates itself above those viewpoints that would regard language as nothing more than what we
want it to mean; from an everyday point of view, language is not yet a

force or a problem. The height of irony is only generated if the emptiness of a way of speaking is subordinated to some higher ideal of a
more sincere speech. When Socrates asks one of his Sophist interlocutors "What is x?" the Sophist often offers a glib definition that Socrates
then pursues to a reductio ad absurdum: So if justice is paying back
what one owes, do you mean that you would return a weapon you borrowed to a deranged man?[17] The Sophist answers no but then cannot
say what he *did* mean.[18]

The point of Socrates' ironic method is not to show that the word
"justice" is *meaningless* but to show that it must mean *more* than we
think. The elevation of traditional irony is achieved by contrasting the
hollowness of what we often say with some ideal of what we *should
mean.* Rorty's critique of philosophy is, by contrast, marked by an
avoidance of the figures of height and elevation that have dominated
the history of irony. Part of this is achieved by his distinction between
the public and the private.[19] If all we have are competing viewpoints,
how can we avoid a philosophy that *recognizes* our perspectival predicament and adopts a metaposition above everyday speech? Rorty's
answer is not to see irony as the *truth* of our being, as a way of understanding meaning in general: "The last thing the ironist wants
or needs is a theory of ironism."[20] Irony can only be a private attitude that creates some space or openness in a necessarily systematic,
rule-bound, and public circulation of speech. Irony can be a style of
philosophical writing, but it can be so only if we separate the fluid,
self-questioning, and mobile speech of philosophy from the public
consensus and truth claims of shared language. On the one hand,
then, Rorty resists putting irony forward as yet one more grand theory
of meaning. Irony is an attitude or question within an otherwise
meaningful system of language. On the other hand, Rorty sees irony
as more than just a figure of speech within meaning. This ambiguity
in Rorty's position about the local or wholesale nature of irony is not

accidental. It has to do with the very structure of irony. On the one hand, irony is clearly a figure of speech within meaning. We could not say that an utterance was ironic unless there were a linguistic stability against which it could be contrasted. On the other hand, once we acknowledge the *possibility* of irony, that we can speak without commitment to what we say, then there is nothing to stop us from raising the question of irony over *any* speech act.

Irony as a Speech Act or Irony as a Point of View?

Is irony a figure of speech that might be explained by a theory of meaning? Or is irony itself a theory of meaning? In the vast amount of literature on the subject a quantitative survey would probably suggest that the latter is the case: irony is frequently described as a position, attitude, personality, point of view, or way of seeing.[21] For the most part, this is how Rorty presents irony. Irony is not a literary manner or style, it is an attitude adopted toward whatever vocabulary one speaks. For Rorty, the ironist recognizes that all we have are our ways of speaking and that "there is nothing beyond vocabularies."[22] Rorty's idea of irony as a philosophical attitude is in many ways in accord with a long tradition (running from Socrates to Kierkegaard and the present) that understands irony as a point of view adopted toward language or meaning in general. However, if we were to begin with current ordinary language usage and some of the recent linguistic and philosophical material on irony, we would be inclined to define irony, like metaphor, as a peculiar type of speech act within language.[23] It is common to say something like, "I was only speaking ironically," which signals that a nonliteral use is being made of a word or expression. John Searle's very brief description of irony as an indirect speech act defines irony in this way: as a specific relation between speaker meaning and sentence meaning.[24] And most contemporary linguistic

analyses of irony begin from a Searlean understanding of speech acts
and context. Like metaphor, irony, it is argued, can be described from
within a theory of meaning.

What this situation seems to suggest is that if we want to understand what irony is we might need to draw a distinction between irony
as a figure of speech and irony as a theory of meaning, and we would
divide examples of irony accordingly. I want to argue, however, that
such a distinction is neither possible nor valuable. Irony is a type
of speech act, but it is one that also opens the question of a theory
of meaning (the relation between language and world). Deciding
whether a particular speech act is or is not ironic will be governed by
just how secure and meaningful we believe everyday speech to be. If,
like Searle, we believe in clear context boundaries and shared understanding, then we will easily recognize the difference between direct
speech acts and irony. But if we think that a theory of meaning is connected with a form of life, then we will have to acknowledge that the
borders of irony will vary with the speaker's point of view. If language
is primarily the first-person direct speech of enunciating subjects,
then irony is perhaps exemplified by statements that we all recognize
as clearly indirect. This is perhaps why Searle begins his analysis from
the proposition "The window is open," which cannot be a true proposition if the window is closed and would be recognized as ironic in a
specific context (such as a diplomatic discussion).[25] If, to take the quite
different view of Alexander Nehamas, we regard speaking, particularly philosophical speech, as the performance or production of a certain mask or character, then we will have a much larger class of ironic
statements.[26] The border between the ironic and the direct speech act
will also be less secure, for irony will have less to do with a particular
class of statements and will include any utterance that gives a sense
of depth, the sense that behind the manifest meaning of what the
speaker happens to say there is something more being *said*.[27] Locating

irony is a matter of determining the limits of speaker sincerity. Searle's world of speakers is remarkably literal; for the most part (unless there are clear markers), we all know what we mean, and we do not have to specify particular conditions or contexts.[28] And Searle is clearly frustrated by the untrusting and perverse views of literary theorists who treat utterances as though they were detached tokens freed from a context or distanced from sincere and context-bound speakers. Literary theorists, Searle suggests, tend to imagine their world as a community of speakers who retreat from what they say, as though speech could be thought of as so many material tokens with no connection to the expressive performance of enunciating subjects. In such a world the possibility of irony would haunt all speech. This is not Searle's world. On the one hand, then, there are those who accept all speech and speakers as sincere, with irony being a clearly recognized trope for the purposes of communication. On the other hand, though, there are those who, like Friedrich Nietzsche, see insincerity and dissimulation as the very genesis of speech: "true speech" is just a particularly artful dissimulation. In this world all speech is ironic, even if that irony is never "seen." To ask or determine whether a speech act is or is not ironic is both to raise a question about the borders of a specific context (what counts as a sincere speech act?) and to raise a question about just who "we" recognize as a sincere speaker, one who says what she means.

What connects the two ways of considering irony—the existential (irony as a way of life) and the linguistic (irony as a speech act)—is the problem of *point of view*. The existential understanding of irony as a theory of meaning or *position adopted toward meaning* depends upon some idea of point of view. The ironist views language or meaning in a certain way. The ironist is capable of adopting a distanced attitude toward language, such that whatever language *is* it is not seen as transparent or in complete correspondence with the world. The ironist perceives the difference between what we say and what there *is* not because she has some privileged view of the world but because she realizes the necessary gap between language and world. Ordinary language may never reflect on its status *as language*, but an ironic reflection on what we say is aware that if there is a world, it cannot be reduced to our language game, rhetoric, or context. In the case of Socrates this difference between rhetoric and world is given in the transcendence of the Idea: whatever justice or the good is, it must be more than a token of language. Irony is a point of view adopted toward meaning; it is a specific way of living one's language. It is, if you like, a form of life.

There are two senses in which we can think of point of view: the point of view of the speaker (as attitude, way of seeing, or perspective) and the point of view of the sentence (at its simplest, first, second, or third person). Irony can be understood existentially as the point of view of the speaker, as a way of viewing the world through the lens of mediation. Ironists are aware that what they see and what they say are only the seen and the said and not what *is* immediately. Irony is a perspective that sees only competing perspectives, a look that regards what it sees as thoroughly within a world of appearances, and a way of speaking that regards speech acts as moves of interaction with other speech acts. But irony can also be understood at the level of the sentence's point of view (first, second, or third person). The standard proposition links a subject and predicate and functions as though the original or default position is that of the first person. "S is P" is equivalent to "I assert that S is P." Irony, I would suggest, places a question mark over this seeming equivalence, placing an "it is said that" before the proposition. If, at a women's consciousness-raising assembly, I state that "women, of course, are incapable of reason," then the sentence works with a silent prefix of "It is thought that . . ." Sincere, nonironic speech is the everyday first-person speech of common sense, where

the subject of enunciation coincides with the subject enounced. The
speaker expresses his intent through a first-person proposition. The
speaker says no more than he means, and what is meant coincides
with what is said. Ironic speech, by contrast, is indirect, invoking an
implicit and unstated "they" and *effecting* a no less implicit "we."
("They" say that women are irrational, but "we" know otherwise.)
"We" recognize irony by understanding *more* than what is said. (And
this makes sense of Quintilian's seminal description of irony as "saying other than what is understood.") Those who use the slogans of sex-
ism, racism, or other narrow points of view often do not realize the full
sense of what they say. "Some of my best friends are black" is the statement of a person who says and means that he is not racist, but the *said*
reveals otherwise. "We" all know that this is the statement of one who
is racist. The sentence meaning seems to deliver a different sense from
the speaker meaning.

We can certainly distinguish between first and third person at a
purely grammatical level ("I" or "she"), and we can also distinguish
grammatically between direct and indirect speech. There are clear
linguistic markers. But irony's point of view would seem difficult to
determine at the level of grammar, at least on Rorty's or Searle's account. Indeed, Searle is insistent that this is just where literary theory
has been led astray. The *utterance itself* cannot determine sincerity or
authenticity. This can only be given from the context of meaning and
expectation.[29] Figures of speech such as metaphor or metonymy can
be determined at the level of the "saying." We can use single sentences
or phrases as examples of most tropes: "Richard is a lion" (metaphor);
"My love is like a red, red rose" (simile); "She's no Miss World" (lito-
tes); or "We referred the issue to the crown" (metonymy). The point of
view of irony, by contrast, cannot be explained grammatically or identified, like some tropes, through certain types of proposition such as S
is P, S is like P, S is no P. The point of view of irony is explained socially,

assuming a context of those who recognize a *said* that is other than what the speaker is *saying*. Even clear and famous examples of irony, such as the sentence that opens *Pride and Prejudice*, rely on a distinction between two styles of speaker: "It is a truth universally acknowledged, that a single man in possession of a good fortune, must be in want of a wife."[30] There are those who believe the social norms of the marriage market to be beyond question and those who recognize the absurd rigidity of bourgeois mating rituals.

It would seem, then, that irony could not be explained fully from *within* a theory of meaning. Irony is not a trope or figure of speech within a language game; irony plays with the very borders of the game. If we feel that social rules can be expressed as universal truth claims, then we will not read the first sentence of *Pride and Prejudice* ironically. What counts as an example of irony depends upon just where we draw the boundary between the meaningful and the obviously parasitic utterance, between what can be stated sincerely and what must signal the very absurdity of our language games. If, like Searle, we think that language works through a shared context of exchange and recognition, then we will happily define irony as an utterance that is *clearly recognized by us all* as the opposite of what is being said. But most theories of irony acknowledge a distinction between the ironist's theory of meaning and the literalism of our everyday context. Irony, from Socrates to Deleuze, has employed metaphors of height, precisely because it relies on clear social distinctions and hierarchies. Irony separates those who would sincerely speak in a certain style from those who would hear what is said as ironic. For the provincial petit bourgeois, the clichés of the marriage market are as close as one gets to universal moral principles. The first sentence of *Pride and Prejudice* could be read by such folk as utterly sincere. It can only be read as ironic by adopting a certain height, seeing the point of view of the sentence as narrow or limited. Far from reinforcing the notion of a

language game as being determined through context boundaries and
recognition, most examples of irony test just what counts as a legiti-
mate move in our language game or just what counts as included
within "our" context. The force of the first sentence of *Pride and Prejudice* lies in taking an everyday banality and framing it within a silent "They say that . . ." Far from securing a plural first person, as
Searle seems to suggest, such that all language could be enclosed
within what "we" mean, irony speaks from the plural third person—
a "they." (It also, however, generates a "we" that is highly insecure and
not given or said; "we" may recognize the limits of the first sentence of
Pride and Prejudice, but we are no wiser as to the game, language, or
conventions that this *we* might sincerely perform.)

Irony, then, would be poised *between* a social and a linguistic act. In
part, it could be interrogated at the level of the sentence's point of
view: is this uttered by "us" or "them," by the first or third person? But
this distinction would rely on point of view at the social, ethical, and
political level. The metaphors that have been used to explain irony—
metaphors of elevation, height, ascension, and "high urbanity"—
have as much to do with visual point of view as they do with the point
of view of the sentence. There is the elevated "we" who sees more
than the point of view of the ironic sentence or at least recognizes that
there is more to be seen.[31] This "seeing more" of irony, this heightened
or expanded point of view, is both social and linguistic. The ironic sentence is limited linguistically, speaking in simple propositions, glib
definitions, everyday clichés, and crass banalities: "Justice is the advantage of the stronger"; "It is a truth universally acknowledged, that
a single man in possession of a good fortune, must be in want of a
wife"; "So if all do their duty, they need not fear harm."[32] Irony creates
a bifurcation between a statement that is first person, "shared," literal, and unproblematic and a statement that is indirect, divided, and
semantically insecure. There are those who speak "sincerely" when

they utter received phrases and puerile dogmas, those who believe justice is capable of simple definition and morality is a question of self-evident truths or maxims. To speak with such simple sincerity is to assume an always present context of stable, shared, and recognized meaning. A certain theory of meaning is assumed. To argue, as Searle does, that language works through a shared context that "we" all share is to bring all language back to a community of sincere speakers, all of whom are clear about what "we" mean. And if this were so, irony would be thoroughly explicable at the linguistic level alone. Irony would be fully determinable at the level of context.

But any description of irony as a speech act already raises the question of the relation of language to the world and therefore cannot be separated from an understanding of irony as a particular position, attitude, or worldview. Irony plays between "we" (who see) and a limited point of view, whether this is a linguistic, social, or visual limit. To speak in a certain way is often to "see" less, while limited vision leads to certain forms of sentence. A character with a simple vocabulary can only grasp the world in the most basic of terms. Irony is recognized or generated if a character can only see the world through a single form of expression. Much twentieth-century philosophy has explored the ways in which certain sentence forms are tied to forms of seeing. Edmund Husserl argued that the theoretical regard, the objectifying gaze of the scientist, was already expressive of a certain sentence form (the "S is P" of the doxic proposition).[33] James Joyce's *Dubliners* has long been recognized as a literary work that is exemplary for demonstrating the intimate relation between the limits of knowledge and seeing and the limits of language. Take, for example, one of the short stories from Joyce's *Dubliners*, "Grace." Readers can recognize the limits of the narrative voice (and differentiate between the "saying" of the narrator and the "said" of the "story") only if they do not include the world of faith and the world of business within one single and linguistically homogeneous context. "Grace" is narrated by a speaker who describes commerce through religious metaphors and church rituals in the language of enterprise. The irony only works if faith is *not* quantifiable in terms of settling accounts and securing credits and if it is a category error to describe business as a "calling." The narrative voice of Joyce's short story sees its characters' commercial exploits through the language of the Christian faith: as a dignified "calling" with "offices," a "crusade," and even baptismal metaphors of "brief immersions in the waters of general philosophy."[34] The Christian "message" that concludes the story is expressed in the vocabulary of accountancy: "Well, I have verified my accounts. I find all well." A certain imprisonment within a way of speaking—the reduction of all language to quantification—precludes us from seeing the world of spirit as anything other than a settling of accounts. It is as though a way of speaking, a commitment or sincerity adopted toward a lexicon, will give us a form of life.

The relation between seeing and saying works both ways. Commitment to a way of speaking, such as the language of commerce, leads us to see the world in a certain way. But a way of seeing the world as so much quantifiable matter also emerges in the form of simple propositions. The impoverishment of our language, its lack of élan, is as much the cause as the result of a certain style of perception. If we regard the world as a quantifiable and uniform matter, then we are likely to speak in the grammar of predicative propositions and statements of fact. A way of speaking or style of language is already an existential position or point of view. It is not that we see the world and then form a certain grammar and lexicon. There is already a certain grammar or logic to our seeing. Irony lies, so often, in highlighting the determination of what we see by the grammar of what we say. This is why so much twentieth-century philosophy, at least in the phenomenological tradition, has tied the point of view of the proposition (S is P) to the look of a subject who measures and determines an extended object world.[35] Sentence point of view and visual point of view are intimately entwined. The very notion of first-person literal meaning requires a stable border between the subject of enunciation (saying) and the object of that utterance (what is said). We know an utterance is sincere if what the speaker says is in accord with what we can observe him to mean.[36] The saying and the said are coincident, or sincere, if they accord with the context we see and know. They are ironic if the world is clearly *not* that way. We all know the sentence "The window is open" is ironic, Searle argues, if we can see that the window is closed.[37] We know the first sentence of *Pride and Prejudice* is ironic because it is *not* a universal truth that a man in possession of a good fortune is in need of a wife. Irony is a particular way of speaking that opens the question of the relation between what one says and what (or where) one is. Irony is, therefore, always more than a literary effect. Indeed, irony raises the question of the boundary between literature and philosophy: is what is being said merely rhetoric, or is this a committed truth claim?

Irony as a Speech Act or Performance

The main problem with Searle's account, therefore, is that it assumes the *recognition* and *understanding* of irony through a clear distinction between saying (the speaker's meaning) and what is usually understood (sentence meaning). But does the fact that irony is not necessarily recognizable to all debilitate a contextual approach to meaning and a containment of irony within meaning? Fowler's *Modern English Usage* provides a way of reconciling Searle's context-based approach with one of the traditional demands of irony, that it is saying *something other than what is understood*. On Fowler's account, irony is *exclusive* and depends upon only part of the audience recognizing it.[38]

Restated in Searle's terms, we might understand this theory as one in which an utterance is used in a context where the background assumptions of part of the audience understand the expression ironically, while the different context of the wider audience takes the expression at the level of its usual sentence meaning. Take a line from one of William Blake's *Songs of Innocence*: "Then cherish pity, lest you drive an angel from your door."[39] This "maxim" can only be recognized *as ironic* if the reader or hearer does *not* occupy the context or share the background assumptions of ordinary usage. The phrase employs the conventions of eighteenth-century moral songs and takes the form of a pious, religious platitude. If we do not speak in this context, if we think (like Blake) that the morality of pity is a way of keeping the poor in their place, then we read the phrase ironically. It expresses a moral adage *as an adage*, as a received phrase, as assumed wisdom. In perceiving the phrase's conventionality we recognize its emptiness. We do so, presumably, because we do not occupy the same context. If we were Christian and pious and shared the background assumptions of this way of speaking (a language of duty, pity, and obedience), then we would take the phrase at face value. It is because we recognize the context *as a context* (of conventions) that we do not take part in the sincerity; we read ironically. Irony is, on such an account, explained according to context, the recognition of context, and the clear separation between sentence meaning (the usual use of an expression in a shared context) and the speaker's ironic meaning (which establishes an exclusive context critical of the assumptions of the first context). Irony is a way of speaking that depends upon ordinary meaning and its contextual recognition and the possibility that this meaning might be viewed from another (more enlightened) context that establishes the ironic meaning. So, to say something *other than what is understood* can be explained in the following manner. The ironist uses an expression—from "Open the window" to "And I am

THE MEANING OF IRONY

black, but O! my soul is white"—that *can* be understood according to literal, ordinary, or standard usage but by virtue of context also says something quite different. In Searle's case, "The window is open" might mean "Close the window." In the phrase from Blake, "And I am black, but O! my soul is white" *means* that we are all white deep down but can also be understood as *saying* that much antiracist moral rhetoric assumes that whiteness is still equivalent to humanness.[40]

This explanation of irony as a speech act determined by context does, however, raise the question of the second-order context in which irony is *recognized*. In the case of Blake, if we know that a phrase of this type is being uttered ironically, we do so because we recognize it not as a moral truth but as a way of speaking, as a received assumption, as an inherited or acquired context-limited moralism. But the boundary between the sincere and the ironic speech act is not just an issue to be decided *from* a context. Irony plays between contexts (is this how "we" or "they" speak?), and it also raises the question of just how secure we feel once we recognize ourselves as contextually bound. Certain acts of irony disclose something about the very nature of contextuality. Blake is perhaps the best example here, and not just because many of his provocative and indirect speech acts have become some of the most sincere speech acts of our context. His *Songs* are still taught to and narrated by children in a simple and sincere manner. "Tyger! Tyger! burning bright" and "Little Lamb, who made thee?" are some of the most well known and well loved lines of English poetry. His prophetic book *Milton*, which railed against institutional religion, opened with a hymn that has become the anthem of the Church of England ("And did those feet in ancient time / Walk upon England's mountains green?").[41] Blake's entire rhetorical project was based just on this essential contextual indeterminacy. It is always possible for the voice of radical questioning to become yet one more pious and tyrannical dogma, and it is always possible to revive the innocence, soul, or

spirit in the most rigid and defeatist ways of speaking. Like so many
antisystematizing Romantic poets, Blake's work multiplied voices and
speaking positions not to create an undifferentiated relativism but to
diagnose the force and point of view of what we say.

The following is one of William Blake's *Songs of Experience*. (As a
song *of* experience, it is already an utterance located in a specific voice
or position.)[42]

> Tyger! Tyger! burning bright,
> In the forests of the night;
> What immortal hand or eye
> Could frame thy fearful symmetry?
>
> In what distant deeps or skies
> Burnt the fire of thine eyes?
> On what wings dare he aspire?
> What the hand dare seize the fire?
>
> And what shoulder, & what art,
> Could twist the sinews of thy heart?
> And when thy heart began to beat,
> What dread hand? & what dread feet?
>
> What the hammer? What the chain,
> In what furnace was thy brain?
> What the anvil? What dread grasp
> Dare its deadly terrors clasp?

The literal (sentence) meaning here is clear enough. The poem
asks about the nature of a God who could create the evil ferocity of a
tiger. But if we ask who is speaking, we start to get a sense of irony. The
very terms of the question—the style, rhetoric, and discourse used—
already determine any possible answer. The language (or context) is
clearly that of eighteenth-century natural theology, in which God is
derived from the mechanistic order of existence as some form of divine watchmaker. The irony, we might say, is identified by recogniz-

ing a certain style of thought. From the poem's point of view, the im-
mortal origin of this mortal, finite, and mechanistic world can only be
described using a language of industrial construction. But surely, if
there is a divine origin or creation, it cannot be understood according
to a "nuts and bolts" or "bones and sinews" model of creation. I say the
irony is "clearly" recognized, but this is only so if we do not share the
position or context of the speaker. If we felt confident with a rudimen-
tary and mechanistic understanding of creation, we would read the
poem "straight."

Irony is perceived only with the recognition of the limits of a point
of view. However, the "step back" that reveals such limits does not
take us clearly to another context. Rather, irony works through a peculiar conditional to generate a point of view at the limit of the first
point of view. *If* we understand the world mechanistically, then we
must ask about God in terms of material construction. But in asking
the question this way, in articulating the mechanistic viewpoint, we
see the impossible position created by such ways of speaking. To question God *as if* the world were a machine is to position oneself as a cog
in a mechanism, a position that could in essence never ask the question of divinity or creation. The very way of speaking incriminates or
undermines itself. The ironic utterance leads beyond itself to a critical
point of view. Blake's poem adopts the voice of a speaker who asks
about the character or definition of God but does so from the clearly
defined and closed context of natural theology. But it is the very question of God or divinity that would render any such homely, self-
contained, or thoroughly explicable contexts impossible. If the world
really were a mechanistically determined collection of terrifyingly violent creatures, how could there be any divinity or any questions
about divinity? The speaker of Blake's poem asks about God as though
He could be found at the end point of a chain of construction. God is
already assumed to be the possible object of a scientific and inductive

form of reason. The very style of the language (mechanism) and the grammar of the questions determine the way of seeing: God is the conclusion of a series of questions. The sense of the world lies at the end of a series of causally determined entities. If, as Blake's poetry does, we accurately repeat the "saying" of such confident positions of knowledge or definition, we can see the incoherence of what is "said."

Like so many literary speech acts, Blake's poems are not just articulated within a context; they disrupt and generate contexts. Speech act theory seems to be the best place to start in order to understand irony, for the very notion of the speech act begins from seeing language as more than the communication of information. Speaking is also doing: a performance of social interaction that both institutes and modifies contexts of speakers. Ironic or literary speech acts have the power to give a far more complex account of the speech act than the standard theory of the performative and context allows. If we were to follow Searle's suggestion that ironic meaning is determined by context, then we would have to establish another (second-order) context that is able to see the limits of the first context. In the case of Blake, the context to be recognized would be that of an unquestioning, pious, institutionalized, and religious moralism. The second-order context would, presumably, enable the recognition of irony because of different background assumptions. In the case of reading Blake's moral aphorisms ironically we might say that because we have a different way of speaking and different background assumptions (those of a more enlightened humanism) we recognize the irony. We can see the "speaker's meaning" as opposed to the "sentence meaning" because we share and recognize the context and background assumptions; we know what these assumptions are (we know where we stand), and we know that we are other than, or different from, the context ironically delimited.

But doesn't this context-based theory of irony as a speech act al-

ready suggest that irony is a clear position, and a hierarchically determined position, defined against a first context of ordinary meaning?
More importantly, we might ask what the character of the second
irony-recognizing context is. Is it another set of values, a different set
of background assumptions, or different meanings? Or is it *a different
attitude toward meaning*, a position that recognizes that moral values
must be more than just background assumptions or received opinion?
(What Blake's poetry holds up for question is not just this or that
moral opinion or context but a form of morality that is circulated as
just so much contextually assured opinion.) As I have already suggested, the context of *ironic* meaning, if we are to call it that, might be
a context in which the possibility of shared understanding, meaning,
and background assumptions is opened for question. What irony does,
in showing our moral rhetoric *as rhetoric,* is to raise the question of the
validity or meaning of what we say. It does so not by offering another
meaning. In quoting or repeating what we usually say irony can demonstrate that what we say is often not fully understood (not only by a
limited part of the audience but perhaps by the context itself). It is
possible to imagine a context where moral rhetoric is just incoherent
or meaningless.[43] Blake's irony shows a whole style or context to be
self-incriminating, intending so much more than it means to say, not
aware of what it is *really saying.* To say, "And I am black, but O! my
soul is white," is to display a certain way of seeing or point of view (to
be human is to be white), while what the speaker understands is quite
different. By looking at what is said as issuing from a certain point of
view, ironic repetition also demonstrates that a way of speaking is also
a way of seeing. And in the case just quoted irony also shows that the
way of seeing or point of view is not itself seen. In the case of Blake's
irony most of the *Songs* are instances of moral or religious rhetoric
that accept their way of speaking as so much fact, as simply the way
things are, and that are not aware that what they *say* can often be

understood to mean so much more. Irony discloses the conventional and platitudinous character of everyday facts and common sense, which, once recognized as conventional, seem to lose their status as facts.

If we are to understand or recognize irony, then both the context account and the existential explanation (where irony is a way of life or special context) demand that we identify *who is speaking* or determine the position of the utterance. Locating irony depends upon the attribution of voice and upon knowing *where* the ironic utterance stands. Context is the situation of an utterance. And context, no less than irony, is determined by giving what is said to a specific point of view.

Irony as a Theory of Meaning

I have already mentioned Richard Rorty's definition of irony as a recognition that what we say is really not a representation of what is and that we ourselves are nothing more than our ways of speaking. Irony, for Rorty, is a theory of meaning or language, an attitude toward truth and representation defined in terms of edifying ways of speaking. Irony can be more than a speech act *within language*. For Rorty it is a recognition of the way language works in general. But if we take irony as a possible speech act seriously, it is also the case, as I will argue here, that the performance of irony actually *precludes* Rorty's reduction of meaning (and philosophy) to a style or way of speaking. That is, if there can be an act of irony within a context (a figure or trope of irony), then there will be a difference made between committed and ironic speech. Not all speech could be ironic. A speech act of irony could not occur in a fully ironic context, could not occur if all meaning were, as Rorty suggests, ironic.

Like Searle, Richard Rorty's definition of irony is strongly context-dependent. There is, Rorty argues, nothing beyond our vocabularies. Furthermore, language usage is *all we are*. Irony is, for Rorty, a healthy skepticism of one's own language game, a preparedness to adjust one's lexicon, refigure one's vocabulary, and desist from positing any truth or representation outside language. But if this is the case, if irony is the immanent inhabitation of a vocabulary with a recognition of its contingency, then it follows that irony is *nothing more* than our context, a sense that all we are is context or an accepted style of language use. Accordingly, for Rorty, irony is at one with a form of liberal pragmatism: openness to the plurality of perspectives and the continual possibility of re-self-definition. Irony is the abandonment of any *metaphysical* desire to justify or step outside our context. Irony, for Rorty, is the humbling of philosophy. Through irony philosophy becomes a form of literary criticism or enlightened conversation. We recognize that our ways of speaking are thoroughly textual; we no longer step outside texts but evaluate our metaphysical paradigms according to their literary merit. There is, for Rorty's ironist, no transcendental step back from description to the real but only other possible forms of description.

For both Rorty and Searle, irony is also defined in opposition to a strong sense of justification. For both, irony is a sign of philosophy's maturity and depends heavily on a sense of context and background assumptions. Irony is, for Rorty, a recognition that we are nothing other than our context and assumptions and that questions of justification, foundation, and representation *stop there*—at where we are, at our particular and contingent perspectives. Irony gives us a sense of our specific linguistic locale and debunks any attempts to speak from a God's-eye view of the world. What Rorty and Searle share is a sense of philosophy as a liberation from the misguided and speculative attempt to ground our concepts in some extracontextual foundation. For Searle, irony explains, and is explained by, the way our contexts and background assumptions work. Searle's brief definition of irony occurs in a paper criticizing Jacques Derrida's overly rigorous demand for concepts. According to Searle, concepts have fuzzy boundaries, and it is only Derrida's definition of concepts as strictly defined that leads him to posit the undecidability of meaning.[44] We should not be asking what a word or concept really means, only how it is, and can be, used.

While Derrida's work has not dealt with the issue of irony explicitly, he is an exemplary figure in the history of ironic philosophy. Socratic irony relies upon differentiating the force of a concept from its everyday definition: we use the words "justice" and "friendship" and "virtue," but when pushed for a definition we seem incapable of capturing the necessity of these concepts. Derrida, in line with the Socratic tradition that insists on the impersonal force of concepts, also insists that there is a certain lawfulness to what we say and that this law lies not in any speaker's decision but in the structural possibilities of meaning. If I use a concept, then it can only work if it intends some sense that would be recognized in more than one instance or more than one context. Meaning is essentially tied to iterability; it is essentially repeatable and can be repeatable only because it is inscribed, marked, or traced out through some system of differences. To recognize "justice" as a word or concept and not just as noise, there must already be a system of iterable marks—the systemically differentiated phonemes or letters of a language that allow me to recognize the various sounds as a specific instance of a word. Before meaning or intent—or the performance or act of speakers—there is already a repeatable system of marks and sounds. This gives us a more radical notion of the performance or force of speech, for what we can do with words (and what words do) depends upon a "context" or structure of forces that lies well beyond social function or intent. The concept's capacity to intend—to refer to a sense that can be recognized as both what you and I say—relies on iterability, an already differentiated system of marks or traces through which meaning's repetition can be expressed. The sounds or marks are already systematized, differentiated, or iterable. Iterability is not repetition, for it makes repetition—recognizing something as the same—possible. Not only are our contexts of intention and performance made possible by a structure of forces and differences that *precede* intent, but the performance of meaning also opens a future. A word can only be meaningful if it intends some future fulfillment of sense. "Intentionality," for the phenomenological tradition that extends from Husserl to Derrida, characterizes both perception and language. To see a thing *as a thing* is to anticipate or intend its future fulfillment in a series of perceptions: that it will be there for me, and others, beyond this present intuition. Similarly, to speak is to invoke a sense that is not just what *I* say but what you must take me to mean. When we speak we do not just exchange sounds or signifiers, we take those sounds to be tokens of some sense that exceeds their particularity. To speak, then, is to rely upon *the ideal of a sense* that would be recognized beyond any private meaning and beyond any local context. (Derrida refers to this as "the concept of the concept.") We must be able to mark or trace what we say, render it repeatable, recognizable, and transportable to a future context. A concept only works with this ideal of sense, of a meaning that a future speaker would be able to repeat, recognize, and reinvoke. Any single meaning or sense is meaningful only in its anticipation of being repeated, and this is possible only if there are iterable marks that allow a sense to move from context to context.

While Searle insists that concepts are contextually located and are only meaningful according to the intentions and rules we recognize in any specific instance, Derrida argues that a concept cannot be located *within* a context. The very possibility of a concept—the possibility of meaning—relies upon a word working across contexts. There must be a force or law to a concept that allows me to recognize it as meaningful. Meaning is not just this use of the token—not just the move in a conversation—but an intention of what this sign is a sign of. For Derrida this means that concepts must have strict boundaries. We cannot just use them in one way here and in another way there, for they can only be used at all if they intend a sense above and beyond any single use or context.[45] It is just this force of concepts that provides a lot of the power of deconstructive method. Derrida can look at how a concept works in a text such that what the text *wants to say* is belied by the force of the concept's *said*. When Michel Foucault wants to write a history of reason, for example, Derrida shows that the very force of what Foucault *says* must undermine his project. Foucault wants to write a history of reason, but the very meaning of "history" and "reason" precludes such a project. The concept of "history" *must mean* a recognizable, repeatable, rationally ordered, and coherent objectification of what is historicized.[46] If this is so, reason cannot be located *within* history, for meaning, time, and objectification are themselves modes of reason. You cannot write a history of reason precisely because the concept of reason is not one concept among others but a concept that must already be in play in any possible argument. The writing of history itself is an act of reason and cannot delimit reason.

Foucault's text can be deconstructed because he uses concepts such as reason and history that have a force that exceeds what Foucault wants to say. If these concepts did not have such a transcontextual force, it is hard to imagine that Foucault could say anything at all. According to Derrida, this force of the concept is both philosophy's possibility and its impossibility. Philosophy is possible only if we ask the question of the concept, What *is* truth? This cannot be answered by pointing to instances of true statements ("two plus two equal four" is true; "snow is white" is true) but only through some grasp of truth *in general*, or just what this concept of truth *means*, not some particular that it points to. But this force of the concept, its inability to be exhausted by any given instance, its capacity to be repeatable in just one more context, also renders philosophy impossible. We could never fully determine what this concept means, precisely because a concept only works if it is open to future sense.

For Derrida, though, such impossibilities are not only valuable, they are necessary. "We" are placed within this impossibility. In speaking or even in experiencing a world, we operate from the ideal of sense, from the Idea of what remains present above and beyond the pure present of any speech act or perception. Of course, such a world in general or complete sense and presence could never be given. Speaking and perceiving *intend* a world or sense that lies beyond any closed context, but such an intention remains necessarily unfulfilled. Unfulfilled because, as Derrida insists, a concept intends—from within a system—that which exceeds all system and location. For Derrida, then, philosophy cannot be domesticated or determined by any context, even though it will also only be made possible from some context. It is the strictness of philosophical concepts—the very power of the concepts of truth, reason, justice, and so on—that will always disrupt and exceed any context or structure. Our *use* of concepts— what we want them to say—cannot exhaust what our concepts might *do*, their possible effects in other contexts.

One of Derrida's main problems, Searle insists, is his failure to see the difference between "use" and "mention." We "use" a concept or phrase when we want it to have its conventional force. Here the concept's meaning is tied to just that function it usually serves. If I am a priest and I say, "I now pronounce you man and wife," then I am using that phrase to perform a certain act—marriage. And we recognize the use because we recognize the context. But if I am acting in a play, or describing a ceremony, or citing an example for linguistics, then I am *mentioning* the phrase. Again, this is determined by context. Use would be tied to when a concept or phrase is uttered sincerely, while mention would be the "empty," "parasitic," or "secondary" quotation of use.

From a deconstructive point of view, however, the distinction between use and mention is just the sort of dichotomy that the structure of concepts renders problematic. To tie the genuine *use* of concepts to certain contexts is both to beg the question and to miss the essential structure of concepts. The distinction between contexts of use/sincerity and parasitic contexts (such as fiction and stage plays) begs the question of how we recognize such contexts: how do we know whether this is a context of sincerity or quotation? Contexts cannot decide what is a use or mention, precisely because the context itself has to be decided. While it might seem clear to distinguish between the use of a phrase in a social ritual and its repetition on stage, is it so clear in the majority of cases? If I say, "Women are the guardians of the planet," am I *using* the phrase (speaking as an ecofeminist) or am I *mentioning* it (speaking ironically as a postmodern feminist, sure that "we" will recognize just how worn out such ideas are)? An appeal to context might help, but it might not, for the context of *who* is speaking—the serious user of the phrase or the ironizing mentioner—is just what is being questioned. Second, and more important, a concept's function is always undecidably poised between use and mention. If a concept were *just* its use and nothing more, each concept would be tied to its specific and unique utterance. But a concept is meaningful only because it transcends use. It can only be used effectively if there is an element of mention, if there is an element that we recognize as not being just what *I say* but what *we mean* when we use a word. There must be both the dimension of mention—such that what we say is repeatable, quotable, exchangeable—and a dimension of use—such that those sounds we recognize are also taken to be what this speaker intends or wants to say. Derrida insists that we can only *use* concepts precisely because they have a force that our usage cannot govern. The capacity for a term to be "mentioned"—quoted outside of its original context, freed from the private intent of any speaker—is precisely what makes any use possible. There is an essential irony at the structural root of concepts; when we speak we use a system that precedes all use and that can therefore have effects that exceed all intent. Any use is "mentionable": capable of being heard or repeated in other contexts.

For Searle, however, irony is not produced through the concepts we use having effects that exceed what we want them to do. Indeed, Searle uses the example of irony to show that we all know exactly when a phrase is being used and when mentioned. If we accept that concepts differ according to contextual articulation, then, Searle insists, we forgo the pure ideality of concepts. We have to give up the idea that concepts have *a* meaning. What we gain, though, is the capacity to recognize a concept according to its use (and not any putative ideal content). For both Searle and Rorty, then, a certain comfort is attained by modifying philosophy's claims, and this modesty can be achieved through the recognition of irony. In irony we see that utterances are neither grounded nor tied to meaning beyond context. Irony is nothing other than a recognition of context. Once we give up the Socratic and unanswerable question (what *is* x?), then we no longer seek a meaning that would be elevated above specific instances of language use. For Searle, we do not need to appeal to the *meanings* of concepts, precisely because we recognize concepts as something we *do* rather than as lofty objects that have a power of their own. Irony is just another way of using the tokens of our language. We decide irony, according to Searle, on the basis of a clear misuse of language, a phrase being employed against the run of our background assumptions. If I say, "The window is open," when the window is closed, then I am not employing the standard use. Obviously, there is another context such as that of diplomatic discussion that makes sense of the utterance. It is the context of our background assumptions and standard usage that allows us to determine whether a phrase is ironic or sincere.

Total Irony

But what if irony were directed toward that context or background? How, then, would we know whether a speech act were ironic? In modern irony, for example, it is not clear who is speaking, whether it is the point of view of an ironically delimited way of seeing or whether it is *our* accepted context. The whole point of many modern forms of irony is that we *cannot know*, nor could such knowledge be gained by appealing to context. This is because what is in question is precisely our background assumptions *as assumptions*. Take the following example from Gustave Flaubert's *Madame Bovary*: "She already felt in her heart that inert submissiveness that is to many a woman both the penalty and atonement for her adultery."[47]

To read this sentence as sincere we have to accept this way of speaking, recognize this context *as ours*, and concur with the background assumptions. To read ironically, the context of the utterance or the way of speaking or usage is taken *not* to be ours. We see it as a particular style—in this case, bourgeois provincial moralism. But if we see it *as not ours*, does this demand that we have another context and are located elsewhere? In writing *Madame Bovary* Flaubert mentioned, "quoted," or indirectly uttered the language of (bourgeois) assumptions and conventions in order to emphasize their conventionality— their assumed or unquestioned moralism. When the obscenity trial concerning the novel spent considerable time trying to determine the morality of Flaubert's position, the irony was compounded. If we are sure of our morals, conventions, context, or background assumptions, then surely we can recognize when they are being flouted or attacked. What the trial revealed was the instability of recognition and context. Was Flaubert's text a scandalous romance of adultery? Or was it the moral description of a woman who had read too many romance novels? The very existence of the trial undermined the self-evidence, security, and conventionality of context.[48] As Searle has argued, irony may be decided by where we are in relation to context and background assumptions. However, if we start to read our own background assumptions as assumptions, or if our context appears as only ours, or if where we are starts to look like a mannered style or way of speaking, then we may have *irony without being given another context within which our irony could be located.*

An ironic statement is recognized *as ironic* because it is not used conventionally and does not agree with the context in which it is uttered. But in a case of complex irony, such as Flaubert's, where the mention or quotation concerns the security of linguistic context itself, we are less sure that we can recognize irony. To employ Searle's language, the distinction between use and mention is less secure. Irony raises the question of whether a phrase is being *used*—in the form of a committed assertion or belief—or *mentioned*—such that the phrase is uttered as an instance of a way of speaking. The recognition of a phrase as a use or mention depends upon but also determines our beliefs and the character of our context. Sincerity is not some pregiven entity or mind-set that determines the difference between use and mention, for sincerity is nothing other than the decision between what counts as used rather than merely quoted or feigned. Flaubert's *Madame Bovary* might be read as the committed and sincere use of novelistic romance-speak, or it might be read as a parody or mention of such speech. The irony lies in the fact that how the novel is read— as use or mention—decides where we are. To decide that a speech act is indirect demands that we know what our context is. But how is this determined? Is this determination contextual? Irony might, then, be defined not so much as an indirect speech act but as the inability to decide on whether the act is direct or indirect, being used contextually or mentioned as a "quotation" of context.

Complex irony is frequently a combination of the context-bound character of an utterance as well as a recognition of that context as our own *and* a sense of the inadequacy or merely contextual status of the utterance. Irony is, as it were, the use of context and convention to demonstrate the inescapable limits of our background assumptions. This is why irony so often concerns statements of fact and moral truth. Both these types of utterance depend upon being more than convention. Irony demonstrates the inevitable *conventionality* of our language of facts and morals; at the same time, irony also demonstrates the unavoidable predicament of having to continue to make truth claims. This is why irony can often direct itself to those utterances that present themselves as thoroughly aware or at home with their contextual contingency. It is the speaker who is thoroughly at home with conventions and platitudes who is the easiest target of irony. Who could be less sincere than one who has no doubts regarding the utter security of his context, one at home in language and assumptions? At the same time, one who had no commitment to language at all would be neither sincere nor deceptive and would be free of the question of irony. The very idea that one might recognize one's context and merely quote its utterances is given in Rorty's ideal philosopher. This ideal suggests that one might successfully differentiate or distance oneself from one's linguistic point of view. But if something appears as just a point of view or as the reiteration of what we all acknowledge as expected and unremarkable convention, then it loses its force or power of being used. We might suspect that a phrase is being uttered ironically not because it is so obviously untrue—as in Searle's case of the open window—but because it just seems so trivially true. It is when an artist does not dissimulate but simply states what "we all know to be the case" that we are led to suspect irony. It is because Blake's moralism is so obviously "moral" or agreeable that we are prompted to question what Blake is saying.

Reading ironically, then, is perhaps akin to reading poetically: attending not just to the reference or propositional content of words but also to what those references and propositions "say" about our linguistic contexts. We open a work of contemporary literature, and the first sentence is a simple proposition. We do not need to read the work through any complex lens of postmodern parody to understand that the sentence is saying more than it says. Take the first sentence of Raymond Carver's short story "Neighbors": "Bill and Arlene were a happy married couple."[49] What is being said here is not just the sense of the simple proposition or the information that the sentence expresses. The story opens by establishing a particular tone or point of view. There is a certain simplicity to the way of seeing that is formed through the story's grammar and diction. This is a world of married couples—social units that can be described as "happy." And happiness is used here not to describe the characters' psychological state, for the story goes on to list their dissatisfactions in the way we list items on a shopping list. "Happiness" here is a convention or marker for a certain social type. The words "happy couple" point less to the content than to what is conventionally or trivially described as "happy," in this case, an ordinary and unremarkable suburban married couple who live their lives with a sense that they might have "a fuller and brighter life."[50] The simple proposition is "saying" more than it simply says. Its sense of what it really says is, perhaps, "This is the language and world of simple propositions." Carver's story is written from a point of view that describes the world through subject-predicate propositions, describing couples in terms of the objects they do or do not possess. The referent of the story is, perhaps, linguistic simplicity itself. Carver's work is neither clearly ironic nor sincere. Carver writes his stories in the sparse, simple, and unquestioning language of the characters he describes. The point of view of his narration is neither the omniscient point of view of high realism, where the narrator can describe, judge, and compare the psychological states of each character, nor is it a clearly ironic voice, in which what the character says clearly indicates its opposite, or in which we can locate the narrative voice in a distinctly recognizable context. If, as in Carver's stories, the context (and language) is that of everyday life and ordinary America, how are we to know whether to read these sentences as sincere and within "our" context or as "mentions" of the language of "happy couples"? An uncontentious sentence is often (but not always) the clearest mark of irony, for once a phrase has been used to the point where it is beyond question it can start to sound like nothing more than mere mention. In the case of Carver's stories we might ask, Are these narratives an attempt to capture and express the true speech of who "we" are, or are they tales deliberately restricted to the point of view of a specific context that we might recognize and delimit?

The target of irony is often a way of speaking in which morality is nothing more than the assumed meaning or ordinary language of one's context. What this suggests is that the performance of irony cannot be accounted for from within a context or theory of so-called ordinary usage. It is just when we feel a comforting sense of ordinary usage—that what we say and what we mean are clear and unproblematic—that irony can take hold. Irony demonstrates the limits of our context and the ways in which our context itself, or the meaning of what we say, exceeds what we understand or recognize our context to be. Isn't our use of the phrase "happy couple" just more evidence of how distant we are from knowing the meaning of happiness? If there are certain words that circulate freely, sincerely, and without question in our context, isn't this because they have lost all their force of use, becoming eminently mentionable? Far from being determined by the security of our context, irony renders contexts insecure by drawing attention to the disturbing banality of linguistic stability.

Modern Irony

The Conditional

In modern irony it is precisely attribution, position, or point of view that is rendered problematic.[1] The question of *who is speaking* is essentially undecidable. As I argue in the next chapter, Socratic irony often operates by invoking both the force of a concept and its conditional. *If* there is any meaning to the word "justice," then it cannot refer to mere power. *If* there is such a thing as beauty in itself, then it would have to refer to an Idea and not a beautiful thing. *If* certain of our concepts are to have any meaning (if we really *mean* to talk about justice, truth, or beauty), then we cannot just offer a simple worldly definition. It is the emphasis on conditional structure that is modern, an emphasis on what it would mean *if* there were such Ideas—whether or not such Ideas have a reality. We may be unsure as to whether there will be anything that answers to the concepts of God, immortality, or freedom, but we are troubled by the thought of those concepts nevertheless. The status of the conditional itself is historical, for we seem to be indebted to certain conditions. *If* there were to be any justice (if we could fulfill the promise of such concepts), then we would have to live up to a sense that we have inherited from the past. Do these concepts we have received still have any meaning? Can we still talk about freedom?

It was Kant who felt that if we were to talk meaningfully about God, immortality, or freedom, then we would have to understand the peculiar nature of conceptuality: that there are certain concepts whose reality we can think but not know. Kant is crucial to the history of modern and Romantic irony precisely because of his own ironic position. Kant is perhaps "responsible" for both the critical insistence of philosophers like Searle and Rorty, who stress the limits of knowledge, and the speculative force of philosophers like Derrida, who emphasize the exorbitant force of concepts to extend beyond all present knowledge. On the one hand, Kant insists on the limits of what can be known or said; any attempt to describe or intuit God, freedom, or immortality would belie the necessarily supersensible nature of what these concepts intend. On the other hand, the very fact that these concepts have such a meaning—the very fact that we can think the supersensible—is evidence of a human soul capable of *thinking* beyond this world. Kant argues that the very meaning of certain concepts gives us evidence of what lies beyond the sensible. If we can think of God, immortality, or freedom, then this demonstrates our power to extend our thought beyond sensible intuition. Kant's most important conditional concept was that of freedom: *if* we can think of a pure freedom, *then* we ought to act *as if* we were self-determining. The very concept of freedom is evidence that there is a soul who can think of what lies beyond worldly determination. The concept or thought of freedom both reveals and institutes the moral agent. It is after we have formed a moral law, such as "act from duty alone," that we realize we must have been free; the very fact that we can form a concept of duty demonstrates our supersensible being, our humanity, or our capacity to think beyond this pathological or sensible world. Such concepts do not refer to experienced objects within our world; they provide (and demonstrate) a power of thinking beyond this spatiotemporal world. Our *experience* is not extended by such concepts (we do not encounter the supersensible as an object), but we nevertheless are forced to admit its reality: "the supersensible was not mere fancy and . . . its concepts were not empty. Now practical reason itself, without any collusion with the speculative, provides reality to a supersensible object of the category of causality, i.e., to freedom."[2] If we have the concept of freedom, then there must have been some spontaneous origin for its genesis.

In Romanticism this conditional structure of the concept is fleshed out through poetry and the necessarily finite attempts to grasp the infinite. If there is an infinite or absolute, then it could not be expressed within a poem or representation. The very *limit* of the work of art opens a feeling but not an articulation of the unlimited. From Socrates through to Kant and Romanticism, the irony of the concept works to give a sense of that which exceeds the concept. If the concept of the absolute is to have any meaning, then there must be that which lies beyond all conceptuality. If the way we use the word "justice" has any meaning, then there must be a sense that lies above and beyond our ordinary usage, for we use the word as though it referred to some sense or ideal that transcends contingent instances. Modern irony, however, often recognizes this force of the concept—we use some concepts as though they were more than just tokens in a conventional exchange—but raises the possibility that perhaps those tokens that we use to signify such depths of meaning cannot be freed from convention. To return to the structure of the conditional, we might say that modern irony opens with the antecedent—if there is truth it must lie beyond the banality of everyday rhetoric—but abandons the possibility of a consequent. It does not follow that such an authentic truth has any reality or existence. All we can do is feel the limits of banality, never arriving at sincerity.

The difference between the Socratic and modern conditionals that govern irony can be gathered by comparing Flaubert's description of the artist (which we will examine later) with Socrates' description of the distinct and nonempirical location of the soul. For Socrates, if philosophy is different from sophistry, then it must appeal to a "said" or "meaning" that is more than just the force or use of what we say. And if the philosopher is different from the Sophist, it is because he lives according to his soul and wisdom. What characterizes wisdom is its capacity to purify the *real* senses of courage, temperance, and justice from the "vulgar conception" of virtues, which is governed by mere exchange:[3]

> Every seeker after wisdom knows that up to the time when philosophy takes it over his soul is a helpless prisoner, chained hand and foot in the body, compelled to view reality not directly but only through its prison bars, and wallowing in utter ignorance. And philosophy can see that the imprisonment is ingeniously effected by the prisoner's own active desire, which makes him first accessory to his own confinement. Well, philosophy takes over the soul in this condition and by gentle persuasion tries to set it free. She points out that observation by means of the eyes and ears and all the other senses is entirely deceptive, and she urges the soul to refrain from using them until it is necessary to do so, and encourages it to collect and concentrate itself by itself, trusting nothing but its own independent judgment upon objects considered in themselves, and attributing no truth to anything

which it views indirectly as being subject to variation, because such
objects are sensible and visible but what the soul itself sees is intelligible and invisible.[4]

For Socrates it is the philosopher who can be freed from the imprisonment of his own person, capable of a viewpoint that is no longer tied
to vision of this sensible world, and able to view the intelligible. But if,
in modernity, it is no longer deemed to be possible to attain this vision
of the invisible, then we can at least strive for the point of view of the
artist: not one who sees the invisible but who becomes invisible. We do
not overcome the locatedness of our vision by ascending to the super-
vision of philosophy; instead, we become one with the visible. We no
longer aspire to some exalted realm of the supersensible; rather, we
reach a point of "infinite impassivity" that frees us from personality.
And we do so by being *nothing other* than the personalities or points
of view that we narrate. The author becomes, then, an imperceptible
distance from the characters he presents. If it is impossible to purify
one's soul to the point of complete rarefaction, seeing what lies above
and beyond this world, then one can at least immerse one's soul within
the world. Flaubert defines the author as necessarily other than any
described position. The artist is not confined to personality; he is freed
from the particularity of viewpoint only by presenting a series of personalities with absolute fidelity and imperceptible distance. The artist's separation is effective and impassive but visible nowhere: "An author in his book must be like God in the universe, present everywhere
and visible nowhere. Art being a second nature, the creator of that Nature must behave similarly. In all its atoms, in all its aspects, let there
be sensed a hidden, infinite impassivity."[5]

What has happened, historically, between the Socratic purification
of the soul and Flaubert's "infinite impassivity"? In both cases, the
ironic viewpoint transcends the world of confident definitions in
which one term can be exchanged for another. Socrates' interlocutors

do not recognize that if this world has any value, then it must be valued in terms of some end—the wisdom of the soul, which cannot be reduced to one value among others. For Flaubert, art is not just the depiction of competing viewpoints or voices, for any such description of located positions also produces the artistic viewpoint as the impersonal and God-like medium through which all voices are expressed. For Socrates, irony leads us away from worldly definitions and values to the higher value of the soul. For Flaubert, there is no heightened position; rather, the soul of the world—infinite impassivity—is present everywhere, elevated only by being irreducible to any one position. What unites the Socratic and Flaubertian modes of irony is just the impossibility of reducing the world to a collection of perspectives or viewpoints. If we can recognize a perspective or point of view, then we also already recognize its limit. Either we ascend to some position above such vision (the contemplating soul of the philosopher), or we aim to encompass the totality of all possible points of vision through the impersonality of art.

Irony is, from the point of view of this modern problematic, a sense of the inevitability of perspective or position alongside the impossibility of reducing an utterance *to* a perspective or position. Any described perspective or point of view—any delimited context—already suggests a "higher" position from which that point of view is seen *as point of view*. But this elevation or step back, by its very ironic nature, cannot be determined as simply another viewpoint. It is a sense of the banality and inadequacy of any mere viewpoint. This "sense," however, is itself only achieved through techniques of point of view. Irony, then, is a literary effect, a manifest demonstration that any position is at once the specifically determined style of a point of view. But it is also a recognition that we can never fully recognize ourselves *as a point of view*. Modern literary irony is also, therefore, a modification of the ironic conditional: if what is uttered or said is always located as a point of view or perspective, then the manifestation or sense of point of view raises the possibility of that which precedes point of view. For Flaubert this ironic distance is given in the artist's absence (rather than the Socratic personality or position). Flaubert's work is at once the fulfillment and the critique of ironic elevation. This is nowhere more apparent, or necessarily and essentially *unapparent*, than in Flaubert's own critique of the possibility of irony.

Bourgeois Irony and Stupidity

Richard Rorty has clearly tied irony to contemporary liberalism and pragmatism. If one forgoes a metaperspective and acknowledges the provisional nature of one's own self and world, then one will live in a state of ironic self-revision. Flaubert, well before Rorty, had also recognized a certain irony in everyday bourgeois life. The enlightened man of modernity is neither committed to faith nor burdened by dogma; for modern man, books and ideas are only valuable for their free and untrammeled exchange. In *Bouvard and Pécuchet* Flaubert charts the journey of two provincial souls who consume the corpus of Western knowledge, freely substituting one schema for another, moving from astronomy, to metaphysics, to poetry and drama. All is of equal value, and Bouvard and Pécuchet remain committed to the increasing consumption and proliferation of ideas as a journey to the truth. If they read enough botanical manuals, they will become successful gardeners; if they add to this a grounding in the history of theater, they will become accomplished performers; and the ultimate aim will be the synthesis of all this reading in a proper and comprehensive grasp of the whole of life. Their endless consumption and regurgitation of "knowledge" is directed toward some truth always within view but never achieved. What separates Bouvard and Pécuchet from the fully enlightened ironist is their *belief.* The Rortyan ironist devours one possible system after another, moving from world-view to worldview but with none of the sense of encyclopedic inclusion or truth that motivates Bouvard and Pécuchet. There is a clear irony in the literalism of Flaubert's characters, who adopt one metaphysical system after another in search of the real. But there is also a haunting irony in the novelistic point of view that is elevated above such literal commitment. The narrator of the novel is so obviously free from the risible commitment and sincerity of Bouvard and Pécuchet. But how authentic is this narrating voice? How confident can we be of our separation from the literalism and stupidity of Bouvard and Pécuchet?

If these characters are so clearly the objects of irony, it is because they are blind to the limits of point of view. They read the texts of the Western canon as though they provided direct access to the real, *as though truth were simply a matter of consuming and accumulating knowledge.* To accept and ironize the manifest stupidity of Bouvard and Pécuchet demands that we have a more appropriate image of good thinking. But there is much in Flaubert's work to suggest that it just this belief—that we might be above and beyond the committed viewpoint of bourgeois literalism—that is truly ironic. Is it possible to view the world as though it were no world at all but a mere perspective, way of seeing, or image? Wouldn't this just be an intensified version of Bouvard and Pécuchet's bourgeois gullibility? Both characters adopt and abandon viewpoints like so many commodities, shifting from project to project, accepting failure and disappointment, and assuming new schemes in a perpetual project of self-renovation. If Bouvard and Pécuchet's simple credulity can be delimited ironically, what is the position from which they are viewed? Is it any more reassuring to confidently recognize Bouvard and Pécuchet as gullible believers; on what truth would such confidence be based? Are Bouvard and Pécuchet the simple objects of irony? If this were so, then the somewhat derisive narrative voice would be sincere. Flaubert would be speaking as a latter-day Rorty, finding those who are committed to their language games eminently laughable. But if the narrative voice is itself an instance of point of view, say, an enlightened character who can dismiss Bouvard and Pécuchet's impassioned search for truth as absurd, then the irony is not so much elevating as alarmingly disconcerting. What if there were an *essential stupidity* to all thinking, such that to think demands that we be lodged within some form of rigid convention? Stupidity could no longer be delimited to character types, and the ironist who felt herself to be other than the stupidity of the world would merely be blind to the conditions of her own seeing.

For Gilles Deleuze and Michel Foucault this was precisely the genius of *Bouvard and Pécuchet*. Whereas philosophers imagine a universal subject of good sense who represents us all, Flaubert was capable of exposing the "categories" of thinking that were random, chaotic, and "malevolent"—incapable of being grasped by the subject through whom thinking takes place. What is truly original is not the transcendental subject whose a priori logic precedes all rhetoric but a stupidity that is bound by all sorts of improbable connections and dogmas. Philosophy has always imagined thought to be active and benevolent, able to synthesize itself in full awareness and contemplation of itself. Stupid thinking, by contrast, is a *passive synthesis*, for thought is made possible by a process that is "digestive"—not inert so much as *entirely free*, not even subjected to the laws of reason. According to Deleuze, the best literature (Flaubert, Baudelaire, Bloy) is haunted by the problem of stupidity:

> Everything becomes violence on this passive ground. Everything becomes attack on this digestive ground. Here the Sabbath of stupidity and malevolence takes place. Perhaps this is the origin of that melancholy which weighs upon the most beautiful human faces: the presentiment of a hideousness peculiar to the human face, of a rising tide of

stupidity, an evil deformity or a thought governed by madness. For
from the point of view of a philosophy of nature, madness arises at the
point at which the individual contemplates itself in this free ground—
and, as a result, stupidity in stupidity and cruelty in cruelty—to the
point that it can no longer stand itself. (*DR*, 152)

The attempt to tear thought away from the triteness of rhetoric always risks falling into banal indifference, some image of a present and
reliable good sense. Against the standard appeal to a subject who precedes the difference and chaos of this world, both Deleuze and Foucault cite a more radical transcendental program. There is no transcendental soul or subject who must be presupposed as the sublime
author or origin of the categories of thought. The categories or differences within which thought is immersed are *singular*: the consequence of mishaps, ad hoc connections, divergent passions, and unreliable attachments. Far from being "other" than categorical thinking,
art should be a "total immersion" in stupidity in order to uncover "the
sudden illumination of multiplicity itself":[6]

Thus we court danger in wanting to be freed from categories; no
sooner do we abandon their organizing principle than we face the
magma of stupidity. At a stroke we risk being surrounded not by a
marvelous multiplicity of differences, but by equivalences, ambigu-
ities, the "it all comes down to the same thing," a leveling uniformity,
and the thermodynamism of every miscarried effort. . . . Stupidity is
contemplated: sight penetrates its domain and becomes fascinated; it
carries one gently along and its action is mimed in the abandonment of
oneself; we support ourselves upon its amorphous fluidity; we await
the first leap of an imperceptible difference, and blankly, without fever,
we watch to see the glimmer of light return. Error demands rejection—
we can erase it; we accept stupidity—we see it, we repeat it, and
softly, we call for total immersion.[7]

Literature exposes stupidity by expressing a certain style or "distribution" of thought that is prior to the distinction between truth and

error and prior to the active synthesis of the subject. If we read Flaubert as simply ironic, then we would have to see his narrative voice as
other than the limits of his manifestly stupid characters. But the irony
would be more complex and more confronting if there were no point
outside the "boundless monotony" of *Bouvard and Pécuchet*.[8] Stupidity, for both Deleuze and Foucault, is not a manifest error that can be
corrected; it is the very shape or style of thought that cannot be contested and that is beyond argument or decision. When we confront the
"acategorical" thinking of *Bouvard and Pécuchet* we are brought up
against the impersonal difference or multiplicity from which thinking emerges. Flaubert's total immersion in the style of thought of his
characters provides an irony so complex that it is difficult to decide
whether the voice of the text is or is not one of absolute sincerity. By
repeating stupidity with such fidelity Flaubert does not so much delimit and subordinate the thought of his characters as disclose a transcendental stupidity that conditions all thinking and speaking. (Like
the German Romantics' definition of irony as "transcendental buffoonery," the confrontation with foolishness by Flaubert is not an act
of elevation so much as a recognition of the complicity of any ironic
height with the depths of stupidity from which it emerges.)

   The problem is even more intense in Flaubert's "A Simple Heart,"
a tale that describes the ingenuous Félicité's religious devotion to her
dead stuffed parrot. The third-person narration of the story describes
Félicité's life, not from her own point of view but from a distanced and
more enlightened position. The narration details how the "little circle
of her ideas grew narrower and narrower" and describes the prayers
she offers to her parrot as "idolatrous" (*TT*, 46). The story concludes
by judging the absurdity of Félicité's vision: "A blue cloud of incense
was wafted up into Félicité's room. She opened her nostrils wide and
breathed it in with a mystical, sensuous fervour. Then she closed her

eyes. Her lips smiled. Her heart-beats grew slower and slower, each a little fainter and gentler, like a fountain running dry, an echo fading away. And as she breathed her last, she thought she could see, in the opening heavens, a gigantic parrot hovering above her head" (*TT*, 56).

The literalism and sensualism of Félicité's belief could only be ironically delimited by a speaker who regarded such devotions as simple and idolatrous. But such a viewpoint would be blind to what makes its supposed superiority possible. It must assume the possibility of a proper or nonidolatrous use of religious representation. At one point the narration confidently explains that "to minds like hers the supernatural is a simple matter" (*TT*, 39). The narrative makes much of her stupidity, contrasting her with the other characters, who are aware of Félicité's incapacity to imagine the supernatural at a sufficiently abstract level. At one point Félicité is unable to understand why, when shown a map, she cannot see exactly where her nephew is living: "And Félicité—whose intelligence was so limited that she probably expected to see an actual portrait of her nephew—could not make out why he was laughing" (*TT*, 36). Who is speaking in this narrative voice? The story is recounted by a speaker who feels confidently distanced from the simple-mindedness of Félicité, one who can define her religiosity as "idolatrous" and her conception of the supernatural as limited. If we accept the point of view of the narration, then we recognize the irony of Félicité's credulity. We would know that the image of the parrot is ironic, for spirit cannot be represented in the form of a stuffed bird. But this recognizing viewpoint—the viewpoint that dismisses Félicité's simplicity in the same way that it delimits Bouvard and Pécuchet's stupidity—would require a distinction between the simplicity and literalism of the characters and the enlightened viewpoint of the narration. Ironizing Félicité's literalism, the narrative suggests that one might not be caught up in the stupidity of concrete images of spirit. But far from being clearly and recognizably distinct from the simplicity of the ironized characters, the voice of narration is itself open to irony precisely in its confidence of recognition. When the narrative refers to "minds like hers," to the limits of her intelligence, or to the idolatry of her belief, it speaks through a certain assurance of expanded comprehension. The irony lies not so much in the obviously false worldview of Félicité but in the very idea that one might confidently purify thought of all its simple and stupid images.

When Flaubert describes the artist as "infinite impassivity," he is not describing a God-like viewpoint that would oversee and judge the limits of worldly characters. It is just this belief—that one might confidently be other than the world of simple belief, passively elevated— that characterizes the bourgeois man of science and cynicism. The artist is not in an elevated position, judging his characters from on high; and the voice of the novelist is not a voice of judgment. The novel speaks *through* the world, faithfully expressing its simplest apprehensions, its stupidities, and its naïveté. The artist is nowhere only by being everywhere. The artist does not recognize the irony of a limited context by appealing to a higher context that "we" share, for there is no "we," no point of recognition, that lies outside the narration. The viewpoint of the artist could only be truly God-like by refusing such a location of recognition. This is a God not of detached judgment and moralism but of eternal and immanent production. If the artist, like God, is to be absolute, he cannot be other than what he creates, for an absolute can have nothing other than itself. There must be no difference between viewpoint and viewed. It is the simple and unmediated apprehension of Félicité that is, if anything, closer to the pure expression and nonplace of the artist than the self-assured bourgeois for whom she is an object of irony.

Irony and Immanence

The ontological, or perhaps theological, idea of "infinite impassivity" is given form not so much in the content or ideas of Flaubert's tale but in his style. (And this suggests that style and the way we apprehend being are closely allied if not mutually constitutive.) The impassivity can only be *infinite* if it is nothing other than itself. An *act* is necessarily finite, for it presupposes one who acts or an agent outside the action. A *speech act* also presupposes a distinction between the activity of saying and what is said. But in infinite impassivity there must be a thorough coincidence between actor and act, the one who speaks and what is spoken. There must not be a subject who then acts but pure act—which would perhaps be better expressed not as activity but as impassivity. And, as infinite, this would be expressed in a meticulous style: not a speaker who then expresses meaning but a saying that is nothing other than itself. The sentence must not be the activity *of* some subject, as though agent and action were separate and finite. Flaubert's "infinite impassivity" takes up an idea that was expressed explicitly by Spinoza but has had a number of Spinozist advocates who were also significant for the history of irony, including Friedrich Nietzsche, Herman Melville, and Gilles Deleuze. Spinoza's philosophy of immanence argued that if we took the idea of God seriously, then He could not be some point outside creation, for then He would not be infinite. He can be nothing other than creation itself. It is only a limited intellect and the impoverishment of our ordinary ways of speaking and thinking that lead us to imagine a God who then creates. For Spinoza, "whatsoever can be perceived by the infinite intellect as constituting the essence of substance, belongs altogether only to one substance: consequently, substance thinking and substance extended are one and the same substance, comprehended now through one attribute, now through the other."[9]

Friedrich Nietzsche took up this idea of immanence with his notion of eternal return: a creative whole that has no point of origin or
end, no external principle, and no identity other than the repetition
of difference. For the tradition of immanence that runs from Spinoza
through Nietzsche to Deleuze, life is not an object or being capable of
being judged or represented. Language is not a proposition about the
world; it is itself an event of a world that is nothing more than its becoming. It is only the reactive intellect that sets itself above or beyond
life, imagining a "higher world." For Nietzsche, there is no being that
grounds appearance and becoming, no soul or substrate that lies
behind worldly events. It is our peculiarly nihilistic or life-denying
grammar that leads us to posit some "x" behind appearances or some
subject who then acts.[10] Nietzsche is often invoked to refer to the irony
of postmodernism, where all we have are masks without real persons,
appearances without truths. But the real force of Nietzsche's argument lies in a certain critique of irony. Nietzsche is modern precisely
because he does more than insist on the inability of thought to achieve
some final truth; he challenges the way in which concepts such as
"truth" produce some ideal beyond life. The very notion of "appearance" or "mask" still suggests some real that lies out of reach, just as
irony suggests a "said" that is concealed behind the saying. But for
Nietzsche we have to rethink the whole concept of appearance; appearance *is* truth. There is appearing, and from this we (reactively)
posit some "x" that/who appears.[11] Like Spinoza, Nietzsche's philosophy affirms immanence. Speech is not some act of representation
added on to the world, speech itself is an event of the world's own force
and becoming.

Flaubert's free-indirect style is within this project of immanence
and is, therefore, both a fulfillment and a problematization of irony.
Traditional irony maintains a commitment to a truth beyond speech,
however fragile such a commitment may be. What differentiates tra-

ditional from modern irony is the immanence and innocence of the
latter. For modern irony, while speech may be inherently finite and
limited, this should not lead us to presuppose some infinite that lies
out of reach. For Nietzsche, the eternal is not some timeless and undifferentiated absolute but the repetition over and over again of specific, finite, and singular events of becoming. What is eternal—the
only Same—is the power of difference or becoming to do away with
any identity. A style or literature at one with immanence and eternal
return would, therefore, strive to do away with the illusion of a subject
who then speaks, a world that is then predicated. Subject and world
would be at one with their own becoming, nothing more than the
styles through which they are expressed.

We often think of writing as the limiting inscription of a real world
that is self-present and undifferentiated; speech and writing dissect
and atomize a world that is otherwise restful and identical. Flaubert's
modern irony or free-indirect style, like Derrida's later deconstruction, takes all the features that are usually ascribed to writing and extends them to being in general. Only writing or style can express an
"*infinite* impassivity" that has no being, substance, or foundation outside its own becoming. This becoming is not the active intention *of*
some agent; it is impassive because of its lack of any being or subject.
Writing is not the activity of some subject who encounters a world, nor
is it a system of differentiation added on to a passive world. For Flaubert great writing *is* the world. For this reason, writing cannot be
placed *within* a context; contexts and positions are effects of a far more
general writing.

If first-order irony delimits a speaker within a broader context of
recognition, the modern irony of Flaubert resists this site of recognition. The artist's point of view is reducible neither to the characters
nor to the voice of narration, and in this resistance of finite location
the artist is nowhere. Flaubert's "A Simple Heart" is, in keeping with

the tradition of irony, written in a tone of confident righteousness, for, as we are so often told, irony relies on an elevated "we" who can see the limits of certain styles of voice. But in "A Simple Heart" irony is as much the story's object as its mode of speech; Flaubert is ironizing irony, for the very style of voice that would be elevated above the simplicity of Félicité is made explicit when the point of view shifts to the other characters in the tale. The narrative voice that refers to those who judge Félicité uses the limited and unquestioned conventions of their own speech. Describing a retired solicitor, the following sentence is narrated without quotation marks: "He lived in dread of compromising his reputation, had a tremendous respect for the Bench, and laid claim to some knowledge of Latin" (*TT*, 23). In adopting the very language of propriety that would be spoken by a man who distinguishes himself from others by being able to "lay claim to some knowledge of Latin," Flaubert repeats the speech of everyday life in all its rigid moralism. The point of view of the artist is not, as in high realism, elevated above the text in an omniscient narration that would speak *about* the style of its characters. The style of the text is the style of the characters themselves, and the artist is nothing other than the pure repetition of the very manner of banality, style disclosed *as style*.

Ironic Possibility

To what extent is the Flaubertian ideal of infinite impassivity possible? Is the total immersion in style capable of freeing itself from the traditional moral elevation of irony? The very belief that one might be *nowhere*, that one might be in a position of open self-definition, and that one might not be thoroughly condemned to the banality of one's own conventions becomes the object of irony in James Joyce's repetition of Flaubert's description of the author. Stephen's celebration of the artist in *A Portrait of the Artist as a Young Man* is a classic descrip-

tion of the distanced point of view of the ironic author; at the same
time, it is ironized as yet one more naive belief in the possibility of an
invisible or transparent point of view: "The personality of the artist,
at first a cry or cadence or a mood and then a fluid and lambent narrative, finally refines itself out of existence, impersonalizes itself, so to
speak. The aesthetic image in the dramatic form is life purified in and
reprojected from the human imagination. The mystery of aesthetic
like that of material creation is accomplished. The artist, like the God
of creation, remains within or behind or beyond or above his handiwork, invisible, refined out of existence, indifferent, paring his fingernails" (*P*, 336).

How do we know that this passage is ironic? We might claim to
know that this use of imagery is ironic by appealing to a broader understanding of Joyce's novel and its position in literary history. But the
more forceful irony of *A Portrait of the Artist as a Young Man* precludes the confidence of knowledge. The novel constantly complicates
any position of elevation by describing its murkier origins, a technique that will be expanded in Joyce's *Ulysses*, in which the voices
of the church service and advertising slogans or bodily noises and
the language of romance fiction are intertwined to disclose a certain
rhythmic and stylistic complicity. In *A Portrait of the Artist as a Young
Man* it is not just Stephen's pompous aestheticism that is delimited
and described as emerging from the very depths of life. The novel is
dominated by images of mud, slime, scum, and grease alongside images of holy water, baptismal immersion, and purification; the overarching "image" is the ocean itself, in which purity and impurity or
height and depth are no longer strictly divided. Stephen's definition of
the artist can be explained as ironic through context. The rest of the
novel describes his continual failure to leave Dublin and conventional
religion. Far from being able to exist in a nonposition of impersonality,
the desire to remain "above life" is seen to be yet one more of Ste-

phen's affected and adopted styles. The novel itself plays with Stephen's own contextualizing, ironizing, and delimiting rhetorical ploys—all his attempts to comprehend and enclose the perspectives and sincerities of others. The standard incorporeal and supersensible metaphors of irony—of flight, elevation, and purification—are juxtaposed throughout the novel with images of slime, viscosity, grease, immobility, and an all too visceral corporeality. Long before Derrida formulated the notion of quasi-transcendentals, Joyce had demonstrated that any attempt to think some transcendental point above and beyond particularity would have to borrow its form or image from brute and contingent particulars. Throughout *A Portrait of the Artist as a Young Man* Stephen's attempts to place himself in a position of supersensible abstraction are described through the very images of the debased materiality he would deny. In the above passage Stephen has described the artist to be like God "paring his fingernails," but the image of nail filing is tied to a whole series of images in the novel—of ivory, whiteness, coldness, lavatory basins, and dampness—that confuse the spiritual with the sensual (*P*, 180). As a child, Stephen had already made sense of the world of religion through the limited images of concrete life and received phrases. His later appeal to a God-like abstraction that would set him apart from life draws from the very images he had earlier borrowed to make sense of figures of the Virgin Mary:

> *Tower of Ivory*, they used to say, *House of Gold*! How could a woman be a tower of ivory or a house of gold? Who was right then? And he remembered the evening in the infirmary in Clongowes, the dark waters, the light at the pierhead and the moan of sorrow from the people when they had heard.
>
>   Eileen had long white hands. One evening when playing tig she had

> put her hands over his eyes: long and white and thin and cold and soft.
> That was ivory: a cold white thing. That was the meaning of *Tower of Ivory*. (*P*, 199)

> And one day Boyle had said that an elephant had two tuskers instead
> of two tusks and that was why he was called Tusker Boyle but some
> fellows called him Lady Boyle because he was always at his nails, par-
> ing them.
>   Eileen had long thin cool white hands too because she was a girl.
> They were like ivory; only soft. That was the meaning of *Tower of Ivory*
> but protestants could not understand it and made fun of it. (*P*, 204)

Stephen's continual, inflated, and self-absorbed condemnation of convention and banality comes to appear as one more convention. But we can only read this conventionality of Stephen's position through the context of the novel as a whole. Stephen regards himself, like a God-like artist, to be "apart in every order" such that "all ages were as one to him," elevated in silence: "This was the call of life to his soul not the dull gross voice of the world of duties and despair, not the in-human voice that had called him to the pale service of the altar. An instant of wild flight had delivered him and the cry of triumph which his lips withheld cleft his brain" (*P*, 295, 301).

The very images of Stephen's elevation and distance recall the ear-lier tired phrases—*Tower of Ivory*—that had once appeared to him as so much noise. He sees his muse and image of flight with "thighs, fuller and soft-hued as ivory" (*P*, 305). Stephen's images of flight and eleva-tion have to borrow from the very sensualism he would hold in disdain. But the irony lies in the *essential* nature of this borrowing. The novel is a series of revelations—by Stephen—of the limits of one series of con-ventions and images after another. But the dream of God-like artistry is perhaps the most limited precisely in its declaration of complete elevation and limitlessness. What could be more clichéd than the language used to describe Stephen's liberation from convention? "His soul was swooning into some new world, fantastic, dim, uncertain as under sea, traversed by cloudy shapes and beings" (*P*, 304). Significantly, however, Joyce's novel does not offer a superior aesthetic against which Stephen's romantic striving can be measured. Stephen's aesthetic distancing from the parochialism of Dublin seems both necessary and impossible, for any distance attained is always *distance from* (and therefore never outside the context it delimits). Recognizing where one is and then locating oneself elsewhere depends upon misrecognition. To see oneself as ironically detached from a context requires a blindness to one's position at the limit of that context. *A Portrait of the Artist as a Young Man* is a tireless critique of ironic elevation, but it can only be read as such critique if we recognize a certain irony. Stephen's romantic striving to be freed from tradition and sensualism needs to be read as just that, *Romantic*. And this Romanticism is not detachable from a received language—of swooning, destiny, and the soul—and an investment in a certain type of female body (the birdlike muse figure that appears to him as an apparition of his own soul [*P*, 303]). The condition for Stephen's elevation is a blindness to the rigidity of the *images* of elevation. One achieves the height and recognition of irony through an unrecognized imaginary medium.

The Ironic Imperative

The power of *A Portrait of the Artist as a Young Man* lies in Joyce's demonstration that our most meaningful phrases and images—of the soul, religion, art, and revelation—appear at first as purely assumed or as mere background. As a child Stephen hears the refrain of "*Tower of Ivory*" as so much invasive noise. Nevertheless, taking part in the convention of these phrases and images demands that we see them as

more than assumptions. To adopt a convention one needs to see and
live it as more than merely conventional. Stephen can only come to
hear what these phrases mean if they are taken to be more than what
is merely circulated and repeated. The novel begins with the mere
sound of other voices but concludes with an ambition to fly above and
beyond all merely received tradition. In this regard Joyce's modern
irony sustains the critical force of Socratic irony. The rhetoric of soul
and the spirit only makes sense if it is more than rhetoric. But, as
Joyce's novel demonstrates, the necessary attempt to give some sense
to what we say is always contaminated by figures and phrases that are
borrowed, received, or assumed—somehow not fully "ours."

If it is the case that meaning is a question of convention and background assumption, then once this background is revealed *as assumed*
it often no longer appears to be ours. At the same time, it is not clear
where else "we" could be. From the complications of modern irony in
Flaubert and Joyce we might argue that irony is—contra Rorty—far
from being an accommodation to the limits of our language; it is,
rather, a ceaseless awareness of limitation. Now we might want to object, as Rorty does, to the second step of Socratic irony. We might agree
with the *question* of irony—we should always challenge our contexts—but disagree with the implied (Socratic) answer that if our
contexts or rhetoric cannot be grounded, then we need to find another
way of speaking. If our everyday usage and rhetoric cannot give us the
essence or ideal of justice, should we just assume that no such essence
exists and that justice *cannot* be justified? For Rorty, we ought to recognize that our ethical lexicon *is* just a lexicon and that it might be edifying to adopt a rhetoric in which terms like truth, representation, reality, and so on would not lead us into the deluded belief that our
vocabularies might be legitimated. The Sophist's ultimate bewilderment and defeat might then be avoided.

For Rorty, then, it is the delusion of "representation" that allows So-

cratic irony to succeed. Only if we think that there is some reality that
really corresponds to our propositions and concepts can we see the
Sophists' merely conventional definitions as inadequate. Searle, similarly, believes that it is only because literary critics have contracted an
unreasonably strict definition of concepts from Derrida that they cannot see that language is nothing more than its contextual use. This
suggests that we might remain within our language—as use, force,
and convention—without striving for justification. Only a metaphysical perversion of everyday speech would demand that we know what
we really mean. For Rorty and Searle, it is only because there are those
who feel that concepts must have some transcontextual meaning that
irony can generate some high ideal or "said" above what we say. Such
grandiose metaphysical gestures would depend upon an (illegitimate)
distinction between the Sophists who merely use the words of their
language game and the metaphysicians who refuse to reduce meaning to use and exchange. Socratic irony is made possible by what Rorty
would refer to as a "representationalist," "realist," or "metaphysical"
theory of meaning. Concepts such as justice, truth, wisdom, and so on
resist being defined according to everyday definitions, but it is still assumed by the "metaphysical" philosopher that something answering
to these concepts exists. What is at stake in Rorty's pragmatic intervention in philosophy is whether speech can be accepted as an ongoing
and open language game (a thoroughly nonhierarchical irony), or
whether the very act of speaking does not open a more troubling irony
as to just *who* is speaking and what is the force of what is being *said*.

If we wish to define irony within a theory of meaning we have to
understand what irony means, how it is understood, how it is recognized, and the context within which it operates as ironic. In the case of
the examples offered in the first chapter it is possible to explain some
second-order context that would enable the recognition of the utterance *as ironic*. Searle's indirect speech act is understood as indirect be-

cause of the circumstances in which it is uttered; Blake's moralisms might be recognized as ironic if "we" know better; while Socratic irony achieves its force because the Sophist himself concedes defeat. In many ways what makes irony recognizable in these instances is the possibility of attributing the speech act to a speaker, type of speaker, or position. The possibility of attribution is necessary if we are going to see irony as a specific *act*. The difficulty of attribution, alongside its necessity, is typical of the modernist irony of Flaubert. Like Socratic irony, Flaubert faithfully follows the language of received opinion to a kernel of incoherence, to a point where the speakers say more than they mean. On the one hand, Flaubert's style is positioned within a certain limited way of speaking; on the other hand, such limits extend beyond definite characters. Flaubert's *Madame Bovary*, for example, is written in a combination of the language of bourgeois, provincial moralism and late-nineteenth-century romance novels. Flaubert speaks this language in the third person in the form of description and therefore does not place quotation marks around the "quoted" style. Consider the following description of Emma Bovary from Emma's point of view and given in the hyperbolic and mawkish language of the fiction she reads:

> Only in her love did she suffer; through the thought of that she felt her soul escape from her as a wounded man in his last agony feels life flow out through his bleeding gashes.
>
> Night was falling. Some rooks flew overhead. All at once it seemed as if the air were bursting with little globes of fire, like bullets, flattening out as they exploded. Round and round they went and finally melted in the snow amid the branches of the trees. In the centre of each the face of Rodolphe appeared. They multiplied, clustered together, bored into her. Then everything vanished, and she saw the lights of the houses glimmering through the mist far away.
>
> And once again the deep hopelessness of her plight came back to her. Her lungs heaved as though they would burst.[12]

The irony of *Madame Bovary* is clear enough if we can identify the style of the narrative and attribute it to a specific way of speaking or point of view. But the style of Flaubert is marked by a characteristically modernist shifting point of view. And deciding just how modern Flaubert is will come down to a question of irony. Has he already anticipated the irony of Joyce's *Portrait of the Artist* such that *Madame Bovary* already displays the absurdity of believing one might transcend the banality of rhetoric? We might say, then, that the joke is on Joyce. He writes as though he were ironizing the Flaubertian ideal of the infinite artist, but he could only do so because he did not see that Flaubert was himself being ironic. We might also say that it is only possible to read this hyperirony into Flaubert after Joyce. But what does this tell us about literary history and self-recognition? Perhaps texts do not just follow each other in time, progressing to ever more refined elevations of irony. A modern text might make us question just how sincere all those high works of literature really were. (Imagine, Jorge Luis Borges suggests, reading *The Imitation of Christ* as written by Joyce, or reading *Don Quixote* as a twentieth-century novel.)[13] This would give us literature and irony as eternal return: the newness of literature would not lie in being different from its predecessor. The *whole* of literature is repeated with each new creation; a truly new work pulverizes the "context" of literature in general, forcing us to re-read every work anew. Irony is just this power to displace the limits of context and sincerity, such that we are no longer so sure that we really know what "we" meant. And this movement of temporal and ironic displacement can occur within a single work.

Consider an earlier passage from *Madame Bovary* in which one of Emma's lovers, Léon, has decided to quit the delusions of romance sentiment and empty language. We might say that he has adopted an ironic attitude to language; he now sees that beneath the rhetoric of passion there is nothing more than debris or, to use Rorty's language, that there is nothing beyond vocabulary:

> Léon had finally promised not to see Emma again. Now he was sorry he hadn't kept his word—seeing all the trouble and the gossip that the woman might still draw upon him; not to mention the banter he had to endure from his colleagues round the stove every morning. Furthermore, he was about to become chief clerk. It was time to be serious. Accordingly he was renouncing the flute, elevated sentiments, and the imagination. Every bourgeois in the ferment of his youth, if only for a day or minute, has believed himself capable of a grand passion, a high endeavour. Every run-of-the-mill seducer has dreamed of Eastern queens. Not a lawyer but carries within him the débris of a poet.[14]

The narrative is still written in the style and point of view of the character described. But is it ironic? Is the position or point of view limited? Are we inside or outside this way of seeing? In the case of Emma we can identify the received or assumed character of her language and way of seeing. Here, perhaps, we are less certain. Who speaks in the final phrase? Is this the way of speaking of an ironically delimited character, one who naively believes that by becoming a chief clerk he is no longer bourgeois but now serious? Or is the attitude to language and meaning here ironically enlightened? We would read the passage ironically if we felt some distance or difference from the voice of Léon. But we read it "straight" if we, like Léon, have the attitude that it is *Emma's* style alone that is received, otiose, jejune, and banal. We can read this as sincere if we are at one with Léon's "seriousness" or read it ironically if we concur with the final voice that judges him to possess nothing more than the mere debris of a poet. And at what point in this passage does the voice shift from Léon's own seriousness to the voice that judges him as laughably typical? It is narrative situations like this, where we cannot be sure whether this is or is not our context, that open the question of irony. If we cannot know for sure who is speaking, then we cannot know whether the utterance is one we ought to recognize as ours. Is what is said part of the second-order context of irony—the exclusive position of the ironic author and the ironically aware audience? Or is it a way of seeing, an ironically delimited style?

The Autonomy of Meaning

What this question of attribution does is demonstrate the uneasiness of accepting our ways of speaking as inherited, received, or assumed. For once we "recognize" that we might not know if we mean what is said or might not know whether what is said is *ours*, we are forced to ask about the way our language relates to the world. Once we cannot answer the question of who is speaking (is this "our" context?), then we also begin to wonder about our context *as* a context, as an *assumed* background. Irony is, therefore, the opening of a question of meaning. Is what is said *meant*? Or is what is said an ironic repetition of a way of speaking that does not know what it means? What irony frequently brings forth is that in order for something to mean, or be intended, it must be taken as more than just a received way of speaking.

According to Michael Dummett, "there is a general convention whereby the utterance of a sentence, except in special contexts, is understood as being carried out with the intention of uttering a true sentence."[15] The question that follows from Dummett's description of this convention is *how* we might recognize such a "special context," a context where what is said is *not* taken to be the utterance of a true sentence. The possible solutions, I want to suggest, cannot be sorted out *within* a theory of meaning; what we understand as a "special context" and the possibility of its recognition are determined by our theory of meaning. (There have been philosophers from Socrates to Derrida who regard all contexts as "special contexts": it is always *possible* to question just what we mean. And even everyday usage must appeal to concepts that cannot be easily reduced to context. But there are perhaps no fewer philosophers for whom such questioning contexts are extremely rare. Searle and Rorty, among others, insist that ordinary usage proceeds without Socratic questions, without the imperative to ground our concepts or question our sincerity.) We will read an utterance as an instance of irony if we do not recognize or assume what it assumes, if it is not our way of seeing the world, if it is not the way our language relates to the world. To take a way of speaking as an object of irony—to place it in a special context—is not to ask about its meaning but to ask how what is meant is being said. Is it another unquestioned commonplace, or is it intended as true? What counts as a true intention if all we have is a language that is never ours but always, to some extent, received or "quoted"?

And if we cannot be sure whether an utterance is ironic, then we are forced to ask ourselves about our context and assumptions and about our way of speaking. As Donald Davidson has argued, there is no linguistic sign or convention to signal sincerity: "But nothing is more obvious than that there cannot be a convention that signals sincerity." It follows, then, that "the plight of the actor is always with us. There is no known, agreed upon, publicly recognizable convention for making assertions."[16] Nor could there be such a sign or convention, for such a sign itself could always be quoted, used insincerely, or uttered ironically. The impossibility of such a sign is connected to Davidson's insistence on the *autonomy of meaning*. If something is *meant*, if an utterance is to be taken *as meaningful*, it must be more than a convention. The phrase "snow is white" has the same *meaning*, whether it is uttered in a stage play or a ski manual. The very possibility of a word's meaning is its ability to be used in more than one instance and more than one context; the meaning of a word must be the same whether it is used in quotation, dissimulation, or irony. Irony, then, cannot be a question of the meaning of what is said (nor could such meaning be determined by context). Irony, rather, follows from the problem of meaning's autonomy. When we read ironically we are not questioning the meaning of the sentence or phrase or of what is *said*; we raise a question about that *saying*. Is the speaker merely quoting, mentioning, or parodying what is said, or is there a sincere coincidence between saying and meaning?

To read ironically is to take an utterance as saying something other or more than what is meant (by the speaker) or understood (by the limited audience). Socrates' Sophists use the word "justice," but the meaning of justice already exceeds any account they can give of it. Blake's speakers use words like "pity" but do not understand that the very meaning of pity demands submission and resignation. The speaker of "The Little Black Boy" fails to realize that his definition of equality—we are all white really—actually signifies inequality. It is because language is meaningful, or capable of referring to a sense that is always more than any particular utterance, that we are haunted by the suspicion of irony. No meaningful word or phrase can be exhausted by a single use or context. Modernist irony, however, is directed to ways of speaking in which the autonomy of meaning— its necessary capacity for quotation and feigning and for exceeding the speaker's intent—becomes the object of irony itself. If all ways of speaking can be feigned and spoken insincerely, what constitutes an authentic way of speaking? What is it to mean what one says?

Can We Mean What We Say?

There are two possibilities. The first is that we accept all language as convention, as nothing more than the assumption of a way of seeing.

We accept that our point of view is *our* point of view. But is it possible, as Rorty suggests, to remain at this first level of irony? This would demand seeing our ways of speaking as received and contingent, as having no privileged relation to the world.

Irony, however, demonstrates the frustrating difficulty of this first solution. The very possibility of irony—that we see our context and assumptions *as assumptions*—opens the question of just what we mean and to what extent what we say *is ours*. If literary irony has typically been the description of a way of speaking as assumed, received, inherited, and limited, then it opens the possibility of another point of view, one that questions the *assumption* of context and raises the possibility that we might mean what we say. Irony, ironically, has encouraged just the sort of "metaphysical" or "realist" striving that Rorty demands ought to be eliminated from philosophy.

This brings me to the second possible answer as to how we recognize irony and how we know whether what is said is meant. Irony is a perpetual possibility of any speech act. Irony raises a question about the very style of our context. What happens when our context—after decades of Rorty-style philosophy—starts to appear as nothing more than style? Would we still call it *our* context? Could we say that we *mean* what we are saying? The very impossibility of knowing for certain whether what is being said is or is not ironic follows from the fact that, by virtue of the autonomy of meaning, we often feel what is said is *not ours*, but we have no other position or context to which we could appeal. As Wittgenstein, Derrida, Davidson, and any number of philosophers who have attacked "private meaning" argue, language is not something that *allows* meaning to be shared. Meaning is essentially autonomous, distinct from any private or singular act. In order to recognize an utterance as meaningful its terms must be *recognizable*—already given as ours. But for the very same reasons, the essentially already-given nature of language will mean that what we say can never be fully ours. It will always have a passive, received, and in-herited quality.

Irony is, then, the very potential of the *eternal monotony* of what we say, for in order to speak we must already borrow a voice from else-where, neither uniquely our own nor flowing from the present. Take the following example from *Madame Bovary* in which Emma's lover, Rodolphe, is seen as limited precisely because of his own "ironic" view of language, precisely because he is "a man of much experience":

> He had listened to so many speeches of this kind that they no longer made any impression on him. Emma was like any other mistress; and the charm of novelty, gradually slipping away like a garment, laid bare the eternal monotony of passion, whose forms and phrases are forever the same. Any difference of feeling underlying a similarity in the words es-caped the notice of that man of much experience. Because wanton or mercenary lips had murmured like phrases in his ear, he had but scant belief in the sincerity of these. High-flown language concealing tepid af-fection must be discounted, thought he: as though the full heart may not sometimes overflow in the emptiest metaphors, since no one can ever give the exact measure of his needs, his thoughts or his sorrows, and hu-man speech is like a cracked kettle on which we strum out tunes to make a bear dance, when we would move the stars to pity.[17]

The final sentences of this passage shift from the ironized point of view of the character to that of the narrator. But can any reader feel confident that what is said is being meant or that the meaning is what is really being said? Is the final "position"—that an ironic attitude to meaning naively assumes that all we have is our empty vocabulary—being uttered seriously? Or is Flaubert speaking ironically? Is the idea of a wordless passion that would move the stars to pity a naive belief in some prelinguistic point of view? Or is Rodolphe's rather Rortyan irony seen as an impoverished, passionless, and empty view of lan-guage? It is in this undecidable character of irony that we realize that irony is not only multilayered and therefore contextually insecure; irony also detaches the phrase from the speaker's position only to ask the question of position more rigorously. Is the speaker speaking in a genuine case of use? Is the speaker merely "mentioning" what is said? Is what the speaker genuinely says capable of being read as a mention, as yet one more banal repetition of received phrases (despite its serious intent)? Reading irony is a matter of determining the possible positions opened up by an utterance and the subsequent question of who is speaking.

The levels or positions of irony might, therefore, be described as follows.

1 First order: the debunking and parodying of received ideas and opinions unaware of their conventionality (for example, the description of Emma through the language of tawdry romance-speak or Blake's repetition of eighteenth-century moralism). Here we see that "Who Speaks?" can be clearly answered by attributing the phrase to a limited context or way of seeing.

2 Second order: the debunking of the first-order ironist who believes he can situate himself outside convention and assumptions (for example, Léon, who sees his rejection of Emma's rhetoric as the height of mature seriousness but who still has a thoroughly bourgeois way of seeing, or take, for example, the narrator of "A Simple Heart," who confidently believes that Félicité's simplicity and idolatry can be securely contained). Here the "distance" from received ideas and the banality of ordinary language is itself seen as an assumed style.

3 The final (yet interminable) level of irony parodies the very idea that we might understand ourselves ironically. Any elevated viewpoint that regards language as mere convention or assumption suggests a certain freedom or autonomy in relation to our assumptions.

(In the case of Rodolphe, the belief that language is always empty ignores the inevitable commitment of our language.) What is ironized is the self-confidence of any final ironic enlightenment, for such enlightenment suggests, to use Rorty's way of speaking, that we might inhabit a language game with a sense of its contingency and conventionality. It suggests that we *assume* our background in the way that we assume a costume or style and that such assumptions could equally well be discarded.

An irony lies in the very belief that we might accept what we say as mere convention and assumption and that we might not be disturbed by its status as assumption. Most of our background assumptions, conventions, and contexts—including those of truth, self-definition, and ethics—only work or are assumed by being seen as more than assumptions. Irony is in this sense parasitic. Irony does not just show that our ways of speaking and seeing are conventional and assumed; it shows that once they are recognized as assumed they no longer seem to be "ours." Once they are seen as conventional they seem to lose their conventional force. Irony shows that there is no position outside our ways of speaking at the same time that our ways of speaking seem to demand just such a position.

In conclusion, then, we can see that Rorty's explanation of irony (as self-definition and the recognition of our own contingent language game) is undermined by the equivocation of voice in irony itself. Irony often reveals that our perspective, point of view, way of seeing, or position is not our own. It demonstrates the opacity of our own perspective and the fact that our capacity for self-definition is neither a question of definition nor fully determined by a self. In contrast to the many examples of simple irony given in linguistic analysis, where it is clear who is speaking, complex irony removes any specific quotation marks from an utterance. Irony places the possibility of quotation over all our speech. This possibility, however, is not an accident added on to an otherwise owned language. Irony—the possibility that what we say might be read for what it *means* rather than what *we* say—is the very possibility of meaning. To speak a language is already to be other than ourselves; it is a demonstration that *what is* and *what we say* are always more than our perspective.

It is in this regard that irony opens the question of meaning. If the possibility of quotation haunts all we say, then our utterances are never fully determined by context. How we mean what we say and the position or context given by what we say can always be questioned by an ironic "step back" from our background. By questioning what we say, irony questions *where we are* (our position) and (as a consequence) *who we are*. The idea of meaning—that what we say is a communication, extension, explication, or expression of what we intend—is disrupted or torn apart by the repetition of irony. The possibility of the feigned, quoted, or dissimulated repetition of the speech acts of our own context was, early on, recognized by Searle in *Speech Acts*. Existing without commitment or sincerity, he argues, would be much like adopting an anthropological point of view: "Of course, you can speak in *oratio obliqua*, and thus avoid the commitments of speaking straight out. You can even employ the forms of speech for speaking normally and still be speaking in disguised *oratio obliqua*, or what you called the detached anthropological sense. But notice that this is really quite irrelevant and does not show that there are different senses of the words involved, or that the original statement was a concealed evaluation."[18]

Of course, anthropological detachment *is* quite irrelevant if we are sure that it is not the point of view *we* are adopting and that this point of view can be contained within what Searle refers to as "certain contexts."[19] But in the final case of modern irony that follows it is precisely point of view that is in question, and it is the questionable nature of point of view that precludes the determination of context. Consider the progressive (and progressively unclear) passage of irony in James Joyce's short story "The Dead."

The story opens with a classic instance of free-indirect style: "Lily, the caretaker's daughter, was literally run off her feet."[20] The way of deciding irony in literary criticism is usually to ask who is speaking. Here, as elsewhere in *Dubliners*, we can recognize the irony because of a misuse of language. One cannot be *literally* run off one's feet. Who is speaking? As elsewhere in *Dubliners* the language is that of inarticulate, limited, and parochial Dublin; it is the language of received ideas and unquestioned moralism.[21] The peculiarity of "The Dead," however, lies in its increasing and indeterminate layering of irony. The central character of the story is a writer and freethinker who adopts a superior point of view in relation to what he sees as Ireland's confinement within nostalgia and sentimentalism. Gabriel is the sort of figure who would clearly recognize the irony or limitation in the way of speaking in the previous *Dubliners* stories. But the position of ironic contempt adopted by Gabriel is itself ironized. His point of view depends upon a separation between his own way of seeing and the limited and nostalgic provincialism of Dublin. The first irony of the story occurs when his sophisticated or elevated perspective is given as not so separate after all. His own point of view is described in the patronizing, overwritten, sentimentalist rhetoric of intellectual superiority, of someone who has read too much late-nineteenth-century literary prose. Consider the following description of his wife—not in quotation marks: "She was walking on before him so lightly and so erect that he longed to run after her noiselessly, catch her by the shoulders and say something foolish and affectionate into her ear. She seemed to him so frail that he longed to defend her against something and then to be alone with her. Moments of their secret life together burst like stars upon his memory."[22]

The irony of this passage can only be recognized by seeing the specific style or mannered tone of Gabriel's way of seeing. Caught within his linguistic reverie, Gabriel fails to realize that his wife, as he describes her, is dreaming of a former lover. This would not be a problem for a context account of irony; we can still identify the context and style of Gabriel's rhetoric. The problem begins to emerge as we move further into the story. Gabriel himself comes to see the irony of his position: "A shameful consciousness of his own person assailed him. He saw himself as a ludicrous figure, acting as a pennyboy for his aunts, a nervous, well-meaning sentimentalist, orating to vulgarians and idealizing his own clownish lusts, the pitiable fatuous fellow he had caught a glimpse of in the mirror."[23]

Gabriel recognizes the conventional and rhetorical nature of his character. The above passage, although narrated from the third person, adopts Gabriel's point of view, and so the critique of Gabriel's empty oratory is a self-critique. But the narration of the story then moves to what is possibly another voice. However, it is not clear who is speaking. Gabriel's own position is framed; he is no longer seen as separate from Ireland's past or from those around him. He recognizes his own way of seeing as included within the Dublin he thought he viewed from an elevated perspective. But it is not clear whether the voice of the following sentences belongs to Gabriel or some third-person narrator. It becomes impossible to differentiate what Gabriel recognizes as his own context from what the narrative voice ironically delimits as merely contextual. What is even less secure is where the third-person narration of Gabriel's position is located. The narration describes the impossibility of a distance from one's past and conventions, but it does so in the language of convention; the final narrative voice is also highly stylized and literary, and it signals its own rhetorical excess through the use of the word "swooned."

His soul had approached that region where dwell the vast hosts of the
dead. He was conscious of, but could not apprehend, their wayward
and flickering existence. His own identity was fading out into a grey
impalpable world: the solid world itself, which these dead had one
time reared and lived in, was dissolving and dwindling.

. . . Yes, the newspapers were right: snow was general all over Ireland. . . . It lay thickly drifted on the crooked crosses and headstones, on
the spears of the little gate, on the barren thorns. His soul swooned as he
heard the snow falling faintly through the universe and faintly falling, like
the descent of their last end, upon all the living and the dead.[24]

Gabriel loses his world, his sense of locatedness, and the security of
his conventions. His assumed background, to use Searle's language,
seems to be just that: *assumed*. What results is not Rorty's cosy sense of
contingency and self-definition but the impossibility of knowing just
what our position is. The voice that deflates Gabriel's grandeur is itself, we might suspect, ironic. But how would we *know*? If we could
adopt a separate or "elevated" point of view, we might see the conclusion of "The Dead" as one more instance of a style unaware of its thorough conventionality. But if we *recognized* the irony in this way and
contextualized the final paragraph, where would we stand? In a nonironic position, free of the naïveté of believing in our own style?
Wouldn't that be ironic? As Searle had argued in *Speech Acts*, "the
price of a really consistent application of the 'detached anthropological standpoint' would be an end to all validity and entailment."[25]

By asking who is speaking and then rendering the answer uncertain, irony demonstrates that prior to any intention there is the space
of position or point of view. In order to speak or intend one must be
given a style or possible position. But as a *speaking* position, a position
that departs from or expresses itself, this point of view or perspective
is neither definitively localized nor absolutely open. We must speak—
locate ourselves in a language that is not fully ours—and recognize

that who we are is nothing other than this sense of location. All irony's metaphors of height, elevation, transcendence, and seeing are subordinate to a *positing* that can be neither reduced to a linguistic metaphor nor comprehended in any literal sense. We can only speak of the height or elevation of irony through figures of speech, but we can only think the concept of a figure of speech through metaphors of spatial distance and difference. In *saying* that irony is "saying one thing and meaning another," we use a certain way of speaking that divides the speaking self from the spoken word. It is this gap between saying and said that gives us a sense that "behind" any utterance there is one who *speaks*. But these very spatial metaphors—a "gap" between saying and "said," a meaning "behind" what is said, a point of view that "sees" what we really want to say, or the idea that we "inhabit" language as a "background"—cannot just be seen as figures *we use* to express what *we mean*, for the very idea of meaning is possible only through these figures. Can it be said that there would be any sense of a "we" or a "user" of language without these spatializing tropes? It is not just irony but the very notion of speech in general—as the expression of one who precedes and governs meaning—that relies on a gap or distance between what is said and the one who speaks.

This is why irony and the history of Western thought are, according to Gilles Deleuze, governed by the question of "Who speaks?" (*LS*, 107). And it is also why irony has been theorized alongside a history of meditations on the soul. It is the soul that precedes the action or event. It is the depth of speech, or the intimation of meaning, that almost inevitably posits an expressing soul. The specific act or performance of irony within a context of speech draws attention, at least for some of the speakers, to the distance between the speaking subject and the "said" that makes all meaning possible, the autonomy of meaning. In order for a sign to *mean* it must be taken as more than itself; it must be taken as the sign *of* some sense, the signifier *of* some

signified, or the expression *of* some subject. Language cannot just be
the free exchange of tokens, for language can only be meaningful if
those tokens are taken as the expressions of some meaning for which
exchange takes place. Any specific or singular token can signify, not
just if it stands in for some presence but also only if we have some sense
of language in general, a notion of one who speaks, of human signification, or of the depth of meaning: "only language as the pure potenti-
ality to signify, withdrawing itself from every concrete instance of
speech, divides the linguistic from the nonlinguistic and allows for the
opening of areas of meaningful speech ... To speak [*dire*] is, in this
sense, always to 'speak the law.' *Ius dicere.*"[26] "We" can have a sense of
who "we" are only through the collective context of speech; but speech
is only possible with the notion of a "we" to be expressed, a law that
allows what we say to be taken as a sign of what we mean.

In irony a specific act of speech works to highlight this gap that enables speaking in general. This is the necessary gap between the law-
ful language that we speak and the specificity or singularity of the one
who is speaking. In irony it is always possible to question whether
what the subject is saying is what is meant. We have no sense of this
"meant" without the saying, and yet the saying never exhausts meaning. Irony—that way of speaking that draws attention to speaking—
both draws speech to its point of view and discloses any point of view
as effected from the speaking system. It is because the language we
speak *is a language* that there is always a dimension in any speech act
that is not the speaker's own. At the same time, the only sense we have
of the speaker is given through the speech act. Irony is, at once, the
impossibility of *self*-definition as well as the unavoidability of the self
as position. To define ourselves we must speak through a system that
would be recognized by others; we must therefore be positioned
within a context. Irony, in keeping with the Socratic tradition, is a performance of two sides of the philosophical question: the responsibility

of our inevitable locatedness within a context and the inadequacy of context to answer our deepest questions.

This can be seen in one final example of irony, from Searle's "Literary Theory and Its Discontents": "I will argue that if you get certain fundamental principles and distinctions about language right, then many of the issues in literary theory that look terrible deep, profound and mysterious have rather simple and clear solutions."[27]

Just as Socrates' irony depends upon the Sophists' belief that the question of justice can be solved by offering an everyday definition, so a certain irony might lie in the claim that sorting out the distinction between use and mention or type and token will solve our "profound" problems of meaning and interpretation. If we cannot work out whether what is being said is a use or a mention, and if we, accordingly, do not believe that the entire field of literary criticism can be sorted out by way of Searle's "half a dozen principles," then we might think that there is something absurd, limited, or ironic about what Searle is saying. We might also feel the same way about Searle's guidance regarding these principles: "Perhaps we can refute all of them." "But I also have to tell you in advance that there are certain rules of the investigation."[28] Who is the "you" here? In order that what Searle *says* be what Searle *means*, Searle will also have to determine, in advance, the position of his audience. Is this at all certain or determined when what he says is being distributed in the journal *New Literary History*? After all, Searle is pointing out that it is only from a position of literary criticism and not philosophical "principles" that we might have been led astray by bad philosophical arguments such as those of Derrida. Searle appeals, then, to a literary audience capable of recognizing itself as *merely* literary when confronted with a clear explanation from a philosopher. Isn't there a certain irony here?

3

Socrates and the Soul of Philosophy

Socratic Irony

The foregoing chapters have already raised the possibility that irony is more than an event within a language game; it is also a position that challenges the idea that language can be reduced to a game. Throughout the history of irony and the meditation on the Western tradition of irony, Plato's Socrates has operated as an ironic inkblot test: we read into Socrates just what we see to be the limits of the Western tradition. It is for this reason that I have decided to consider Socrates after a reflection on modern irony, for the very decision as to the meaning of the figure of Socrates will depend upon our own commitments.

Socrates functions either as a nostalgic model of philosophy as engaged praxis—before we fell into merely cognitive or theoretical arguments—or as the beginning of philosophical slavishness, for it is with the Socratic method that we become subjected to "truth." Kierkegaard explored Socrates against Hegel in order to argue that irony could free us from the strictness of conceptual truth. Rorty, by contrast, suggests that it is the Socratic style of irony, which insists on the ineffability of certain concepts, that leads us into metaphysical illusion. Of course, this is not an accidental disagreement. Socratic irony only works if it opens the question of the *possible* reality of concepts; it ceases to be ironic if it offers clear and unquestioned definitions. The problem in reading Socrates lies in the force of the irony: does the Socratic question lead us to a higher order of truth beyond definition, or does it demand a more humble acceptance of what counts as a definition?

Socratic irony is more than just a figure of speech. It is an art of the soul or existence, a mode of personality that is elevated through a commitment to concepts. When Socrates encounters the Sophists (who believe that moral concepts mean nothing more than what we want them to mean), the dispute centers (or decenters) on the very nature of moral meaning. When Socrates asks for the definition of a concept, such as justice, the Sophists have no shortage of definitions, definitions they have received from others or definitions that seem to suit their present purposes. And when Socrates responds he, too, seems to appeal to nothing more than the way in which our concepts are used. When Thrasymachus argues that justice is the advantage of the stronger, Socrates does not counter this with another definition. He merely extends what Thrasymachus has already said: if you *say* that justice is the advantage of the stronger, would you also *say* that those in power who use their advantage to act (unwittingly) against their own interests are still acting justly? If justice is paying back what you owe, would you say that returning a weapon to a deranged man is an act of justice? Can you really mean what you have just said? "So tell me, Thrasymachus, was this what you intended to say, that the just is the advantage of the superior as it appears to the superior whether it really is or not? Are we to say this was your meaning?"[1] Socrates tries to show that our use of a concept, or what we say, is never exhausted by what we (think we) mean.

The specificity of Socratic irony, according to Gregory Vlastos, lies in a change of meaning to the term *eirōnia*. And it is this shift that constitutes the Socratic "contribution to the sensibility of Western Europe" (*S*, 43). Originally used to signal deception or willful misleading, Socrates redefines irony by "creating something new for it to mean: a new form of life" (*S*, 29). Irony is not defined or explicitly theorized by Socrates but is *performed* through the production of "a previously unknown, unimagined type of personality" (*S*, 29). According to Vlastos, the new character of irony is summed up by Quintilian, for whom irony is saying "something contrary to what is to be understood" (*S*, 21). Vlastos argues that irony marks a difference between what would be known or understood in an utterance and another meaning that is "true" in a moral or ethical sense. Quintilian's definition implies not only a doubleness of meaning, a distinction between saying and understanding, it also suggests a clear hierarchization. The ironist says something that is both "to be understood" (sentence meaning) but enables this understanding to be contrasted with what she is really *saying* (speaker's meaning). If she *says* something other than what is understood, she must rely on a standard understanding (how "we" normally understand such an utterance), and then she must be able to say something else.

Not surprisingly, then, it is through this separation that irony is often defined as a position or personality. And it is perhaps also not surprising that this position or personality (from Cicero to Kierkegaard and Deleuze) is described in terms of depth, height, distance, and hierarchy. The ironist is superior. This is what makes Socratic irony (for Vlastos) an instance of "complex irony"; it is not just deceit or dissimulation but relies upon a different point of view: "In 'complex' irony what is said both is and isn't what is meant: its surface content is meant to be true in one sense, false in another" (*S*, 31). According to Vlastos, this play of truth values explains the irony of Socratic ignorance. Socrates is, at one level, speaking truthfully when he claims to know "nothing." Unlike the Sophists, he has no easy definition of virtue, justice, the soul, or truth, and in this sense his claim to ignorance is true. But there is a higher knowledge or truth that renders Socrates' claim to ignorance false, or ironic. Socrates is only ignorant if we accept the Sophists' own confidence in definitions as knowledge, for Socrates cannot offer such definitions. In this sense Socrates indeed knows "nothing." The function of irony, however, is not to convey everyday knowledge but to open a path to a "higher" truth. Such a mode of truth would not be that of definitions or knowledge but the sort of wisdom that begins precisely from knowing nothing, from questioning without appeal to an already given convention or context. Such a path to truth would be ethical, having more to do with forming oneself as a being who questions rather than the possessor of so many facts. Moral truth is unique precisely because its way of being known is crucial to what is known. There is a specific form or mode of moral truth quite distinct from content. Moral truth cannot be given as a statement, definition, or conveyed meaning; it must be discovered for itself. And the necessity of this discovery can be realized only through self-transformation. It is the *performance* of Socratic irony that enables the interlocutor to perceive his own limits, his own self-deceit. If the interlocutor is initially deceived by Socrates, if he believes Socrates to be ignorant, then it is because he is deceived first of all by himself. The Sophist believes all too readily in a knowledge gained through received opinions and clever definitions. In order to commence the path to moral knowledge the Sophist must challenge himself, not receive another opinion. The character of the truth to which Socratic irony leads would be corrupted if it were imposed or forced or stated in the form of a proposition.

Socratic irony, according to Vlastos, is therefore also irreducibly connected to *erōs* as the path to self-formation. The aim of the dialogues is truth, but the character of this truth depends upon a certain type of soul and its position in relation to everyday experience. Irony is part of an ethics of dialogue and assumes a form of moral knowledge that can only be achieved through a care for one's soul and the soul of the other. Irony, therefore, is saying one thing and meaning another within a quite specific economy of truth, an economy that is determined according to one's position in relation to worldly experience. This is quite different from the simple contextual shift described by Searle with the example of "the window is open." The context in which irony is generated does not just use a figural or nonstandard meaning; it does not rely upon or institute a clear distinction between speaker meaning and sentence meaning. Nor is it akin to Rorty's thorough recognition of linguistic contingency. Socratic ignorance is a refusal of clarity and self-evidence, a refusal of the recognition that "we" all know what "we" mean. The Socratic ironist does not accept *what is*—either rhetoric or things—as exhaustive or immediately given but demands an account of *how we understand or know what is.* Irony is a "step back" from everyday life, a questioning of how the everyday organizes itself. For Vlastos, the ironist's interlocutor can only see the deeper truth of the ironic statement through the development of his own moral autonomy (*S*, 44.), a position achieved through a distancing from accepted or complacent opinions. There is a clear distinction, then, between the dynamic and autonomously achieved truth of the ethical self and the true propositions of everyday life.

This play in truth values can work in two directions. Consider the proposition: (a) "Socrates is not a teacher." This statement is true in that the Socratic method is not one in which moral truths are just given. It is true in an everyday sense. But an irony lies in a perspective from which this statement is also false. Socratic method is a way of bringing the speaker to justified true belief, and in this sense Socrates' disavowal of knowledge and teaching is false. So (a) is true in the everyday sense but false once we become aware of the special mode of moral knowledge and teaching. A slightly different statement—(b) "Socrates has no knowledge"—is quite false in an everyday sense, and his interlocutors constantly express their frustration that Socrates withholds his own opinion. When Socrates defers to the Sophist's superior wisdom he is being *simply* ironic, as if he were saying, "Of course, Thrasymachus, *you* know what justice means." The Sophist knows that Socrates is pretending his ignorance only to lead the Sophist to the point of self-incrimination. The claim that Socrates has no knowledge is clearly false. However, from the perspective of moral knowledge and its unique form, Socrates is truly wise, and this wisdom lies in *not* knowing. So (b) is true once we consider the peculiar character of moral truth, which is not knowledge, and its relation to the soul. It is quite true, from the perspective of moral autonomy, that the Socratic position is not one of knowledge. It is the very character of moral wisdom to be other than knowledge, and this distance from knowledge, or *doxa,* cannot be given but only performed through irony. This is why, in one ironic sense, it is true that Socrates is a teacher: not one who conveys knowledge but one whose very form of life teaches us our own autonomy.

Socratic irony, therefore, inaugurates a form of life or personality. However, it is not just any form of life but one deeply committed to moral autonomy and truth. According to Vlastos, irony is the saying of one thing that is understood as false in the everyday sense but that is true from a moral perspective (*S,* 32), or it is understood as true in an everyday sense but false from the position or perspective of the purified, philosophically trained soul. Socratic irony, for Vlastos, is a question of distinctly different meanings and the truth of those meanings. Furthermore, the distribution of truth values is determined by the speaker's *position*: whether she is within or above everyday meaning. The true meaning of the moral perspective is recognized only when one can see beyond the sense of everyday understanding. Irony takes place here in a moral hierarchy that is also an epistemological hierarchy. It is only with a particular form of life—the Socratic path of moral autonomy—that we can posit another meaning or truth to the ironic utterance. Irony and the truth of irony depend upon a performance and dramatic interplay of voices, positions, and perspectives. But all this drama and interplay has a governing *telos*: truth.

Dialogue and Life

To a certain extent, Vlastos's reading of Socratic irony resembles that of Pierre Hadot, for whom it is not the *content* of the dialogues that is important so much as the art of dialogue itself as a way of life. The philosopher is defined in opposition to everyday life, but for Hadot this opposition is one of perpetual conflict rather than a definitive break (*WL*, 56). There is no distinct truth or moral autonomy to be achieved through dialogue. There is no moral truth other than the dynamic form of dialogue. In this sense, the philosopher's position is *atopos*: not located or positioned at all. He is in love with a wisdom that is beyond the human (*WL*, 57). He is placed beyond any position within the world. However, this love of wisdom, which takes the philosopher beyond the human world, nevertheless begins from within the world:

> For such a man, daily life, as it is organized and lived by other men, must necessarily appear abnormal, like a state of madness, unconsciousness, and ignorance of reality. And nonetheless he must live this

life every day, in this world in which he feels himself a stranger and in
which others perceive him to be one as well. And it is precisely in this
daily life that he must seek to attain that way of life which is utterly for-
eign to the everyday world. The result is a perpetual conflict between
the philosopher's effort to see things as they are from the standpoint
of universal nature and the conventional vision of things underlying human society, a conflict between the life one should live and the cus-
toms and conventions of daily life. (*WL*, 58)

Whereas both Hadot and Vlastos argue that the "truth" of a Socratic exchange is not just some content that might be given in another
form, Hadot's reading emphasizes that the dialogues themselves are
an art of self-formation. The form itself *is* the content; there is no
truth other than the form. For Vlastos, there is a distinct play between
true and false ways of seeing, and it is precisely the function of irony
to illuminate the distinction between the two. Hadot's reading, on the
other hand, does not depend on the recognition of a second (ironic)
sense or meaning in the dialogues but on the temporal exchange of dialogue itself (*WL*, 63). In fact, the point of dialogic irony for Hadot is
missed by modern readings, with their focus on truth. We might say
that for Vlastos the Socratic saying has a truth that can only be decided
when we consider the moral "said" or meaning. For Hadot, the ethics
of dialogues resides at the level of saying alone, and it is only our modern sensibility that posits truth as the *telos* of the dialogues.

For Hadot, not only were the dialogues originally exercises in argu-
mentative method, but these exercises were "therapeutic." The cura-
tive art of philosophy lay not in its revelation of truth in general but in
the act of dialogue as a form of life that directed focus away from the
passions: "For the point is not to set forth a doctrine, but rather to
guide the interlocutor towards a determinate mental attitude" (*WL*,
91). The position of Socrates is not characterized by a separate *sense* or
meaning that can then be accorded a truth value; rather, it is the *posi-*

tion itself that is ethical. And this "position" is essentially mobile and in perpetual self-creation. While the dialogue depends upon a desire for the truth of the *logos*, it is the path, rather than the object, of dialogue that is important. And this path is nothing other than a certain distancing from *life*. This is what connects the dialogues to death. One no longer speaks in order to achieve some external end; speaking takes place for its own sake in a present that is liberated from the demands of desire and outcomes. The dialogues are a meditative focus on the pure present, and they take us away from the desiring time of everyday life (*WL*, 84–85), for desire is futural and essentially oriented to what is *not* given. In this taming of desire the dialogues are also exercises in a loss of self, a preparation for death. For Hadot, "This is nothing other than *the* fundamental philosophical choice" (*WL*, 94). The ethic of philosophy, through the exercise of dialogue, is defined against everyday life and against all the desires that locate the self within the world. In this sense, "to be a philosopher implies a rupture with what the skeptics called *bios*, that is, daily life" (*WL*, 56).

While Vlastos locates Socratic irony in a truth value (or other meaning), Hadot suggests that *the* ethic of philosophy is a distanced attitude toward any meaning. The philosopher recognizes the futility of any worldly value and in so doing *produces herself as a philosopher in a turn away from the human.* Philosophy is a "point of view" constituted in opposition to the everyday: "For Plato, training for death is a spiritual exercise which consists in changing one's point of view. . . . this constitutes a conversion (*metastrophe*) brought about with the totality of the soul. From the perspective of pure thought, things which are 'human, all too human' seem awfully puny" (*WL*, 96). This purely philosophical form of ethics is defined as a negation of content and an *atopic* point of view. This is where Hadot's reading differs most from Vlastos, for it is not *another* meaning or position that the philosopher adopts but a critique of worldly position as such. Like Vlastos,

Hadot regards Socratic irony as crucial to "Western consciousness" (*WL*, 150). But for Hadot, Socrates does not provide a position or truth value so much as a certain absence; he is a mask or "split" figure. The Socratic mask uses rhetoric to show its limit (*WL*, 155, 163). In adopting the discourse of his opponent Socrates submits to the path of discourse only to reveal that language *can only be a mask or position* against which the "existence" of the philosopher is defined. Irony is a revelation through a mask or position. It demonstrates that *existence*—that which separates a philosopher from mere life—lies beyond any identified position. The philosopher does not *have* a position but explores the openness, creation, and self-production of position taking. Irony is rendered possible by adopting the mask of language *as a mask*:

> Here we come upon one of the most profound reasons for Socratic irony: direct language is not adequate for communicating the experience of existing, the authentic consciousness of being, the seriousness of life as we live it, or the solitude of decision making. To speak is to be doubly condemned to banality. In the first place, there can be no direct communication of existential experience, and in this sense, every speech act is "banal." Secondly, however, it is this same banality which, in the form of irony, can make indirect communication possible. (*WL*, 156)

Only with a sense of language's inevitable *banality* can the ironist emerge in his authentic distance from any identified position. So if irony is, to follow Rorty, an acceptance that there is no higher truth or justification for language to attain, this does not mean that we cannot practice a philosophy that is at odds with language. We would accept the inevitably limited nature of all speaking, abandoning the "higher" truths that are sought by those such as Vlastos. But we would nevertheless have elevated ourselves above life and language, not in the position or meaning of truth but in the nonidentity of the philosophic personality. Speaking authentically in dialogue does not entail expressing or arriving at one's position; authentic dialogue is the continual transformation of position. For Hadot, the use of the Socratic mask and the focus on the present in the dialogic art disrupt the possibility of the philosopher's sustained identity. This is what links the ethic of philosophy to death and the retreat from time.

The difference between Vlastos's and Hadot's readings of the ethic of dialogue tells us something about the possibility of irony. If irony were another sense or meaning above and beyond everyday sense as well as a hierarchization of sense, then it would depend upon locating a second meaning elsewhere. Irony, theorized as position or personality, renders this other sense possible through a difference of *speaker's point of view.* The ironist who lives the moral life sees the true meaning of what we say. The concepts of justice, love, beauty, and the soul cannot be proffered through simple propositions but demand a higher way of seeing and speaking. Irony is enabled by recognizing the moral point of view and the autonomy of moral truth, a truth that cannot be received through statements and definitions but must be discovered. On the other hand, as in Hadot, irony is also regarded as a certain absence or impossibility of position that can only be performed but never recognized or identified. It is the dramatic persona, rather than the proposition, that provides the philosopher with a voice. It is only in being other than the viewed persona, or in being a viewpoint that cannot itself be viewed, that Socratic irony manages to elevate itself above mere life. On Vlastos's definition philosophy is ironic through the location of a higher point of view, that of moral autonomy. But if, as Hadot suggests, another point of view is still "human, all too human" for the philosopher as *atopos,* then philosophy will be defined beyond the hierarchy of positions, beyond truth *as a meaning.* This problem connects meaning, ethics, and the task of philosophy with the problem of point of view and the production of point of view with certain modes of "saying." Is philosophy another position within the world that edifies everyday sense, such that the adoption of an ironic attitude will lead the everyday out of itself to a "higher meaning"? Or is the focus on meaningful content still too human and too positive? If this were the case, the task of philosophy would not lie in any position or meaning but in the existential distance from content and meaning.

Both Hadot and Vlastos seem to be reading peculiarly modern concerns into the figure of Socrates. Vlastos's notion of truth values and Hadot's concept of existence both find in Socrates the proper opening of philosophy and the very limit of modernity. Thinking Socrates through the figure of irony, they argue, will free us from an overly simple and "propositional" account of moral judgment. Today, perhaps, we tend to think of all philosophy as determinable through truth values, but Vlastos finds a new mode of moral truth in Socrates that would disrupt a logical truth table, in which the values of truth and falsity are strictly opposed, allowing the sense of propositions to be determined. A "saying" can be both true and untrue. Hadot's insistence on the existence, rather than the arguments, of Socratic dialogue is also a challenge to modernity: philosophy was once an art of life and not an exchange of truth claims. But we also have to note that Hadot's resistance to a certain modernization of Socrates, in which Socrates offers true arguments, is itself highly resonant with modern literary styles. The idea that Socrates is never given as a position within the dialogue and is nothing other than a becoming through the masks and styles of dialogue is so close to Flaubert, Nietzsche, and a modern sensibility that we need to ask how "modernity" is being decided here. This seemingly historical border is also a stylistic border. For Hadot, philosophy becomes lamentably modern when it loses its power as creative and ongoing self-creation, when it becomes rigidly "philosophical." (Rorty makes a similar but conflicting point about modernity: we lose all sense of irony when we see language as a representation of the world.) Vlastos's emphasis on Socrates' specific sensibility is also an emphasis on a new way of understanding truth, a moral truth that our modern logical truth tables are at a loss to explain. How we read Socrates depends, then, on how we understand our fall into modernity. Does Socratic irony represent a Greek past when philosophy was lived as ongoing praxis, as part of a conversation for the purposes of life, or was that irony a now-lost capacity to be freed from the desires and aims of mere life?

Reading Socrates

It is precisely in Hadot's recognition of the impossibility of rhetorical autonomy and language's *essential* banality that the figure of Socrates meets with the modern problem of the posthuman. Is it possible to free ourselves from the attachment to true propositions? Could we see truth not as some content or information that we might be given or discover but as a continual art of self-formation? Irony is at once the recognition of a certain limit (of everyday understanding) and a sense of the impossibility of any such recognition. This can be seen in the following "examples" of Socratic irony. (Of course, the idea of "example" is already ironic, for it is the very nature of irony *not* to be reducible or confinable to delimited figures. The moment we recognize an example of true irony as *the* exemplary figure, we have mistaken irony's form for some type of content.) The following is a scene from the *Symposium*:

> My dear Agathon, Socrates replied as he took his seat beside him. I only wish that wisdom *were* the kind of thing one could share by sitting next to someone—if it flowed, for instance, from the one that was full to the one that was empty, like the water in two cups finding its level through a piece of worsted. If that were how it worked, I'm sure I'd congratulate myself on sitting next to you, for you'd soon have me

SOCRATES AND THE SOUL OF PHILOSOPHY

brimming over with the most exquisite kind of wisdom. My own understanding is a shadowy thing at best, as equivocal as a dream, but
yours, Agathon, glitters and dilates—as which of us can forget that
saw you the other day, resplendent in your youth, visibly kindled before the eyes of more than thirty thousand of your fellow Greeks.[2]

On this occasion Agathon recognizes Socrates' irony and chastises
Socrates accordingly: "Now Socrates, said Agathon, I know you're
making fun of me." In this instance we might see Searle's description
of irony at work. From the context (an encounter with some Sophists),
the reader and the interlocutor recognize that Socrates' disavowal of
wisdom is ironic. Wisdom is *not* to be poured into the soul like so much
wine. Socrates' deferral to Agathon's bountiful wisdom is an ironic
way of saying that for Agathon wisdom is like water pouring along a
line of wool into a cup. If wisdom were of such a nature, then sitting
next to a wise man might enhance one's wisdom, but as this is clearly
not the case, Socrates is being ironic.

However, there are many other passages in the dialogues, including the *Symposium*, in which Socrates' method relies upon his interlocutors not recognizing the irony.[3] In these cases Socrates says
something *other than what is understood*, and he does so in order to
lead his interlocutors through their *own* rhetoric.[4] Furthermore, the
limits of the interlocutors' rhetoric are often not recognized by the interlocutors; the irony is, as it were, never disclosed. The dialogues end
in bewilderment, with Socrates seemingly sharing in the sense of defeat.[5] Here is how Socrates narrates the *Euthydemus*:

Tell me what this fine show is in heaven's name!

Virtue, Socrates! We believe we can impart it—no one in the
world so well or so quickly!

O God! Said I. What an achievement! Where did you find this
godsend? As I said just now, I thought of you two especially as skillful
at fighting in full armour, and that is what I said of you; for when you

first stayed in this town, I remember this was what you professed.
Well, if you now truly have this knowledge, O be gracious—for I humbly
address you as gods, and I pray your pardon for what I said before.
But do you think, Euthydemus and Dionysodorus—are you quite sure
this is the truth? One cannot help feeling doubtful at such a por-
tentous announcement.

Be assured, Socrates, they said, that this is true.[6]

In cases such as this the irony lies in the interlocutors accepting the
usual sentence meaning of what is said; they remain thoroughly confident of their context. Only by accepting Socrates' deferral to their superior powers do the Sophists arrive at a point where the coherence of
their context seems to fall apart. By deferring to the usual or conventional meaning of a term and by accepting what the Sophists say, Socrates then goes on to show that the Sophists *cannot mean* what they
claim their (contextually secure) statements seemed to mean. The
Sophists accept Socrates' wonder and admiration for their powers of
definition. They take the Socratic utterance directly and as contextually secure. When they then go on to give a standard and conventional
definition of virtue, the definition appears as unworkable. How might
we account for this form of irony where the Socratic position only
works by not being recognized and by being other than the contextually determined meaning? There are two possible solutions.

The first is to remain within a theory of meaning as recognized and
contextually determined use. If we were to be charitable to the immanence of Searle's and Rorty's approach we might begin by resisting
any appeal to another meaning. It may be the case that the Socratic
position cannot be accounted for within the *described* context, but the
irony lies in the context of the Platonic dialogue. We, as readers, recognize the irony. The Sophists clearly do not know what justice or virtue *is*. The context here is not the described actual circumstance of
the utterance—the Sophists and Socrates speaking together—but its

transcription and location within the tradition of Western moral philosophy. So neither the Socratic disavowal of wisdom nor the Sophists' claims to define moral knowledge are in themselves ironic. The irony only occurs with the location of these utterances in the context of a dialogue. It is "we," as readers, who allow the irony to take effect. Socrates is able to say something other than what is understood because there is a context of readers who can discern the Socratic irony. "What is understood" is how the *interlocutor* takes the utterance; "what is said" is how that utterance is read in the context of a transcribed dialogue of voices or positions. So when Socrates defers to the wisdom of the Sophists, the Sophists understand the *sentence* meaning (they really are wise), while the reader recognizes the ironic *speaker* meaning, or what Socrates is "really saying." The failure to arrive at a coherent account of virtue clearly demonstrates that Socrates, not the Sophists, is wise. The "what is said" that is different from the "what is understood" does not need to be explained by referring to some private meaning held by Socrates. The ironic sense is not another meaning located outside context. It is the performance or production of a new context (the Platonic dialogue as read by us), and it is this context that determines the meaning of the Socratic utterance *as ironic* within the context of Western philosophy.

The problem, however, with such an explanation is that the performance of irony depends upon locating the ironic utterance within a second-order context (that peculiarly "Western" philosophical consciousness or sensibility bestowed by Socrates). The Sophists' confident definition of our ordinary moral vocabulary is ironically subordinated to the context of the inscribed dialogue. The irony is achieved on this account by a shift of context. Ordinary sentence meaning is now uttered in a situation or context—Western philosophy—where it can be recognized as not being the case. Within the described situation Socrates' statements are taken at face value, as are those of the

Sophists; but from within the context of a Platonic dialogue they are recognized as ironic. But this relies on us knowing what the Platonic context *is*; it relies on us having some sense that "we" can see what is meant in this exchange of voices. Explaining Socratic irony by saying that there is a context of reading philosophy whereby the Sophists' claims are recognized as inadequate relies on *some* notion of a more adequate position, but just what this Socratic or higher position is remains, and must remain, open. Furthermore, the irony lies not just in Socrates' interventions. Socrates is only able to be ironic because there is already a certain blindness in the everyday speech he encounters. There is something internally inconsistent with sophistry. The Sophist makes rhetorical gestures using concepts such as truth, justice, wisdom, and beauty, concepts whose very meaning disrupts the commitment to rhetoric. Can we really say, in any context, that "truth" is merely relative? Would the concept of truth still have any meaning? To say that irony is only the generation of another context or meaning—using phrases differently—precludes the more interesting possibility that the Sophists' rhetoric is *self-refuting*, or that there are forms of sentence meaning that as such yield their own irony.[7]

The types of claims used by Socrates in this form of "intrinsic" irony usually concern moral knowledge. His interlocutors seem more than ready to offer confident definitions of ethical terminology. Justice, friendship, wisdom, the soul, virtue, courage—none of these terms presents any definitional problems for the Sophists. It is not just that the Sophists are self-assured but clumsy rhetoricians and that Socrates' superior skills are recognized in the second-order context of reading the dialogues. The Socratic performance of another context—if this is how we are to describe it—depends upon identifying the limits of everyday definitions and rhetoric. It is, in many ways, a demonstration of the impossibility of locating our moral terminology within a context. It is a demonstration not just of the inadequacy of the Sophists' context but of context as such when it comes to certain types of concepts. When Socrates asks what we mean by justice or virtue or wisdom and he is given a definition, the irony lies not just in the fact that he is given an incoherent definition. The irony lies in the impossibility of definition as such (alongside the confident and everyday usage of terms whose meaning we think we know).[8] Irony in these complex forms can be better explained, I would suggest, not by appealing to a context in which "we" recognize another meaning (a specific speaker meaning). Irony is generated *within the first context through a destabilization of context.* This destabilization concerns the peculiar nature of moral knowledge and the limits of moral terminology (or meaning) as such.

One explanation of Socratic irony depends upon seeing the position, personality, or way of life of Socrates as an attitude adopted toward ordinary meaning. When Socrates asks what justice is, he accepts one Sophist's claim that justice can be defined. He defers to the Sophist's wisdom and by asking what justice means demands that his interlocutor spell out what we intend when "we" use or say the word "justice." The problem with the Sophist's position, then, is precisely that he assumes that our *use* of ethical terms such as justice, wisdom, truth, the soul, and friendship is an adequate account of what these terms really *mean.* The Sophist works on the assumption that the meaning of our moral lexicon is nothing more than what we assume it to be, that justice can be reduced to the way in which it is used. There is, for the Sophist, no distinction between the meaning of justice and his own use and understanding. From the Sophist's point of view, we can understand what justice is if we look at what we say. The Socratic question—do we know what we mean when we use the word "justice"?—raises the possibility that meaning *exceeds* our understanding of our own moral rhetoric. From within the very language of moral rhetoric itself, Socrates demonstrates that *morality in its very usage* is more than rhetoric. There are certain rhetorical maneuvers that can only be used by invoking the idea of what lies beyond rhetoric. The irony of Socrates' position cannot be explained by saying that he possesses a different meaning or superior definition but that the very possibility of definition is questioned once the interlocutor is, upon scrutiny, no longer able to say what he means:

> Tell me, then, you the inheritor of the argument, what it is that you affirm that Simonides says and rightly about justice.
>
> That it is just, he replied, to render to each his due. In saying this I think he speaks well.
>
> I must admit, said I, that it is not easy to disbelieve Simonides. For he is a wise and inspired man. But just what he may mean by this you, Polemarchus, doubtless know, but I do not. . . .
>
> [The dialogue then pursues a number of possible definitions.]
>
> If then the just man is an expert in guarding money he is an expert in stealing it.
>
> The argument certainly points that way.
>
> A kind of thief then the just man it seems has turned out to be, and it is likely that you acquired this idea from Homer and Simonides, seems to be a kind of stealing, with the qualification that it is for the benefit of friends and the harm of enemies. Isn't that what you meant?
>
> No, by Zeus, he replied. I no longer know what I did mean.[9]

In Socratic irony certain terms present themselves as background assumptions (crucial terms of our context), and yet they can also, when interrogated, become thoroughly at odds with ordinary usage or opinion. Socratic irony is, I would argue, the opening of a context through the structure of a conditional. If there is justice, wisdom, or truth, then it cannot be defined or decided as this or that particular understanding but must lead us beyond this present life to what is always so. It is because we use words like "beauty" and "goodness" that we must assume a soul that precedes all worldly knowledge:[10]

If all these absolute realities, such as beauty and goodness, which we are always talking about, really exist, if it is to them, as we rediscover our own former knowledge of them, that we refer, as copies to their patterns, all the objects of our physical perception—if these realities exist, does it not follow that our souls must exist too even before our birth, whereas if they do not exist our discussion would seem to be a waste of time? Is this the position, that it is logically just as certain that our souls exist before our birth as it is that these realities exist, and that if the one is impossible, so is the other?[11]

The "true" position of moral autonomy, as a step back from everyday definitions, is (as the Socratic conditional suggests) the location of a higher point of view, not of another rhetorical position but of a soul that exceeds all rhetoric. Irony tears the point of view of the statement away from the subject of enunciation. When we use the word "beauty," then we *must mean* that which precedes any specific valuation. The uttered proposition leads us to assume a soul that precedes all articulation. If this proposition—concerning "justice," "beauty," or "goodness"—makes sense, then there *must be* a soul that is not itself one more exchangeable term. The conditional generates, rather than designates, the ironist's position. If there is to be an understanding of what we really mean, then it can only be attained by the philosophically autonomous and purified soul.

The Force of Concepts

Once we use a concept, it can take on a force or meaning that can seem to conflict with what we thought we said. (Imagine a tyrant who shrewdly invents the concept of "universal justice" to mask his own will; he thereby opens the possibility that he might be judged in the name of this concept. Whatever its intended birth or genesis, a con-

cept only works if it exceeds that genesis.) Using a concept is always
more than just a single use, and this is because concepts only work or
have meaning if speakers and hearers presuppose some meaning that
we all share, that transcends any singular use. In order to take what
you say as having meaning I must posit some sense that is more than
just the material utterance, more than the marks on the page or the
sound of your voice or the movement of your gestures. I have to posit
some intended sense that is not immediately present and that we both
recognize, and would continue to recognize, in any other use. This
would seem to suggest that the meaning of concepts—or what lies
above and beyond any specific use—might be explained through the
notion of context, shared meaning, or collective use. I recognize the
sound that issues from your voice as having meaning because we have
established certain conventions of recognition. The meaning is not
some hidden or deep sense but just a move in a game with certain expected responses. "Justice" cannot mean just anything (to use this concept is already to be committed to the practices of a language), but this
meaning is just the shared and recognized usage that "we" have. (And
"we" are just this community of users, our identity defined through
shared practice.) But this is precisely where the Socratic challenge begins: if concepts are nothing more than their rhetorical force, how is it
that they seem to operate in ways that we do not recognize, that challenge our conventions, or that make our usage appear incoherent?
(How can we say to the tyrant that what he presents as justice is not
justice? How is it that we feel that we have not yet come up with a via-
ble concept of justice? How is it that these tokens we use seem to demand something from us?) Socrates, like Derrida after him, is no less
insistent that concepts have a meaning and force that transcends not
just what I might want to mean but also human meaning in general.

This is partly demonstrated in the "aporetic" dialogues. There are
concepts that we confidently use and even feel that we can define, but

when our definitions are pushed we do not seem to really be able to say what we mean. More important, though, Socrates puts forward a conditional claim regarding certain moral concepts such that the very existence of the concepts we use is evidence of a more than human power. If the concept of virtue were to have any real meaning, then it could not be defined as just another linguistic token that we pass around and use. The very concept of "virtue" is used to signal a value that is not reducible to contingent values or interested use. If all language is just the expression of force and use, how is it that we use such concepts that seem to challenge the mere assertion of force and interest? (This, according to Nietzsche, is what makes Socrates so fascinating. On the one hand, force seems to be weakened by the invention of moral concepts. The strong become enslaved to the idea of "the good." On the other hand, what an astounding act of force to have invented such life-subduing concepts! What sort of being must the philosopher be—this strange moral animal who can judge life from the elevation of concepts? Is it just rhetoric that invents these antirhetorical concepts, or does the Socratic use of rhetoric indicate that life is more than mere use?)[12] Concepts such as virtue, justice, beauty, and the good refer to a meaning that is more than context-dependent. When I use the word "justice" I am not just saying that I think this is a good act or that I approve. I am referring to an idea that seems to regulate human behavior rather than being determined by that behavior.[13] The very *meaning* of justice relies on it not being context-dependent; we would not call an act *just* that simply obeyed the rules of a given community. We could always ask whether the rules of our communities—what passed as justice—were really just. Telling someone that she is morally wrong is not just a way of telling her that the majority would disapprove of what she does. If concepts such as justice are meaningful, they seem to refer to a higher morality, some soul "in us" that is not reducible to the rules and uses of this world.

The fact that we use such concepts is evidence that we are capable of *thinking*—if not knowing or defining—what lies beyond mere force, usage, and advantage.

Who is speaking, then, when we use concepts like justice, friendship, beauty, and goodness? The voice of the Sophist is always doubled by the voice of the concept, the meaning that exceeds the specific utterance. If our concepts have fallen into vague, derived, and corrupted usage, it is always possible, through irony, to push the speaker beyond what he says to what the concept will commit him to mean. And if concepts can have this power, if they intimate a meaning beyond what we say, then they also evidence the unworldly destiny of the soul. The soul, according to Socrates, is not some object within the world that we might know. On the contrary, the soul is indicated by the fact that there are certain concepts whose meaning we do not fully know but that seem to offer themselves as necessary ideas. Even a philosopher as "modern" as Gilles Deleuze expresses a commitment to the existence of the soul. We cannot reduce the world to the relations and perceptions we have of it; it is always necessary to think the forces or hidden "souls" that give us the very positions and points of view from which we speak and perceive: "the whole world is only a virtuality that currently exists only in the folds of the soul which conveys it, the soul implementing inner pleats through which it endows itself with a representation of the enclosed world."[14]

The (In)Human Soul

The relation between irony and the soul is an intimate one. The connection is made clearly in the Socratic dialogues. Philosophy is a practice of the soul, and as long as we remain within everyday opinion, our souls will be contained within the limits of opinion. There is a clear if not definitive strain in the dialogues that suggests that irony leads us beyond rhetoric to the truth of the soul. In the *Defence* Socrates claims to be unskilled as a speaker and to be a complete stranger to the juridical language of the courts. Socrates also claims that he only possesses the limited form of human wisdom, which—as opposed to the grand claims of the "wise men"—recognizes the limits of the human.[15] However, it is in Socrates' thoroughly human recognition of the limits of human wisdom that philosophers free their souls from association with the body, with things, with the world. Unlike the Sophists, who believe that their human rhetoric exhausts what is, philosophers recognize the human in order to think beyond the human. It is only by recognizing the finite character of human life that philosophers can posit a soul beyond the exchange of worldly values. There must be that for which all value, judgment, and exchange take place—some term that is not yet one more token within life. According to the *Phaedo*, philosophy is not the substitution of one set of values for another but a way of life that reflects upon all value. And it is only in reflection that the soul can pursue its proper journey away from any given or exchangeable thing. The soul in reflection is a radical non-equivalence, not a thing within the world but a reflective separation from the world.[16] And it is only in the life of the philosopher, in wisdom as a purification from everyday pleasures, that the soul is realized. If we recognize that no worldly definition or merely human knowledge can capture the meaning of our most valued concepts such as truth, beauty, and justice, then we also recognize that there is a higher wisdom. The ironic revelation of the limit of everyday knowledge is a demonstration of the soul's disjunctive relation with everyday life. Whatever justice, truth, goodness, and beauty *are*, they cannot be reduced to *this* definition, *this* instance, or *any* empirical instance. There must be some nonworldly source for their being and knowledge. Socrates offers one of the many forms of this conditional structure in the *Meno*: "If then there are going to exist in him, both while he is and while he is not a man, true opinions which can be aroused by questioning and turned into knowledge, may we say that his soul has been forever in a state of knowledge?"[17]

The existence of the soul here depends upon a conditional. *If* these higher realities exist and are known, then only a soul (and not corporeal perceptual knowledge) can explain their knowledge. It is this conditional structure that characterizes irony as a style that delimits knowledge and opens the question of the soul. It is this *question*, from Socrates to Deleuze, that stems both from a commitment to life and a critique of mere life. On the one hand, and in opposition to the avowedly flat irony of Rorty and ordinary language philosophy, we have to say that any event of life poses the question of the force or soul of which that event is an effect. We can always ask about the style or legitimacy of our context and concepts. On the other hand, while critical of any reduction or restriction to mere life, the idea of the soul refuses to posit another value beyond life. If justice and truth have any meaning, then they are not just imposed concepts, imperatives, or rules; they must have a truth or sense that lies in the soul.

If Socrates offers himself as a diagnosis of life (how we read Socrates will determine just what we take life to be), then it is Immanuel Kant who offers the most forceful counterironic challenge. It is only when we are truly modern, Kant insisted, that we will desist from taking flight into the heights of speculation and supersensible intuitions. Enlightenment frees us from enslavement to any posited or revealed "higher" good. Refusing one form of irony (the commitment to a supersensible intuition or knowledge), Kant, *however unwittingly*, generates a peculiarly Romantic irony. This is an irony that can no longer be contained within the personality, existence, or life of Socrates (or any philosopher). It is a *literary* or purely formal irony, an impersonal irony that operates through ideas rather than conversations, and styles rather than souls.

From Kant to Romanticism

Kant

The transition from Kant to Romanticism (and the present) is crucial for irony as a historical phenomenon. We could read Kant's break with Socratic irony as the opening of modernity: Kant refuses any possible knowledge of a "higher" realm of truth. The reason why there seems to be a "beyond" to so many of our concepts is not because our concepts are too worldly and inadequate but because there could be no possible *knowledge* of such Ideas as God, freedom, and immortality. The very meaning of these Ideas precludes their presentation or objectification. For Kant this meant that Ideas of the supersensible could *only* be practical. We can act as if we were free and as if there were a God, but we cannot know or strive to know such objects. The Romantics, famously, ignored this prescription: striving to know what lies beyond life is the necessary fulfillment of life. We could see the Romantic "misreading" of Kant as the necessary step toward achieving full modernity. Kant insisted that our knowledge was necessarily limited to spatiotemporal relations and that we could neither know nor do without what lay beyond those relations. Beyond the things we know are those things-in-themselves that must remain out of bounds for theoretical knowledge. Romanticism extends this perceived incoherence or "gap" in the Kantian critique: if we can think but not know the absolute, then the very limits of knowledge—our concepts and contexts—might come to appear as productive rather than negative. The unlimited or absolute would not lie beyond life and the human but would be created by life's own ceaseless striving. We would begin with the Socratic conditional: if there is an absolute, it can be known only by the soul. Kant would transform this to an "as if": act as if you were a free soul. This would then generate the Romantic sublime: if there is a limit to what we can know, this necessarily raises the question and power of the unlimited. And it may be that the unlimited is nothing other than, and created through, the perception of the limit.

Kant explicitly rejects the Socratic (or Platonic) assertion that nonempirical knowledge is possible. Kant confines knowledge, strictly speaking, to *empirical* concepts. For Kant, even if we have certain concepts (of freedom, the infinite, and God), this does not entail that we should strive to *know* the content of these concepts.[1] From the Socratic conditional—"If there is absolute reality, then it can only be known by the soul"—comes the Kantian "as if." Concepts such as freedom enable us to act as if there really were a soul (which, of course, cannot be known).[2] Unlike the Socratic dialogues, which aim to elevate the soul to a vision of the supersensible, Kant insists on a necessary gap between certain concepts that tell us what we ought to do and other concepts that can be fulfilled empirically or given objective form. It is usual to regard Kant's aesthetic theory as a bridge over this gap. Between the first critique, which insists that we cannot know any absolute or moral law, and the second critique, which insists that we nevertheless have a duty to act from a pure law, there is the power of reflective judgment, which gives us an "as if." What gives us pleasure in aesthetic experience is the viewing of an object as if it were the fulfillment of some universal consensus. In thinking of laws of nature we view nature as if it were governed by some law; in judging beauty we act as if the pleasure we feel were not ours alone but representative of humanity. But the "as if" is not confined to Kant's aesthetic and reflective judgment. In practical or moral judgments we decide to act as if we were free. The imagination of what I might do if I were free enables me to form a moral law that then presents itself as a duty. If I can *think* of what a free agent would do, then I *ought* to do it. In this sense the "as if" of Kant's moral law fills the "vacant place" opened by the first critique, which insisted that pure reason's Ideas of God, freedom, and the infinite could not meet with objects.

We cannot know what man, as a moral being, is. We cannot know an object, such as the free soul, that would lie outside all relations of causality. But we can take the concept of causality, which structures the world we do know, and extend it beyond any known world to think a cause that is not an event within this world. Such a cause would be the imagined but not given freedom of the moral agent. What would we do if we were not motivated by any idea other than that of freedom? We would act as if we were above all worldly concerns. The "as if" of Kant, like the Socratic conditional, enables a structure of irony that is linked to performance (rather than knowledge) and moral autonomy rather than substantive humanism. The supersensible substrate of humanity is not a substance that we are given to see; it is only generated in and through acts of judgment. The soul of the "if" or "as if" is not a thing to be known but an *active capacity* derived from the limit of knowledge:

> Thus reason uses this concept [of freedom, *causa noumenon*, or un-
> conditioned cause] only for a practical purpose, transferring the de-
> termining ground of the will to the intelligible order of things, at the
> same time readily confessing that it does not understand how the con-
> cept of cause can be a condition of knowledge of these things. Cau-
> sality with respect to the actions of the will in the world of sense must,
> of course, be known by reason in a definite way, for otherwise practi-
> cal reason could produce no act. But the concept which reason makes
> of its own causality as noumenon does not need to be determined the-
> oretically for the purpose of knowing its supersensible existence. (*PR*,
> bk. 1, chap. 1, sec. 1, 51)

If we have the concept of freedom, then this is not because we *know*
any free thing (such as the soul). If there is an Idea of freedom, it is
because certain concepts are not fulfilled by knowledge. This gives us
the structure of a conditional. Like Socrates, Kant stresses the positivity of not knowing: if there are Ideas that cannot meet with knowledge, then there must be an origin or genesis beyond knowledge. This
shared conditional structure explains why irony as a feature of philosophy becomes important, after Socrates, with German Romanticism.
Both Socratic irony and post-Kantian Romanticism regard the question or thought of the good, rather than any known good, as primarily
productive and effective. Both Socratic and Kantian philosophy question just how any good might be thought. We might also note that
these are pre- and posttheological epochs: no immediate foundation
for the moral law is given. It is in the absence of any external or evident foundation that Socrates can question the very locus of the moral,
insisting on the self-formative path of the soul. Kant can demand the
necessary construction of law, only because no law or duty is or could
be revealed to us. The very sense of the limit of everyday knowledge is
sufficient. The higher wisdom of ideal truth need only be sensed as a

possibility, "as if." As Kant argues, "The possibility of such a supersensuous nature, the concept of which can be the ground of its reality through our free will, requires no a priori intuition of an intelligible world" (*PR*, bk. 2, chap. 2, sec. 7, 147).

The Soul, Moral Feeling, and Synthesis

Like Socrates, Kant tied his ethics of concepts to the nonempirical nature of the soul and to the apparently inhuman power of concepts. Socrates' target was the Sophists, those who believed that the definition of concepts was contingent and dependent on use. Against mere rhetoric, Socrates pushed the Sophists to acknowledge that the meaning of concepts frequently exceeds use and context. Kant's target was slightly different, not those who felt concepts were nothing more than their use, but those who felt that concepts labeled sentiments rather than strictly autonomous meanings. Moral concepts or ideas, Hume had argued, are merely labels we attach to our feelings. If you act to my disadvantage, then I express my feeling of disapproval by calling your action "bad" or vicious; and if your actions are beneficial, I describe them as virtuous.[3] Our moral concepts might appear to have an objective meaning, but this is only because we form societies and have general rules and regularities for those feelings of praise and blame that we attach to others' actions. We all share the same human nature that will tend toward agreement on praiseworthy (virtuous) or blamed (vicious) actions. Moral concepts were, for Hume and those of Hume's time, expressions of human feeling, and they were moral precisely because of the inherently social nature of human life. Kant's attack on this account of moral concepts, like Socrates' irony, lies in showing that whatever the origin or use of our concepts, our concepts nevertheless have a practical force that extends far beyond their human source.

(Just because the idea of God, for example, arises from human fear or a misguided desire to provide some sort of cause for the universe, this does not mean that the very existence of the idea doesn't tell us something about the power of human thought and how that power can be extended. If we can *think* a supreme being, then we are obviously capable of thinking beyond what is merely experienced sensuously. And this Idea can have a practical force: how would we act or think of ourselves if we admitted the possibility of a supreme being?)

Both Kant and Hume agree that we cannot find concepts in the world and that ideas are the outcome of human synthesis. We do not experience goodness or virtue; we attribute such concepts to what we experience. We do not experience relations such as tallness, nearness, or consequences, but we do synthesize experiences into such relations through concepts. The concept of cause results from the fact that we connect our experiences into some sort of order. (For Kant, this is evidence of our activity in synthesizing experience through the concept of cause; for Hume, it is evidence for the power of experience to produce concepts.) The concept of self or the soul is, similarly, also not something we experience or encounter; it results because we assume from the regularity (or synthesis) of our experiences that there must have been some self or soul who synthesized or who experienced. Kant agrees with Hume that relations and concepts are effects of the synthesis of experience, but Kant insists on the power of these concepts to lead thought beyond human nature. It is true that we connect experiences into a causal order, and it is also true that we then extend this series illegitimately and feel that we must be able to know the cause of all causes. Further, we also tend to abstract the concept of cause from all these instances of causality. But this concept itself does not have an object; it is only *because of this concept* that we have a world of ordered and caused objects. Kant insists that we cannot *know* anything beyond this caused and ordered world but, once we recognize that we have this concept, we can *think* of a cause that would not be located within the determined world. What if there were a being who could cause an action that were not itself caused? Such a being would be free. The *concept* of cause, which applies to experience, enables the *Idea* of freedom, beyond all experience. From this Idea of freedom we can then imagine a moral universe: imagine a world in which we could all act as if we were not caused or motivated by anything other than our pure will.

Whereas Hume and his contemporaries had argued that all human action must be motivated by some feeling, Kant shows how concepts arise that cannot be reduced to feeling or knowledge. The very Idea of freedom enables me to think of an action that would not be motivated or derived *from* feeling. Indeed, far from being derived from feeling, moral concepts actually *produce* certain feelings. Once we think of ourselves as moral or think of the moral law, we are struck with respect. The Idea of freedom allows us to form moral laws: what would we do if we were free from worldly desires? The respect for such an inhuman idea provides a peculiarly moral motivation: a motivation that is not caused by feeling but that follows from imagining that one might act in the absence of feeling. Respect has just this human/inhuman quality. The very fact that I can think of the Idea of freedom presents me with an elevated form of myself as a rational will and not as a causally determined motivated being (*PR*, bk. 2, chap. 2, sec. 2, 123). Neither freedom nor God nor immortality is a concept that we can give an object to; such concepts arise because we extend the concepts we use to organize experience in order to think what could not be located within experience. The fact that we can think such concepts has a powerful force. First, it indicates that we can extend the range of concepts beyond what we are given (and so we have evidence of the "depths of the human soul" from which this synthesizing activity emerges).[4] Second, once we can think such concepts, our moral personality is transfigured irreversibly: "humanity in our person must it-

self be holy to us, because man is subject to that which is of itself holy,
and it is only on account of this and in agreement with this that anything can be called holy. For this moral law is founded on the autonomy of his will as a free will, which by its universal laws must necessarily be able to agree with that to which he ought to subject himself"
(*PR*, bk. 2, chap. 2, sec. 6, 138).

Imagine that I wanted to argue that I was not responsible for an action because my nature (or biology) determined me to do it. I did not
do what was just or right, and I explain this away by saying that human life is determined by passions or interested motives. And so, I
might conclude, concepts like justice and rightness mean (or should
mean) just what our passions or biology prompt us to do, and any attempt to find an objective meaning is deluded. But to argue that our
will is determined and that we could not have acted in some purely rational manner already admits the idea or concept of pure reason. To
say that I could *not* have acted justly, or that we are incapable of some
impersonal elevated justice, admits the concept or representation of
justice. This is the negativity of irony: in denying the concept of pure
freedom I at least give it voice and meaning, saying more than what
I mean to say. Compare this to Rorty's ironist who insists that we are
nothing more than vocabularies: doesn't this produce and admit the
very thought of the limits of our vocabulary, the possibility of another
vocabulary? The moment that we present ourselves as determined
shows that we have some concept of cause or determination, and if this
is so we also admit the possibility—at least at the level of representation—of a pure cause. We can *think* a course of action that is self-
caused. We are not therefore capable of reducing ourselves to mechanically caused beings, for the very concept of causality both indicates
and enables a *power to represent* what lies beyond determination. For

Kant, the very concept of will *demands* the formulation of a moral law. Once we think of a will, capable of decision, we also allow the representation of a will itself, freed from external motivation. The very concept of will—a will that decides on this or that action—presents us with the pure force of decision. A will that was nothing more than decision, or a pure will that was not prompted by any external force, would be autonomous only through the moral law. It would will not just what was desirable for me in my singularity but what would be desirable for any other will. From a worldly act of willing (wanting this or that object) I can then think of will as such: a will that acts not for some end or object but only to be pure act.

There is a difference in kind, not just of degree, between moral and empirical willing (*PR*, bk. 1, chap. 1, sec. 1, 24). A moral will is not directed to some contingent object such as happiness or pleasure. What makes a will moral is its pure formality; only a moral will is universalizable and immanent. What we will in a moral law is not some state within the world such as well-being, happiness, or pleasure. We will the *law*: a will that is not enslaved to any end other than that of willing. For Kant, what reason desires is a will not determined by happiness or pleasure but form. Only a free will has no external object; it wills as such, regardless of any determining or external end. It wills only itself, forming laws that are only motivated by the idea of a pure will. If I act morally, then I act in order *not* to be prompted by any outside object. When forming a moral law I do not act for myself or any person; I form a judgment compatible with *any will*, regardless of ends or interests. When I think of a moral law (such as treating all others as ends in themselves and not means), I also recognize a certain type or grammar of judgment. Only a being who was not determined by this or that particular desire could form a judgment of the form *always act as if...* The universalizing will that expresses itself in the form of categorical imperatives such as "one must ..." or "one ought..." or "always act as if..." recognizes itself as free—as capable of speaking from the point of view of humanity in general:

> Thus freedom and unconditional practical law reciprocally imply each other. I do not here ask whether they are actually different, instead of an unconditional law being the self-consciousness of pure practical reason, and thus identical with the positive concept of freedom. The question now is whether our *knowledge* of the unconditionally practical takes its inception from freedom or the practical law. It cannot start from freedom for this we can neither know immediately, since our first concept of it is negative, nor infer from experience, since experience reveals only the law of appearances and consequently the mechanism of nature, the direct opposite of freedom. It is therefore the moral law, of which we become immediately conscious as soon as we construct maxims for the will, which first presents itself to us; and, since reason exhibits it as a ground of determination which is completely independent of and not to be outweighed by any sensuous condition, it is the moral law which leads directly to the concept of freedom. (*PR*, bk. 1, chap. 1, sec. 1, 29)

We are capable of forming moral judgments. The point is not to find an object that answers to such imperatives—such as *the* good— but to ask about the type of being who is capable of forming such laws. Any being capable of thinking freedom, God, immortality is a being capable of pure concepts; the practical force of such concepts is just the elevated idea of humanity they enable us to imagine:

> Duty! . . . where is the root of thy noble descent . . . ? This root cannot be less than something that elevates man above himself as a part of the world of sense, something which connects him with an order of things which only the understanding can think and which has under it the entire world of sense, including the empirically determinable existence of man in time, and the whole system of all ends which is alone

suitable to such unconditional practical laws as the moral. It is nothing else than *personality,* i.e., the freedom and independence from the mechanism of nature regarded as a capacity of a being subject to special laws (pure practical laws given by its own reason), so that the person belonging to the world of sense is subject to his own personality so far as he belongs to the intelligible world. For it is then not to be wondered at that man, as belonging to two worlds, must regard his own being in relation to his second and higher vocation with the deepest respect. (*PR*, bk. 1, chap. 3, 90)

Now this is all very well, and we might admit that the person who argues that she is mechanically, genetically, or culturally determined must admit that she can, by that very argument, *think* or represent the opposite possibility: that she can act out of pure duty. Indeed, much of Kant's time is spent in formulating examples that allow us to at least think of pure duty.[5] A man may have acted out of good feeling or prudence his entire life, and the consequences might all come out as moral. But wouldn't an action be truly moral if there were no feeling, no prudential considerations, and no human or personal motivation, and yet the man still did what he ought to do? Duty or morality is just this idea of an action that we consider *right* and that we feel ought to be done, regardless of the persons, feelings, or consequences involved. Isn't this the wondrous possibility of the moral: that in the absence of any feeling or worldly reason, someone still performs an act we recognize as good?[6] Any attempt to reduce morality to mere feeling or pathological motives has to deny the practical force of the concept of morality and duty: we *can think* of an action that would be motivated by nothing other than the very concept of its rightness. Such an action would be what we ought to do regardless of our feelings or specific concerns. Kant emphasizes the force of our moral concepts, a force that cannot be reduced to feeling or prudence: "Thus morality must have more power over the human heart the more purely it is presented. From this it follows that, if the law of morals and the image of holiness and virtue are to exert any influence at all on our minds, they can do so only in so far as they are laid to heart in their purity as drives unmixed with any view to welfare, because it is in suffering that they most notably show themselves" (*PR*, pt. 2, 162).

Now, just because we have concepts with this moral meaning, we might still object that there is no proof or indication that we will ever act on or be motivated by such concepts. This is where Kant's ethics of the force of concepts comes in. As in Socrates' theory of the soul, there is a conditional structure. If there were to be morality, it would not be pathologically caused. When we use the word "moral," we do not mean what is advantageous or prudent; we mean that any other agent would also and should also have acted in this way. Kant can obviously prove that we can think or represent the meaning of such moral or nonpathologically motivated concepts. We can think of the dutiful, just, or right action; and we obviously do so even when we try to deny that such acts are actually possible. But there is also a positive dimension to Kant's moral concepts. If morality is the idea of *not* acting on feeling, how could I possibly be motivated to be moral? How do I move from the thought of a free or uncaused act to the execution of the act?

Kant's response is formulated through a notion of moral feeling and its relation to concepts. Most actions are motivated by feeling; I have the interest or desire from which I then act. In the case of morality, however, the feeling does not *cause* the action. From the representation or thought of the action I am then given a feeling of respect. The idea of *not* being motivated by feeling produces its own feeling. This is not a personal feeling—far from it. By being presented with the concept of freedom I am chastened, subdued, submitted to the moral law. Indeed, this law only has its force in *not* being humanly motivated. Its force lies in its detachment from any prudential or sympathetic motive: the very idea of a law elevated beyond mere human interest produces a feeling of respect. I can act as if my actions were not just chosen by me but would be chosen by a pure will unmotivated by particular or pathological considerations: "the moral law in us, without promising or threatening us with anything certain, demands of us a disinterested respect; finally, only when this respect has become active and dominating, it allows us a view into the realm of the supersensible, though only a glimpse" (*PR*, bk. 2, chap. 2, sec. 9, 155).

Kant's moral law is tied to this strange power of moral concepts. The concept of duty, for example, presents us with a representation of what I might do if I could abstract from all my personal motives: "the moral law transfers us into a nature in which reason would bring forth the highest good were it accompanied by sufficient physical capacities; and it determines our will to confer on the sensuous world the form of a system of rational beings" (*PR*, bk. 1, chap. 1, sec. 1, 45). Once I think of myself in this way I recognize a higher form of personality (just as Socrates' commitment to concepts was a way of life). The idea of not acting from feeling produces a higher order of feeling: the feeling of respect, *respect for the self I would be if I were moral, if I were not just a human among other humans but a member of the kingdom of ends.* Such a kingdom of ends would be a virtual community, generated by extending the concepts we already use to then think of a "we" that does not (yet) exist. Such a community would be inaugurated if I could fulfill the concepts of justice, right, law, freedom, and duty— concepts that bear a teleology that takes us beyond the merely human.

Inhuman Freedom

If there is freedom, then it is not something we could know. Nevertheless, the very idea of freedom indicates that we can think beyond causal determination. The very idea of this "beyond" opens at least the possibility of morality. The concept of freedom is therefore practical rather than theoretical. It does not present us with something we might intuit or present in the grammar of propositions (theory). We cannot predicate the soul or freedom, but we can speak in the form of practical imperatives: act as if your action were that of a being motivated by nothing other than the kingdom of ends.[7] The practical force of the concept enables a speech act—the categorical imperative—that is elevated above the force of rhetoric, conversation, and persuasion.

Kant is not just critical of the attempt to reduce moral concepts to their human use and origin; it is not just that the very existence of these concepts is evidence of the supersensible soul. Kant is also demonstrating the practical and effective force of concepts: what concepts *do*, and the law they give us. We can recognize this law both as our own and as ruthlessly inhuman. Only a law not motivated by particular feeling could be autonomous, for it would not be determined by our pathological motives (determined by sensuous objects to which we were related). Autonomy lies in the pure formality of the law; it is a law that applies regardless of any consequences, motives, or feeling.[8] It is only by being other than any human feeling that we can truly recognize this law *as a law* and as an object of respect, elevated above worldly motives and calculations. We cannot know what lies beyond experience, but the very thought of what exceeds experience—what is not determined or presented to us—gives us a representation of a possible kingdom of ends, a world of wills whose only motivation is the will itself. The very concept of will is the opening of morality. In thinking of ourselves as beings who have a will we enable the representation of a moral, rather than a pathological or merely human, law. This law has force only because it is not something that causes my will (like passion or feeling) but is the will's own cause: how would I act if nothing other than the idea of myself as a willing agent were to motivate me? My motive would be *moral*: pure, devoid of particular considerations. Such a law would be my own precisely in being the outcome of my pure will (rather than the specific passions and feelings that are given or that I do not decide). In being my own in this way (not pathological), the law would also be universal. This law that one gives oneself can be formed only if we think above our merely empirical selves and act as if we were not beings of this world. This giving of the law to oneself in order to be other than one's worldly self is a gift enabled by concepts, in particular, the concept of duty:

> The heart is freed from a burden which has secretly pressed upon it; it is lightened when in instances of pure moral resolution there is revealed to man, who previously has not correctly known it, a faculty of inner freedom to release himself from the impetuous importunity of the inclinations, to such an extent that not even the dearest of them has an influence on a resolution for which he now makes use of his reason. . . . there is consciousness of an independence from inclinations and circumstances and of the possibility of being sufficient to myself, which is salutary for me in other respects. The law of duty, through the positive worth which obedience to it makes us feel, finds easier access through the respect for ourselves in the consciousness of our freedom. (*PR*, pt. 2, 167)

From all this we might say that it was Kant who was the first to offer a genealogy of the inhuman. Metaphysics, he argued, had continually adopted a God's-eye view of the world, as though the law or the good determined thought from outside. Plato's Ideas, as the Socratic dialogues make clear, indicate that we often do not mean what we say. The force of concepts seems to exceed what we say; our definitions do not seem to live up to the elevation of our concepts. Certain concepts such as freedom cannot be represented or fleshed out within this world. If such concepts do have any referents, then this would seem to lead to a realm beyond human finitude. Kant's genius lay both in restricting knowledge to what can be presented to us—what is finite and worldly—and in showing how the very structures or concepts of knowledge lead beyond all presentation. From the human point of view, what can be known or experienced would always be presented *to us* and would therefore be related to or other than the act of knowing. For this reason, those objects we *know*—situated in time and space—are suitable subjects for predication, for we always regard them from this or that aspect, addressing them *as* this or that. In knowing such an object we must already have determined it in some way, related to it in some way.[9] But there are also concepts that move us to think what cannot be included within a proposition or definition. If the standard proposition takes the form of "S is P," it is because we are able to describe a being or substance according to recognizable qualities or predicates. But do concepts such as justice, freedom, and the soul admit of such definitions? If we were to spell out the predicates of freedom or the soul, we would, in some way, have determined them as knowable substances. But if there really *is* freedom, then it must be above and beyond any substantive determination. Not a possible object for human viewing, the freedom of the soul must be assumed to be (or have been) that point from which viewing and predication proceed. The human point of view might, then, have this uncanny characteristic: it is that one point within the human world that we are capable of thinking but not seeing or predicating.

Kant's revolutionary move, the very power of enlightenment and modernity, is to demonstrate the thoroughly human generation and the legitimacy of the inhuman. The moral law is, he insists, not reducible to sentiment, happiness, or assessment of any worldly benefits. Like Socrates, Kant will insist that morality's very meaning exceeds any explanation we might give at the level of human feeling. When we talk about an action being moral we do not mean that it is advantageous, prudent, or naturally motivated. And Kant gives us limit cases to show the force, law, and meaning of moral concepts. It may be that for most of our lives our motives, nature, and prudential reason incline us to actions that would also qualify as moral. Kant does not want to dismiss either the existence or the worth of such a felicitous coincidence between human nature and moral judgment. But it is precisely those occasions when we act morally in the absence of prudence or inclination and yet would still call an act moral that tell us something about the meaning, possibility, and function of morality. Whatever our nature or inclinations, it is possible to think of an act that we would call moral *simpliciter*. Such an act is done simply because we *ought*. There is no motive other than the very goodness of the act. The point of raising such a possibility is not to tell us to banish all natural human motives; it simply reveals to us that we can and do think of another type of motive. This moral motive does not lie in any given feature of human nature but is given in and from the law itself. The moral law elevates and prompts absolutely, without consideration of inclination or consequence:

> But if it is an inexorable duty, transgression against which violates of itself the moral law without respect to human welfare and, as it were, tramples on its holiness (the kind of duties which one calls duties to God, because we think of Him as the ideal of holiness in a substance), we give our most perfect esteem to pursuing it and sacrificing to it everything that ever had value for our dearest inclinations; and we find our soul strengthened and elevated by such an example when we convince ourselves, by contemplating it, that human nature is capable of such an elevation above everything that nature can present as a drive in opposition to it. . . . to put everything else down below the holiness of duty and to know that we *can* do it because our reason acknowledges it as its law and says that we *ought* to do it—that is, as it were, to lift ourselves altogether out of the world of sense; this elevation is inseparably present in the consciousness of the law as a drive of a faculty which rules over the sensuous, though not always effectively. (*PR*, pt. 2, 164–65)

The very form of the categorical imperative—act as if your will were not motivated by anything other than the concept of a pure will—liberates human agency from a world governed by subject-predicate propositions. For the most part, we evaluate objects according to this or that value that may attach to them, such that the object and its qualities are tied together or synthesized in the judgment. But the moral law does not attach an external value to duty. Duty is not good because of some external quality or benefit; the very concept of duty or the pure will is immediately elevating. The very *idea* of a pure will—a will not prompted by passion, inclination, or prudence—commands absolutely. And the grammar of the law or the categorical imperative tells us something about the human soul. What being must I be if I can think of this law that would command absolutely? There must have been freedom if human reason could give such a law to itself, if it could speak in such a way. The voice of the law that chastens us, commands us, and elevates us also discloses something of our higher, supersensible, and other than merely human humanity.

The Passage to Romanticism

Kant's pure concepts are inferred from the transcendental synthesis of experience. Concepts such as causality, substance, magnitude, and necessity are not arrived at by generalizing from experience. We only have experience because we have such concepts, concepts that are evidence of a subject who synthesizes but whose transcendental status can only be thought after the event of its own activity.[10] Kant's ethics, like Socrates' conditional that leads to the human soul, depends on excluding the origin or genesis of concepts from the conceptualized or experienced world. The soul as the origin of synthesis is not itself an object for experience. And it is famously the "gap" between soul and world that allows for the thought of the moral law: if there is a power or soul responsible for synthesized experience that lies beyond all experience, then there must be some ground prior to worldly and objective determination.

The Jena Romantics accepted this gap between the subject as a synthesizing power and the concepts that resulted from this synthesis. They followed Kant in arguing that we must assume a soul as the unknowable and unrepresentable origin or birthplace of concepts. But the problem with the unrepresentable, they contended, is that we have to represent it *as unrepresentable*. Irony lies in the retreat of the absolute origin of synthesis from any of its effects. The subjectivity that "we" are is always other than any self of which we are conscious. We have to use concepts in order to signal this absolute that gives us our being as subjects, but we also have to be aware of the essential failure of such concepts. Irony—the performed distance from our concepts—is not something we ever successfully achieve. To believe that we *are* other than the concepts we have used is to fall back on an ever more rigid conceptual determination, for the subject who conceptualizes *is not*. The subject is not a being who then synthesizes the world; the subject must be assumed, after the event, as the ineffable genesis of the synthesis that gives being. It cannot be possible to achieve a position of irony, for subjectivity or synthesis is that which posits or gives itself position. The only way out of this predicament of subjective reification is through the performance of continual self-distancing, a "transcendental buffoonery" always aware of the gap between the subject and persona.

Indeed, this very gap is what enables the idea of the subject. It is not that there is a subject who recedes behind any specific position; it is from the event of receding that subjectivity is performed. This is the crucial—and ironic—difference and distance from Kant. Kant insisted on the possibility of metaphysics through a strict distinction between those objects we can know and predicate and the soul, which can only be *thought* as the ground of moral freedom. The Romantics increasingly recognized that any thought of what lay beyond representation relied on being *other than representation*, produced through negativity rather than underlying positive judgments. Herein lay the importance of *poiēsis*. For Kant, the subject could be *purely practical*: never objectified, and known only through its active effects. Romantic irony recognizes the impossibility of remaining as pure act; there is always the fall into determination or transcendence. The pure act issues in (and is known through) that which it produces. There can never be pure *praxis*—an activity that is always at one with itself, such as the Kantian will. *Poiēsis*, or the externalization and objectification of the act, is not just possible but necessary. For the Romantics, the effect or production of the pure act—the poem—would therefore need to present itself as always other than or inadequate to its creative and dynamic origin.[11]

The Kantian and Socratic idea that the soul lies beyond the limits of rhetoric is given a new intensity in Schlegelian irony. There is, in Schlegel, a sense that the limits of rhetoric do not lie in unfortunately banal dogmas that might be overcome by rigorous metaphysical questioning. Rather, the soul is perceivable only as other than the limit of rhetoric. Rhetoric is essential to the passage beyond the merely rhetorical. In this sense, it is not surprising that irony for the Jena Romantics was defined less through a philosophical dialogue with clearly hierarchized positions (between truth and *doxa*, philosophy and rhetoric, everyday life and existence) and more through the play of voices as such, particularly through the polyvocal drama of irony.[12] The truth of irony was not given a position, form of life, or personality but was seen in what lay beyond any specific position.[13] Not surprisingly, drama—Shakespearean drama—offered a certain exemplarity. The Romantic celebration of Shakespeare does not often make an explicit connection to irony, but it does celebrate Shakespeare's *absence* and *impersonality*.[14] This emphasis on absence itself as truth, alongside the idea that truth is not a proposition but a recognition of the limits of a proposition, also serves to inscribe a boundary between philosophy and literature. Irony is neither a position, nor a statement, nor the description of a state of affairs. It is not given as a form or figure of speech in the way of tropes or other intralinguistic phenomena. As such, irony cannot be a form of philosophy strictly speaking but must be dramatized through voice. If philosophy is a commitment to true speech above and beyond the rigidity of rhetoric, irony begins with the impossibility of just such an elevation. (This explains why irony is dramatic or novelistic for the Romantics and only philosophical in the form of the Socratic dialogue. Only when philosophy was not propositional was it close to the truth of the soul.) At the same time, while irony is not a given position or content, it is not *pure absence*. On the contrary, the Romantics define irony or the limit of meaning as feeling, intimation, sentiment, imagination, or other such dispositions of the soul. This is what connects their work with the practical dimension of the Kantian limit. For Kant, it is in the peculiar *feeling* of the limit of any empirical or affective moral justification that we come to respect the pure form of the moral law. Respect is that feeling we have when our personal and limited feelings are chastened, subdued, and humiliated:

> Thus the effect of this law on feeling is humiliation alone, which we thus see a priori, though we cannot know the force of the pure practical law as drive but only the resistance to the drives of our sensuous nature. This same law, however, is objectively, i.e., in the conception of pure reason, a direct determining ground of the will. Hence this humiliation occurs proportionately to the purity of the law; for that reason the lowering (humiliation) of the pretensions to moral self-esteem on

the sensuous side is an elevation of the moral, i.e., practical, esteem
for the law on the intellectual side. . . . Therefore, respect for the moral
law must be regarded also as a positive but indirect effect of the law
on feeling in so far as the law weakens the hindering influence of the
inclinations through humiliating self-conceit. (*PR*, bk. 1, chap. 3, 82)

We are, to use Wordsworthian language, admonished by the sense
of the limits of any personal sentiment. We feel the limit of any mere
feeling. The possibility that we might *not* follow our present desires—
the "if" of the imperative—is inextricably connected to the higher
feeling of the soul: "the soul believes itself to be elevated in proportion
as it sees the holy law as elevated over it and its frail nature" (*PR*, bk.
1, chap. 3, 81). True morality and the soul's feeling of respect are not
given or experienced but *intimated* at the limit of experience through
the inadequacy of any experienced feeling to be a truly moral, pure
justification.

The feeling which arises from the consciousness of this constraint
[i.e., duty] is not pathological, as are those caused by objects of the
senses, but practical, i.e., possible through prior (objective) determination of the will and causality of reason. As submission to a law, i.e.,
as a command which constrains the sensuously affected subject, it
contains, therefore, no pleasure but rather displeasure proportionate
to this constraint. On the other hand, since this constraint is exercised
only through the legislation of one's own reason, it also contains
something elevating, and the subjective effect of feeling, in so far as
pure practical reason is its sole cause, can also be called self-
approbation with reference to pure practical reason, for one knows
himself to be determined thereto solely by the law and without any
[sensuous] interest; he becomes conscious of an altogether different
interest which is subjectively produced by the law and which is purely
practical and free. (*PR*, bk. 1, chap. 3, 84)

The Kantian moral law depends upon a recognition of our not truly
belonging to this world. The empirical knowledge we have of the

world is inadequate to ground the possibility of that which is given by
pure concepts. There is no worldly recognition possible for the concept
of freedom.

How would such a recognition of freedom, which Kant precludes,
be possible? Not in the knowledge of philosophy or theory but (for the
Romantics) in the feeling enabled by art. Literature is, in one sense,
an exemplary art because the feeling of the limit of knowledge is
given in knowledge's own medium of language. In literature we do
not just read propositions; literature foregrounds the very medium of
speaking and proposing. For the Romantics, while philosophy states
truth in the form of propositions, literature allows us to feel truth at
the limit of the proposing of the proposition. It does so primarily in
the explicit use of language through character, position, persona, and
personality. The absence of the author in a dramatic work becomes, for
the Romantics, a model for the division within the self between articulated persona and the genesis of any possible persona. Whereas Kant
had allowed the higher moral personality to be produced through the
law, the Romantics placed what is other than the worldly self in the
dramatization or vocalization of art. The voice that tears the self away
from the world is no longer that of reason or conscience (*PR*, bk. 1,
chap. 3, 103) but poetry. Not surprisingly, Shakespeare becomes a figure for the manifestation of the "invisible point which no philosopher
has discovered or defined and where the characteristic quality of our
being, our presumed free will, collides with the inevitable course of
the whole."[15]

Unlike the philosophical proposition that speaks from the point of
view of reason in general, the literary work presents itself in the particularity and specificity of its point of view.[16] It is from the singularity of the literary fragment or character that we are drawn to that
point from which any system or general reason might emerge. At the
same time, however, this very singularity indicates that there is noth-

ing other than point of view. The literary point of view, *as singular,* foregrounds its particularity. Whereas everyday speech utters propositions as though they were so much shared and recognized content, the literary use of character, tone, and style draws attention to the subjective genesis of any proposition. Literature is other than *common* sense. Literature is more capable of giving us a feeling or intimation of truth precisely because its manifest singularity indicates the limit of knowledge. German Romantic irony, as "transcendental buffoonery,"[17] is not saying one thing and *understanding another* but saying one thing and recognizing its thorough and necessary banality, that point that is not reducible to understanding. There is no point of general understanding above and beyond the utterance, no subject in general who precedes the creative process of speech, only the particularizing events of singular speech acts. To complete the definition from Schlegel's *Fragments,* irony "is at once self-creation and self-destruction."[18]

To the Romantics, as in the Socratic tradition, irony is tied to the problem of position and self. The peculiar "as if" of the Romantic ironist precludes the moral autonomy of Socratic irony or the Kantian moral "personality." The achieved performance of distance from rhetoric is no longer possible. The soul is not given as a moral practice within the world; it is not the *technē* of a philosophy that would live in opposition to everyday life. As transcendental buffoonery, Romantic irony is a form of self-creation that is at one and the same time self-destruction. Any attempt to be other than a self, position, or persona will always be given as yet one more persona. Self-creation must occur as continual self-destruction. The self is, authentically, not reducible to a position but must, nevertheless, always occupy a position. It is through this problem of position or personality that Romantic irony might be defined against Socratic irony. Whereas the aim and path of Socratic questioning is moral autonomy, Romantic irony perpetually strives to overcome the illusion of the autonomy of the self. The aim is not autonomy—drawing us back to self-formation—but impersonality—drawing us back to an emergence from an absolute that is certainly not our own.

Hegel and Absolute Idealism

Hegel was critical both of Kant's elevation of concepts above concrete existence and the German Romantics' transformation of Kant into a theory of irony. Hegel's response to irony was both an extension and a critique of Romanticism's acceptance of the gap between the unrepresentable soul and the finitude of concepts. We only fall into the predicament of irony, Hegel argued, if we imagine some undifferentiated absolute or supersensible substrate that precedes our differentiating concepts. In doing so, we mistakenly assume the starting point of an unlimited absolute set over against a limiting concept. What we need to realize is that this opposition—between the preconceptual and the concept—is only possible through the very movement or articulation of concepts. The unlimited, undifferentiated, and preconceptual absolute is an effect of concepts. At the same time, the finite and limited concept is only thinkable as the concept *of* what is not conceptual. A concept only works as a concept if it is more than itself. Concepts are always concepts *of* some being. The concept is not some static limit or passive token of the real; it is the real's own way of movement or realization. Rather than assuming some unrepresentable, preconceptual being that we can only grasp through concepts, Hegel argues that being *is* concept. The difference between the concept and the nonconceptual is an effect of the concept. The naive idea that concepts are subjective forms that we impose on the unlimited is also an effect of conceptual difference. This "we" or "subject" who conceptualizes is itself an effect of an absolute that *is conceptual*. The task of philosophy lies in realizing this coherence between the subject and the absolute;

subjectivity is not a position or point that is divorced from an objective absolute. Once we, as subjects, realize that our being is an event within absolute conceptualization, we are no longer other than the absolute; subject and substance become one in absolute idealism.

Kant's idealism is transcendental: we need to presuppose certain ideas in order to have knowledge of being. The idea is a transcendental condition, required in order to think being. Hegel's idealism is absolute: we do not need to presuppose ideas in order to determine being; being is just the progress or absolute negativity of ideas. Time, for example, is not some *form* that synthesizes reality; the real, or being, is itself just this process of temporal idealization. "Idea" has to be taken, therefore, in a more than mental or cognitive sense. An idea is not a human or mental event; it is the negation of the merely actual or inert. All life is a process of ideality and negation, a continual becoming other than itself in order to *be* itself. For Hegel, all movement of life, all action or reaction, is ideal precisely because life becomes or is only by moving to what it is not. This process of becoming or negation only recognizes itself in the self-conscious human idea. Idealism includes not just the negation of concepts in the narrow sense but the "negation" of becoming in general. The animal that consumes another animal "negates" that animal, and what an animal *is* is nothing other than its specific mode of negativity. Idea, therefore, has more to do with *eidos*, or form, in its Aristotelian sense, where form is just the power for a being to fulfil what it is. Life is ideal, and idealism is absolute, precisely because life is nothing other than this self-fulfilling process of realizing form, and the form that is truly self-realizing is the philosophical idea. It is only this idea that recognizes that ideas are not negations of the real world; the real itself is just a becoming through ideas. It is not that there is being, which is then negated by human ideas or concepts. Being is nothing other than negativity, a totality of mutually constitutive relations and differences. There is, therefore, no preconceptual origin of concepts; there is no subject or someone who then conceptualizes. There is a movement of conceptuality, idealization, or negation from which it is possible to think the distinction between subjects and objects.

Irony, from Socrates through to the Romantics, had begun with the disjunction between the concept that we speak or say and the force or meaning of that concept. For Socrates, this disjunction allows philosophy to pursue the concept to its originating Idea or ideal. From the discord between our uses of the word "justice" and its meaning, we must assume some high Idea of justice that animates what we say. The disjunction between speech and concepts leads us to the elevation of the Idea, an Idea that overcomes the contradiction between conflicting uses and senses. For the German Romantics, it is the disjunction itself that evidences an absolute that is inimical to any form of conceptuality. The absolute or Idea does not simply lie outside the concept; the absolute is the effect of conceptual limitation. Romantic poetry and literature therefore aim to intensify the inadequacies of conceptual determination, and so "irony" takes on a far broader definition than specific figures of speech. Romantic irony works by contrasting all the speech we may utter about the absolute and infinite with the meaning or feeling of the absolute. It was against this Romantic celebration of the disjunction between the meaning of a concept and what we think we say that Hegel set his rational history of the concept. For Hegel, what lies beyond the concept is not an empty negativity or undifferentiated absolute but itself a movement of the concept. Any idea beyond representation or concepts is effected through the labor of the concept. It is not that there is an infinite or absolute that our concepts cannot reach. The absolute or preconceptual is posited *from the concept.*

If our concepts appear inadequate, this ought to lead us to extend their domain. We should not think of some preconceptual undifferentiated abyss that concepts then negate or order, nor should we assume some infinite Idea of which our concepts are finite representations. There is nothing other than the negating activity or movement of the concept. The concept is only a concept in *not* being the thing; and the thing *is* what it is only in being other than and determined by the concept. It is from this mutually negating movement that both the preconceptual and the conceptual are formed. In the case of "justice," for example, if our concept of justice can meet with no worldly definition, this is because of an inadequate development of the concept. The response to this conceptual limit or negation ought not to be some Romantic positing of an absolute beyond the concept; rather, negativity needs to be taken up by the concept. First, our concept of justice will have to move beyond its pure form and not just be an empty idea. The definition of the concept will also have to include its worldly instantiation. Second, our world will have to meet our concept. If the Greeks' concept of justice seemed elevated above this world, this was because they had not yet concretized the universal concept. This concretization will occur, Hegel insists, only with his own philosophy, which is an actual realization of the history of philosophy's concepts. Philosophy is not the conceptual interpretation of the world, it is the concrete formation of the world through concepts and the transformation of concepts through worldly activity. Hegel's philosophy explicitly presents itself as a necessary overcoming of the negativity of the concept that opens the history of philosophy.

Socratic dialogue had allowed the concept its own movement and did so through a certain (dramatic) style. The various voices in the dialogue follow and respond to a question, a question that is formed in relation to some seemingly pregiven sense: just what *is* justice? Hegelian dialectic takes a different form, arguing that the sense of the concept is itself effected through the question and dialogue. Philosophy is, then, not the discovery of concepts or meanings that exist prior to some act of knowing; philosophy is the active formation of concepts. This formation is not cognitive but practical; negation begins through the needs of life, our necessary labor and struggle with a world that is other than ourselves, or negative. It is because of the needs of life, the necessity for all life to become and respond to what is *not* itself, that we are never in a state of pure immediacy. Life is mediation and becoming, and for Hegel, becoming is always mediated by what being is not. The seed negates itself in becoming a plant; the human body negates itself in coming to reason. All becoming or life is negation and self-destruction, but a negation that is also the very essence of what each being is. The concept's way of becoming other than itself, however, has this peculiarity: it can reflect upon and recognize its negativity. It can ultimately become, not just in response to what is other than itself but in response to its own movement. We can form a concept of the concept or a negation of the negation. At this point in history, the being of the concept and that to which the concept responds will coincide. We finally have concepts that allow us to think conceptual activity; the content of the concept is the concept itself. In absolute idealism or speculative philosophy what the concept means or represents will be nothing other than conceptuality itself.

For Hegel, the concept has a proper and historical itinerary. Only the concept of absolute spirit can conclude the teleology of the West. Only with "Spirit" will philosophy realize that it does not apply concepts to the world or discover concepts. Philosophy reaches maturity when it recognizes itself as nothing other than conceptual activity. Philosophy does not define concepts, as though there were real and simple predicates that might explain what a thing is. Philosophy is not about definitions of what we already say; philosophy does not tell us what "x" is. The being of a thing—what it is—is not independent of its conceptualization. When a philosopher says that "x is y" she does not just link up already given concepts; she creates concepts through their mutually effective relations. There is, therefore, a crucial and historical difference between mere representations, which simply describe things according to this or that perceived quality, and philosophical propositions, which are aware of their constitutive power, the power to allow being to be. The "is" of what Hegel refers to as a "speculative proposition" does not passively link a subject to a predicate but recognizes itself as an act of conceptual unfolding.

Everyday thinking links concepts as though they were simply tokens there to be used, unaffected by what we do with them or what we say (*PS*, preface, sec. 43, 25). The ordinary "mathematical" propositions of the understanding, Hegel argues, link one already given concept to another. When we say, "The tree is green," we attach a quality to an object, and we could just as well imagine other qualities being attached. The tree might just as well not be green; the relation is contingent, and neither side of the proposition affects the other. The "is" functions like a simple plus sign; it has no ontological meaning. In the speculative proposition, however, the "is" is not just a link between two preexisting terms. There are only two terms, only the difference between a substance and its attributes, because of the labor of the proposition. When we say, "The absolute is spirit," for example, the relation is necessary and productive. The absolute is realized or recognizes itself through such propositions. The absolute can only *be* through spirit, and spirit can only recognize itself properly through the concept of the absolute. The proposition no longer passively synthesizes already given identities; "absolute" and "spirit" come to be what they are only through the speech of philosophy, which both separates and unites them in the proposition. The "is" effects the relation of difference and identity that constitutes the two terms (*PS*, preface, sec. 60, 37): "The philosophical proposition, since it *is* a proposition, leads one to believe that the usual subject-predicate relation obtains, as well as the usual attitude toward knowing. But the philosophical content destroys this attitude and this opinion. We learn by experience that we meant something other than we meant to mean; and this correction of our meaning compels our knowing to go back to the proposition, and understand it in some other way" (*PS*, preface, sec. 63, 39).

Hegel therefore identifies his own dialectic with a certain style of proposition. To say that the "real is rational" is not just to describe a certain feature of the real. The proposition performs or effects the unity it describes. There is a "real" only insofar as there is some rational recognition of the real. In itself, or without articulation through propositions, the real would not *be*. It is not just that the real requires reason and concepts. Reason, in order to be reason, also requires this real that seems to be other than itself. Only after having made statements about the world can reason realize itself as that which allowed the world to come to recognition. The speculative proposition that the "real is rational" allows both rationality and reality to recognize their own becoming in and through philosophy. Philosophy does not accept and use concepts. It allows concepts to fulfill and realize themselves through a proper mode of articulation. In the case of defining what justice is, for example, we need to see this "is" not just as the adding of predicates to a subject; the passage from subject to predication is the very movement of justice itself. A just state would be one in which the very act of defining justice was essential. A just state does not accept the concept of justice as some already given and external law that we then define; a just state is one that determines for itself what justice is. Only then, Hegel insists, does the concept come to maturity.

Anti-irony

The problem of Romantic irony, Hegel argued, lay in never reconciling the subjective principle of conceptuality with the objects that it recognizes as necessarily different from itself. Irony withdraws into itself, surveying the entire world, values, and others from on high, from a position of never realized absence. Rather than being the great post-metaphysical and leveling liberation that contemporary ironists claim it to be,[19] Hegel regarded the ironic retreat into the subjectivity of concepts as the very end of the political. If, as the Romantic ironist insists, all we have are concepts that point to a real we never grasp, then everyday thinking in terms of judgments and values would have to be dismissed as naive. Only the elevated ironic artist who lives in a world without meaning or value has gathered the true principle of existence. He must distance himself from the belief and commitment of those engaged in life. The problem with this, Hegel argues, is that the ironizing artist can no more believe in his own soul than he can in the reality of the world, for both assumptions would posit some being beyond mere representation.

Since Hegel, irony has often been celebrated for just this reason; true ironic distance precludes even a commitment to oneself. The ironist recognizes even his own character as yet one more effect. The ironic artist would therefore be nothing more than a series of masks, personae, and appearances, his soul having no being other than a purely formal principle. The ironizing artist is therefore elevated above those who still maintain character, values, and commitment, and for Hegel, this is where the conflict and impossibility of irony are unmasked:

> I live as an artist when all my action and expression in general, in connection with any content whatever, remains for me a mere show and assumes a shape which is wholly in my power. In that case I am not really in *earnest* either with this content or, generally, with its expression and actualization. . . . When the *ego* that sets up and dissolves everything out of its own caprice is the artist, to whom no content of con-

sciousness appears as absolute and independently real but only as a
self-made and destructible show, such earnestness can find no place,
since validity is ascribed only to the formalism of the *ego*.

    True, in the eyes of others the appearance which I present to them
may be regarded seriously, in that they take me to be really concerned
with the matter in hand, but in that case they are simply deceived,
poor limited creatures, without the faculty and ability to apprehend
and reach the loftiness of my standpoint.[20]

Hegel goes on to anticipate Nietzsche's theory of nihilism in his critique of the Romantic artist who abandons the reality of values but
who nevertheless maintains a yearning and striving for those values:

The next form of this negativity of irony is, on the one hand, the vanity
of everything factual, moral, and of intrinsic worth, the nullity of everything objective and absolutely valid. If the *ego* remains at this standpoint, everything appears to it as null and vain, except its own subjectivity which therefore becomes hollow and empty and itself mere
vanity. But, on the other hand, the *ego* may, contrariwise, fail to find
satisfaction in this self-enjoyment and instead become inadequate to
itself, so that it now feels a craving for the solid and the substantial, for
specific and essential interests. Out of this comes misfortune, and the
contradiction that, on the one hand, the subject does want to pene-
trate into truth and longs for objectivity, but, on the other hand, cannot
renounce his isolation and withdrawal into himself or tear himself free
from this unsatisfied abstract inwardness.[21]

Like many contemporary antipostmodernists or anti-ironists, Hegel recognized that the attempt to free oneself from any founding
value would lead to self-contradiction and self-loss. But Hegel's answer to the predicament of irony lies not in reasserting the preconceptual real and the substantive character of the subject but in recognizing the common origin of subject and object. Both subject and the
world from which the subject appears to be divided are effects of the

concept. The concept has a force and reality that far exceed the mere persona of the human artist. Recognizing this force of concepts beyond human praxis demands moving from art to philosophy, from a sense of the absolute's emergence from a singular point (of the subject) to the speculative point of view that grasps the general emergence of all punctuality. We have come to realize—and here Hegel agrees with the Romantics—that art is no longer an adequate expression of the truth of the world.[22] Art is not cognition or representation. Art's "truth" lies in disclosing not the world or reality but the specific movements or articulations of conceptuality. Art is the singular or subjective expression of the universal. (And Romanticism expresses this most acutely through the failure of its own universal concepts to meet with objective fulfillment; such a failure is positive in that it intimates the unlimited only from art's manifest limits.) But in modernity, according to Hegel, we demand a higher truth than the singular inscriptions of the universal offered by art. We must move beyond the perceived end of art not by affirming art's necessary failure and self-enclosure but by realizing the universal power of conceptuality. If we think of art's universal possibility, we will confront not just the specific expressions of concepts but conceptuality as such—or what art *is*: "Art invites us to intellectual consideration, and that not for the purpose of creating art again, but for knowing philosophically what art is."[23] Any concept of that which lies beyond the concept, including the "aconceptual" concept of art, is nevertheless only given through the concept. We must overcome the end of art, not through the self-limitation of irony but in the recognition that even an ironic inference of the nonconceptual is only possible through concepts.

Philosophy arrives at maturity, or arrives at Hegel, when it no longer tries to find a preconceptual origin or reality that would match our concepts. Concepts are not forms we attach to objects; they are not ideas that float above existence. Existence *is* conceptual. Being is just this presentation of itself to itself. There is just conceptualization. Being—anything that we say "is" at all—must be understood through the "is" of a speculative proposition. Everyday sentences speak as though there were beings that were then predicated: "the tree is green"; "a cat is on the mat." But the "is" of the speculative proposition is not a static link between beings; it is from the "is" that being is thinkable, conceptualizable or *is* at all. Being would not be being without its own conceptual articulation; the "is" is being's own way of being.

Hegel does not just make this assertion *about* speculative propositions. He is telling us not just how we must speak and write philosophy but also how philosophy has always been possible. We have only had philosophy, even in its unfulfilled forms, through the power of the concept. Hegel is, on his own account, merely drawing out what philosophy and conceptuality have been all along. He argues, like Socrates and Kant before him, that if we follow what we already *say*, then we will ultimately recognize what we *must mean*. Philosophy, the universal, and the concept are inescapable and all consuming. If we wanted to reject all generalizing, concepts, and metaphysics, we might just point to "this" here and demand a recognition of being prior to all predication or conceptualization. But the word we use for the most minimal particular—"this"—is precisely the most general and universal of concepts, capable of repetition and reference well beyond the punctuality of "this" here. Any appeal to the brute particular that lies outside the concept must use the *concept* of the particular. This is why, according to Hegel, the person who thinks he is talking at the level of sense-certainty is actually already intending the universal: "What we say is: 'This,' i.e. the *universal* This; or, 'it is,' i.e. *Being in general.* Of course, we do not *envisage* the universal This or Being in general, but we *utter* the universal; in other words, we do not strictly say what in this sense-certainty we *mean* to say, and since the universal is the true [content] of sense-certainty and language expresses this true [content] alone, it is just not possible for us ever to say, or express in words, a sensuous being that we *mean*" (*PS*, sec. 97, 60).

From the fact that we speak at all we are already within the universalizing movement of the concept, already carried away from the singularity of any point of view or context: "When I say: 'a single thing,' I am really saying what it is from a wholly universal point of view" (*PS*, sec. 97, 60). At the same time, when we articulate a universal concept we do so from some particular concrete point. (And this is just the function of art; it is the recognition of the singularity of any concept's presentation: "For the work of art should put before our eyes a content, not in its universality as such, but one whose universality has been absolutely individualized and sensuously particularized.")[24] Certain speculative concepts, however, overcome this distinction between the event of articulation and the universality of the concept's claim. The concept of the "absolute" and the concept of the "concept" lead us to the position of self-recognition. *If there is an absolute*, then there can be nothing *other* than the absolute; there cannot be an absolute and *then* its concept. The very meaning of the (speculative) concept of the absolute precludes us from positing something beyond its domain. There could not be a being who then had a concept of the absolute, for this would locate an act of thought in opposition to the absolute. It lies in the peculiar nature of this concept of the absolute to change the very way we must think of concepts: not as tokens or labels but as the way in which being *is*. To *be* absolute the absolute would have to be at one with its conceptualization and its becoming. There could not be an absolute and *then* the thought, concept, or representation of the absolute. The absolute, to be absolute, must just be that which conceptualizes, realizes, and becomes itself. It could not be a being that *then* becomes, for then becoming would be added on, and the absolute can have no addition; it must *be* its becoming. If "we" think through the very concept we already have of the absolute, then we *must mean* that "we" are nothing other than this absolute conceptual power coming to recognition. And this must tell us something about who "we" are: reason is such that it forms concepts—of the absolute—that demand reason's self-recognition.

Hegel's style, in opposition to the Romantic attempt to sustain the gap between the subject who speaks and the persona that is articulated, extends infinitely—beyond an opposition between the "saying" of the concept and the concept's sense (or said). The "end" of philosophy will be that moment of full recognition when the saying and the said are united, when the voice who speaks is at one with the content spoken. This drive for unity of voice accounts for the extraordinary difficulty of reading Hegel. His writings, like Socratic dialogue, seek to follow the movement of the concept. But the concept is no longer fixed in some idea above and beyond the world, and the voice or point of view of dialectic is no longer divided between the Sophist's confident definition and the Socratic question. Rather, Hegel's own sentences move from a certain limited understanding of the concept to a higher or speculative meaning. Once a concept is voiced at a certain level it is forced to move beyond itself. Hegel undertakes the movement of philosophy through the adoption of a limited point of view, only then to see how truth emerges *necessarily* from naïveté. It is not enough to find truth ready-made. Any simple dismissal of error—any opposition between truth and error—would leave something outside truth. "We" need to be united with the very genesis or articulation of truth, which would also include all errors and opinions as moments on the way to truth and recognition:

The necessary progression and interconnection of the forms of the unreal consciousness will by itself bring to pass the *completion* of the

series. To make this more intelligible, it may be remarked, in a prelimi-
nary and general way, that the exposition of the untrue consciousness
in its untruth is not merely a negative procedure. . . . [When] the result
is conceived as it is in truth, namely, as a *determinate* negation, a new
form has thereby immediately risen, and in the negation the transition
is made through which the progress through the complete series of
forms comes about of itself.

   But the *goal* is as necessarily fixed for knowledge as the serial progression; it is the point where knowledge no longer needs to go beyond itself, where knowledge finds itself, where Notion corresponds to
object and object to Notion. (*PS*, sec. 79, 50–51)

The main difficulty, in reading Hegel, lies in working out *who is
speaking* or the point of view of the sentence. Most of Hegel's sentences have an implicit "as it were" function. A sentence will use a
concept in its limited sense and pursue this sense until the concept is
expanded to include a broader definition; but this does not then establish some higher or more stable viewpoint. The concept is then pur-
sued until its subsequent limit and negation. The use of point of view
is crucial for Hegel's *Phenomenology of Spirit*. The work oscillates between two points of view: the speculative point of view, which Hegel
prefaces with the use of "our," "we," or "for us," and the limited point
of view of the passage or movement of concepts, which is attributed to
a certain "stage" or "level" of consciousness.

Consider the following development of concepts from the notori-
ously difficult "Force and Understanding" sections of the *Phenomenology*. On the one hand, Hegel describes certain attitudes of consciousness, attitudes that are produced *from the very meaning of
concepts*. We begin, Hegel argues, with the concept of sense-certainty:
we know what a thing is because we receive it through the senses. But
this very concept leads to a dialectic; if we receive things through external sensibility, then what we have is not external at all but only in-

ner perception. And so, Hegel continues, consciousness "now" understands the world as inner perception, but this perception is taken as
some sort of thing or object: "This unconditioned universal, which
is now the true object of consciousness, is still just an *object* for it;
consciousness has not yet grasped the Notion of the unconditioned
as *Notion*" (*PS*, sec. 132, 79). Consciousness is not fully reflective; it
still relies upon some "universal" that is simply given or unconditioned such as "perception." It still has some concept that lies outside
of itself: consciousness explains itself through the concept of perception. In the speculative point of view, however, this concept of "perception" would be seen as consciousness's own. No *object*—such as perception—can explain or lie outside experience, for any such object
would result from experience. This means that consciousness cannot
be a *thing* that explains all other things. Consciousness is not something *about which we might have a concept*. It is the movement of the
concept. Hegel's speculative viewpoint emerges from the description
and delimitation of other viewpoints: "For us, this object has devel-
oped through the movement of consciousness in such a way that consciousness is involved in that development, and the reflection is
the same on both sides, or, there is only one reflection" (*PS*, sec. 132,
79). Consciousness is nothing more than the movement of a certain
style of proposition. If it is the nature of consciousness to posit something other than itself, this is because consciousness is a conceptualiz-
ing movement. It is not as though there is Being that then passes
through conceptualization. (Such an argument would rely on a concept—being—that precedes all concepts.) Being is not that presence
that is then re-presented in concepts. Being is nothing other than the
presentational movement of the concept: a movement that—when
grasped—cannot be explained by any *thing* but must remain as a
movement.

Infinite Negativity

This stress on movement is the heart of the speculative viewpoint that, for Hegel, overcomes the finite negativity of irony. Irony acknowledges a gap between our concepts and any thing we might offer to fill them: it separates the voice that speaks of, say, "justice" from the higher meaning of justice—a meaning that elevates itself above all saying. For Hegel, this gap between the concept and the real can be sublated when "we" see that what is other than our concepts is effected through *our* concepts. We should not be striving for a pure universal justice beyond all determination, for when we reflect on such strivings we see that they rely on the very determination they seek to eschew. The speculative viewpoint, unlike irony, does not place itself at a higher level than everyday conceptual thinking, as though there were some higher realm beyond the world. Hegel's position of speculation is, he insists, a consequence of moving everyday experience to the conclusions entailed by its implicit concepts. Any individual or limited standpoint, by its very nature, implies the speculative viewpoint (*PS*, preface, sec. 31, 18). Everyday "understanding" is already capable of recognizing a relation of negation between concepts and world, of recognizing the limits of its concepts. But what needs to be grasped is the opposition between understanding and the world, or how it is that our understanding seems to be set over against what is not itself (*PS*, preface, sec. 31, 18). We only have the limits of "understanding" or rigid conceptuality because there is the negating movement of reason. Whatever negates or is other than consciousness must not be seen as an empty "beyond" or an ineffable absolute that chastens consciousness, as in irony. Consciousness, as concept, is just this movement, separation, mediation, or negation that "gives" the difference between being and concept. Like so many descriptions of traditional irony, Hegel describes this emergence of speculation as the result of a dissolution, from within, of the comfortable, the familiar, and the everyday: "Quite generally, the familiar, just because it is familiar, is not cognitively understood. The commonest way in which we deceive either ourselves or others about understanding is by assuming something as familiar, and accepting it on that account; with all its pros and cons, such knowing never gets anywhere, and it knows not why. Subject and object, God, Nature, Understanding, sensibility, and so on, are uncritically taken for granted as familiar, established as valid, and made into fixed points for starting and stopping" (*PS*, preface, sec. 31, 18).

Against this "everyday" analysis of the limits of concepts and their differences (an analysis that merely looks at the world as some already differentiated or "positive" thing), the higher life of Spirit looks the differentiating power itself squarely in the face. This is a counterironic mode of look or point of view, not a point of view "hovering" above the world. This is a look that grasps itself looking. The ironic look that negates the world as something "other" is transformed into a look that recognizes itself (and what "is") as *nothing* other than the power of negativity:

> But the life of Spirit is not the life that shrinks from death and keeps itself untouched by devastation, but rather the life that endures it and maintains itself in it. It wins its truth only when, in utter dismemberment, it finds itself. It is this power, not as something positive, which closes its eyes to the negative, as when we say of something that it is nothing or is false, and then, having done with it, turn away and pass on to something else; on the contrary, Spirit is this power only by looking the negative in the face and tarrying with it. (*PS*, preface, sec. 31, 19)

The philosophical position of Hegel's *Phenomenology* relies, therefore, on a certain style of point of view. Spirit emerges as a seeing that sees itself. Irony is overcome by recognizing that the gap between the use of a concept and its extension is an effect of the concept itself: "Thus what seems to happen outside of it, to be an activity directed against it, is really its own doing, and Substance shows itself to be essentially Subject. When it has shown this completely, Spirit has made its existence identical with its essence; it has itself for its object just as it is, and the abstract element of immediacy, and of the separation of knowing and truth, is overcome" (*PS*, preface, sec. 37, 21).

In this rejection of positivity, Spirit must not regard itself as a finite point of view that overlooks what is other than itself. Rather, Spirit must be that which generates point of view from itself in order to grasp itself. Irony, by contrast, would be the fall of spirit into positivity, a misrecognition of itself as a specific existence, style, or position, rather than the absolute possibility of any position in general. This is why Hegel's *Phenomenology* is written from two points of view and articulated through sentences that produce a second (higher) point of view from the first: "What is, for the Understanding, an object in a sensuous covering, is *for us* in its essential form as a pure Notion" (*PS*, sec. 164, 102).

We might say, then, that Hegel is critical of a Kantianism that would simply accept the point of view of the subject and then subordinate all philosophical questions to the limit of this finite point. For Hegel, any finite point of view that looks upon the world must be extended to the point where the world is nothing other than its own appearing. There is not an (object) world that then appears to a subject. There is just appearing, and from this opening of the speculative look in general subject and object are differentiated. This is why style is so important for Hegel, if not for Kant. Kant accepts the transcendental viewpoint of the subject, the point from which his critique is written. Hegel, however, argues that it is just the production of this viewpoint, through certain ways of using concepts, that philosophy must render transparent. How is it that we can have these concepts that seem to invoke the absolute? The subject cannot be posited as the explanation of such concepts, for the subject is only effected from conceptuality. Philosophy must become aware of itself as an event of saying. Philosophy is neither literature nor art; it is, necessarily, in excess of any single concept or event of speech. It is the recognition of that power of conceptuality in general from which any speech act derives.

Post-Romanticism and the Ironic Point of View

Irony and Authenticity

According to many contemporary scholars, Socratic irony is the inauguration of a peculiarly Western sensibility, a sensibility that we might—at the risk of anachronism—describe as authentic. Authenticity is just that resistance to recognizing one's self as a fixed or determined being within the world. It is the *non*presentation or absence of the Socratic soul, through the donning of masks, positions, and personae, that allows the Socratic subject to remain above and beyond any of his worldly interventions. But there is also an irony in this attempt to remain other than any perceived self, for Socrates can only be the soul *behind* the mask *through* the mask. To see the self as successfully other than its performances, to believe in the achievement of authenticity, is to risk once again falling into static self-recognition. Any sense of the self beyond the limit must remain ironic and provisional, as a sense rather than a cognition of the self. To recognize the limits of the self is both an act of humbling irony (which sees the self as effect of persona) and a rejuvenation of autonomy (through the *recognition* of this effect). This play between self and persona, between recognition and concealment, precludes the possibility of a final ironic *position*.

For Paul de Man there is an endless oscillation of irony that demands "the transition from anthropology to the field of language and, finally, of literature" (*RCC*, 12). No theory of man can account for the play of irony, for irony is a rejection of any definition of thought as a thing within the world. It is a rejection of anthropologism. In its Romantic form, however, it is also (as de Man asserts) a move to the field of language: that point where thought or consciousness finds its worldly limit and possibility. For Hegel, the very form and style of speculative philosophy allowed language to lead us beyond the limits of the understanding to self-recognition. In speaking, we already move beyond our merely human selves to the point of view of reason in general. Like so many post-Hegelians, de Man recognizes at one and the same time this universality of language alongside the impossibility of universal recognition. There is no style that is successfully speculative, no sentence form that does not create a bifurcation between the subject that speaks and the subject that is spoken about. When I say "I," Hegel argued, "I say in general all 'I's'; everyone is what I say, everyone is 'I,' this singular 'I' " (*PS*, sec. 102, 62). I can only resolve this tension by becoming "everyone," by recognizing in myself that absolute movement of spirit and humanity. Literature, however, is the insistent rejection of this universal personality, and it is so precisely through the punctilious use of persona.

According to de Man, any utterance is essentially intersubjective. By speaking, one both offers one's meaning and acknowledges that this meaning is also (as communicable) not one's own. Structuralism, for de Man, stems from this "built-in discrepancy within the intersubjective relationship" (*RCC*, 12). The structuralist solution to the vertigo of language ownership is that of "conceiving a metalanguage without speaker in order to remain rational" (*RCC*, 12). Like Hegel, the structuralists insisted that naively sticking to our personal or "I" viewpoint could only lead to contradiction; we only have an "I" because there is already a language that speaks through us. If there is to be meaning, we must eliminate subjects and intention and move toward a structure that can be shared. Meaning, as shared structure, may be a structuralist answer, but it is also, de Man insists, a form of inauthenticity, an absence of self, a "hiding behind a screen of language" (*RCC*, 12). In removing point of view, the structuralist has removed the *moral* problem of the discrepancy between meaning and interpretation. The structuralist cannot account for the ethics of reading and speaking: that we posit some sense behind what is said, and that when we do so we decide, interpret, and position ourselves. The very notion of point of view, which the structuralist has eliminated, draws attention to the position of the speaker, both within language and in relation to the world. It is this problem of point of view that de Man, commenting on the structuralism of René Girard, regards as *the* problem of literature (a problem that also marks a break with anthropology):

> There can, indeed, be no narrative without point of view—but an intentional theory of the novel will have to turn this truism around and ask instead: since the correlative of all narrative is the constitution of a "point of view" to be occupied by the narrator, what then is the subjective necessity that prompts the creation of such a privileged viewpoint? Instead of showing that point of view exists for the sake of narrative—which is tautological—one should ask how and why narrative (in itself useless) exists for the sake of point of view. (*RCC*, 14–15)

The awareness of point of view, in contrast to structuralism's emphasis on system, is given in ironic literature. It is only through the linguistic event of narration that points of view are effected. The transcendental self that narrates is necessarily other than any of its narrated selves but is given as transcendental only in *not* being the self narrated. The subject of enunciation is essentially split from the subject enounced. In everyday language and grammar we act as though the subject that speaks were adequately expressed in its propositions. For de Man, language begins in just this desire for unity: to speak *what one is*. A manifestly literary narration is, however, an awareness of the everyday self's necessary inauthenticity. In narration the self presents itself *as a character*. It is the explicitly objectified, transcendent self of character that can then, by negation, indicate the authentic self that is other than any narrated persona. For de Man, ironic self-consciousness is authentic precisely because it acknowledges that any description of the natural empirical self will always be other than the transcendental subject, will *always* be a fall or a loss. The peculiarity of literature lies in the refusal to overcome this fall or loss. Literature moves beyond the erotic desire for self-unity and recognizes the loss itself as constitutive. Desire for unity is the first step in the achievement of authenticity; the self narrates itself in order to recognize itself. But authenticity is only fully realized when aesthetic consciousness recognizes the necessary nature of the self's disunity or separation. Literature and style must be recognized as transcendental, with the "fall" into character or persona being a *felix culpa*. Neither authenticity nor the transcendental subject would exist without this loss.

De Man is critical, therefore, of the inauthenticity of a Romanticism—such as early English Romanticism—that would posit a "natural" self above and beyond any of its limited narrative acts. It is literature, not the natural man, that is transcendental and originary. It is only after the event of narration that we can lament the fall or limitation of that self *that narrated*. Herein lies the specifically ethical temporality of narration. Only with the properly literary (reflective) recognition that a described unified self is the effect of an act of narrative description is authenticity achieved. The irony of narrative demystifies the autonomous self of early Romanticism by constantly oscillating between "natural man" and his fictive inscription, neither of which exists outside its separation through narration. Overcoming Romanticism is, for de Man, overcoming the "conception of the self as the pole of a subject/object relationship" and the "belief in the unity of a world of correspondences" (*RCC*, 102, 108). The irony of literature, and its ethical dimension, lies in this explicit and creative doubling of the self through the narrative creation of an "other self that overlooks the former self caught in the world" (*RCC*, 110). That is, ironic literature demystifies and destroys, rather than intimates, that self that precedes any narrative positing. Irony is irreducibly temporal, for it is only with the initial description of the worldly self that the higher point of view can be established *as having been.* And irony is hierarchical and ethical only through this temporality. Irony sustains and creates the gap between a subject that is other than the self that was described, thereby producing a past or original self that will always remain about to be. Ironic consciousness is a "permanent duality" in which any supposed correspondence between self and nature or self and world is demystified, seen as an effect.

Most speech and narrative, de Man argues, operates at the naive level of allegory, as though our language corresponded to some outside world or nature. Allegory relies, therefore, on the assumed difference between word and world. This very idea of allegory or correspondence that allows our speech to be meaningful already rests on a prior act of nonallegorical narration, the narration that separates point of view from the world. There must, therefore, be some transcendental narrative of allegory, a "story" or temporalization that places a world prior to its linguistic description. An original fiction, figure, or trope positions a viewing and speaking subject in opposition to the world. There can only be a nature that corresponds to our point of view *after* narration has given "us" point of view. "We" narrate and predicate nature in order to establish a world that is other than our selves and in so doing produce a describing and predicating self. Nature always appear as "ours" precisely because we only have nature through the acts of narration that also constitute us as subjects. The art of irony lies in exposing the necessary failure of allegory and correspondence:

> For nature speaks a language that is all too familiar, not by itself, since the otherness of authentic nature resides in an area that no language can reach, but because we can endow nature with the illusory correspondences that originate in ourselves . . . correspondences now become an obstacle to authentic poetry, a way to hide the predicament of the self by a pseudo-objective myth that manipulates nature for the purposes of self-deceit . . . .
> Irony [by contrast] is the device by means of which the excessive naturalism of the correspondences is exorcized and renounced in the hope of achieving a truly allegorical style, no longer dependent on references to entities that lie outside the self. (*RCC*, 113–14, 116)

A "truly allegorical style" occurs when irony has demystified everyday allegory. We begin from the naive correspondence, and difference, between word and world (allegory). Irony foregrounds the word's power to produce this duality. A truly allegorical style is then hoped for: an allegory in which what is other than the sign or word is no longer some preexisting "entity" but narrative's own effect.

Literature as Transcendental

De Man's idea of the opening of literature as the possibility both of the self and of authentic reflection provides a way of thinking irony as crucial to the tension between philosophy and literature. Literature is not a discipline or body of work within the world; there can only be self and world through an "original" event of narration. Such an origin is transcendental, never viewed in itself, perceived only in its retreat. Point of view, de Man insists, is a transcendental literary effect. There would be no speech without the idea of *one who speaks*, and this necessity of point of view relies upon narrative in general. Irony lies in exposing the literary production of that point of view that we naively believed to originate from the author. There are only authors and speakers after the event of narrative. And if point of view is a necessary condition of all speech, this leads us to de Man's conclusion about the transcendental status of narrative. If meaning demands one who speaks, then meaning also demands the production of speaking positions through narration. Only irony—and not philosophy—is capable of grasping the genesis of point of view. While literature explicitly performs point of view, philosophical speech would remain at the level of allegory, always speaking as though our language adequately doubled some outside world. This inauthenticity of philosophy would apply even to those ironic or contextual positions put forward by Searle and Rorty. The idea that there is nothing other than contexts or language games *refuses the essential inauthenticity of language.* "Contextual" approaches suggest that we might abandon the idea of language's truth and become nothing more than our linguistic personae. De Man, by contrast, insists that in order to read the narrated self we necessarily see any character as other than, or a fall from, an original self or subject. Character, self, or persona is always a mask for the original subject, a subject that is only effected in not being at one with any narrated character. Irony does not abandon this original self, but it exposes this "origin" as an effect of the fall into language. Without the idea of language's fallenness or inadequacy we could not read signs or texts. Language can only be meaningful or make sense if it refers to what is other than itself. But this outside or world to which language must seem to refer is effected through the event of language; any reference to context or world must present itself as that which language came along to name. For de Man, there is no question that irony could amount to abandoning the transcendence of language. By its very ironic nature language is always other than itself and always creative of a self that it immediately destroys. Language can only *be language* through allegory and irony: through the idea that language is always the sign of what it is not (allegory) and through the recognition that this otherness or negativity that limits language is only given through language (irony).

But irony is not just a transcendental possibility of meaning. De Man also argues for the historical pertinence of literary self-consciousness and the recognition of irony. There is a certain epoch—the modern—capable of recognizing a transcendental effect that was there all along. It is only after Romanticism and all its *aporias* that we can authentically realize that the self that supposedly exceeded all narrative was actually an effect of narration. We are then compelled to move from the allegory of the proposition, where our signs express or reflect what is true, to the irony of literature, where our speech is aware of its production of temporality, selfhood, and sense. It is precisely because the genesis of such production can only be perceived *after its fall into determination* that all authentic speech, including philosophy, must be ironic. This raises the question of the relation between philosophy and literature and philosophy and epoch. De Man's conclusions seem to suggest that philosophy can only achieve its end in becoming ironic, in recognizing that the truth, origin, and ground that it has always sought were actually the effects of rhetoric and the temporal syntheses that rhetoric makes possible. If point of view is transcendental, then de Man's insistence on the "primacy" of narrative is well founded. There can be no successful articulation of the subject or speech in general; there can only be singular self-aware or ironic speech acts. Philosophy could only free itself from irony and

rhetoric if it were capable of thinking beyond point of view and beyond the temporality of narration.

It was this task—of thinking the limits of personal point of view—
that dominated the philosophy of Søren Kierkegaard. De Man's work
is at once the distillation of all the problems of authenticity and viewpoint raised by the existential tradition; at the same time, rereading
this tradition allows us to see just how de Man arrives at the transcendental temporality of narrative and what possibilities have been fore-
closed.

Kierkegaard and the Concept of Irony

Kierkegaard's work *The Concept of Irony* is both a meditation on Socrates and an ironic use of Hegel's idea of absolute infinite negativity.
While Kierkegaard's work does seem to grant literature an essential
status within philosophy, unlike de Man, he nevertheless sustains a
commitment to a peculiarly philosophical irony and the delimitation
of rhetoric. In *The Concept of Irony* this task takes two general forms.
First, Kierkegaard states, against Hegel, that irony itself is infinite
negativity. Irony is not overcome by confronting an absolute negation
that separates the ironizing subject from his world; there is no negativity without irony. Second, irony is properly philosophical, for it is
only in irony that we are capable of a style that separates the subject
that speaks from any of its personae. Kierkegaard, no less than Hegel
and de Man, is quite aware of the problem of point of view. Whereas
Hegel insists that limited viewpoints necessarily lead us to grasp the
absolute emergence of all punctuality, de Man argues that such an
absolute is an effect of rhetorical limits. What makes Kierkegaard's
Concept of Irony so interesting (and so ironic) is its liminal position
between these two possibilities. On the one hand, like Hegel, Kierkegaard shows how any point of view necessarily generates the specula-

tive viewpoint that overlooks and is other than any finite point. We can never remain within rhetoric. But like de Man, and against Hegel, Kierkegaard also recognizes that this negation of particular viewpoints is infinite or interminable: we never achieve that speculative point of view that grasps viewing in general.

Kierkegaard begins his *Concept of Irony* with an analysis of Socratic irony and its capacity to move from the use of concepts to the Idea. When Socrates detaches a concept from its everyday utterance, he leads us to the possibility of the Idea, a meaning that, according to Kierkegaard, is "absolute infinite negativity." It is this negativity of the Idea that delimits the specific personality of our existence. The Idea is given negatively, as what lies beyond the finitude of our existence. Because we *live* the difference between the worldly concept and the Idea that lies beyond the concept, irony elevates us above our finite point of view (*CI*, 154). It is in this manner of elevation that Kierkegaard describes Aristophanes' Socrates:

> Whether he is in a basket suspended from the ceiling or staring omphalopsychically into himself and thereby in a way freeing himself from earthly gravity, in both cases he is hovering. But it is precisely this hovering that is so very significant; it is the attempted ascension that is accomplished only when this staring into oneself allows the self to expand into the universal self, pure thought with its contents. The ironist, to be sure, is lighter than the world, but on the other hand he still belongs to the world; like Mohammed's coffin, he is suspended between two magnets. (*CI*, 152)

From this elevation of the Idea, we are brought back to the specific finitude of our point of view. It is as though our point of view, or our world, were suddenly being examined from above. We do not occupy that higher position, but the historical figure of Socrates gives us an intimation of this philosophical height. Seeing one who lives as though he were other than this world allows us to feel the limit of this world and its possible "beyond." This is why, for Kierkegaard, Socratic elevation is a form of hovering or suspension; one is never fully above and beyond the world but always in a relation of relative height. The ironic point of view is not an otherworldly or speculative overcoming of this world, nor is it a commitment to the immanence of narrative or rhetoric. Irony is always an elevation *from* this world, and this elevation is only possible through the concept. The concept is both meaningfully used within this world and dependent on a higher Idea that can never be given. It is the concept that offers infinite negativity. One does not simply negate this world from a higher viewpoint. Height is enabled by concepts that are both within and beyond the world. To use a concept is to invoke an *impersonal* force or meaning, and irony is the manifestation of this impersonality. But impersonality can only be achieved as a delimitation of personality. The ironic point of view allows the concept to speak through the self, as other than the self. Socrates does not elevate *himself*; it is only in following the negativity of the Idea that Socratic impersonality becomes the very height of personality in general, a personality that lives impersonally.

Kierkegaard is insistent that this ironic point of view within which concepts are thought ought not collapse into a positive, determined, or reified self that could be delimited as a thing within the world. The power of the Socratic position, according to Kierkegaard, is its capacity to sustain a certain "height" or "hovering." Whatever the world is, it can never fulfill the demand of the Idea. But this Idea does not indicate, as it did for Plato, an existing realm of Ideas toward which the worldly soul can successfully ascend (*CI*, 153). Kierkegaard makes a clear distinction between Plato's assertion of a realm of Ideas and the Socratic irony that sustains itself in a relation of absolute infinite negativity toward the Idea. The ironic position is at once directed toward the Idea, but the ironist also acknowledges the limits of his own worldly position or *existence*. Socratic existence is simultaneously aware of its worldly location alongside its capacity to attest to a point of view "above" that location. The "above" is, however, effected from, rather than preceding and overseeing, the worldly viewpoint. On the one hand, the concept is used in everyday dialogue. On the other hand, it is possible to exist in such a way that one's concepts are open to question. It is this predicament of existence that places one in an infinitely negative relation to the Idea and that admits of no sublation in the Hegelian sense. Not only does the Idea "hover" over dialogue, never capable of being grasped from within the exchange of voices, but the Idea's negativity is also effected from the very limits of voice. Indeed, there is much in Kierkegaard's work that suggests that it is not that there *is* an Idea that is then grasped inadequately in dialogue; rather, from the very movement of dialogue a negativity is generated. The Idea does not lie in some pure position beyond the limits of voice but is effected from the limit.

There are, therefore, two starkly opposed positions regarding the limits of the Idea. The first is Platonic/Socratic: there are ideas that our concepts can only grasp in limited form. The second is Hegelian: it is only because of the delimiting movement of concepts that we are able to think of some pre- or supraconceptual Idea. These two possibilities also open the question of temporality and epoch. Do speech and conceptuality inaugurate time and thereby allow for the Idea of a sense or subject prior to speech acts? Or is there a flow of real time that can only fall into the rigidity of fixed speech? Does irony disclose or create the temporal gap from the origin? And is "our" epoch the privileged site for these questions of recognition? What makes Kierkegaard important in relation to these questions is that he allows them to remain unanswerable. Kierkegaard does not simply affirm a presence that is elevated above our concepts (Plato), nor does he include all that is within the movement of representation (Hegel). Far from producing a theory of voice and world, Kierkegaard places himself within the personality of Socrates. In this performance of personality it becomes impossible to decide whether it is speech or the Idea that is temporally originary. We cannot *say* that the Idea precedes and grounds speech, for this very act of saying gives the Idea through speech. But we are no less able to reduce the Idea to speech, for speech only works if there is an Idea toward which it is directed. It is personality alone that can deal with this contradiction. *The Concept of Irony* traces the emergence of a certain type of personality: a personality that recognizes itself not as a thing within the world but as a way of relating between one's worldly existence and the (nonworldly) concepts of that existence:

> situation was immensely important to Socrates' personality, which must have given an intimation of itself precisely by a secretive presence in and a mystical floating over the multicolored variety of exuberant Athenian life and which must have been explained by a duplexity of existence, much as the flying fish in relation to fish and birds. This emphasis on situation was especially significant in order to indicate that the true center for Socrates was not a fixed point but an *ubique et nusquam* [everywhere and nowhere], in order to accentuate the Socratic sensibility, which upon the most subtle and fragile contact immediately detected the presence of idea, promptly felt the corresponding electricity present in everything, in order to make graphic the genuine Socratic method, which found no phenomenon too humble a point of departure from which to work oneself up into the sphere of thought. (*CI*, 16–17)

What needs to be understood in all this is not just Kierkegaard's difference from Hegel but the ways in which this difference is effected from different styles of dialectic and point of view. Much has been made of Kierkegaard's use of personae in his other works. While *The Concept of Irony* is not written in an explicit persona, Kierkegaard establishes the movement of his argument from the personality of Socrates. What Kierkegaard traces is not any Socratic position—propositions or statements—so much as the style through which the Socratic point of view is achieved. *The Concept of Irony* is a book about the Socratic viewpoint that at the same time resists a stable viewpoint, always speaking through Socrates. The "position" of *The Concept of Irony* is not that of a philosopher making statements about the world. Kierkegaard rehearses and foregrounds the very possibility of the philosophical statement. Like the Socrates he describes, Kierkegaard hovers above this text: listing readings of Socrates, quoting philological studies at length, comparing Plato's and Xenophon's portraits of Socrates. The irony of this book lies not only in its topic but also in its excessive volubility. Like Hegel, the history of philosophy, for Kierkegaard, is not just a series of statements. What Socrates presents us with is the very *existence* of the philosopher as one who recognizes and lives the difference between the Idea of philosophy and the worldly grasp of that Idea. From that gap the philosopher can see himself as more than a point of view within the world, as existing toward the possibility for viewing the world in general.

Grasping Socrates as an historical possibility means that we must not reduce the force of his existence to being a mere vehicle for the explication of concepts. Socrates must be more than an object of philosophical activity, for he exists as a subjective power or potential. He offers Kierkegaard the challenge of a certain style: not to be present within the text as some expressed self but to remain everywhere absent. Irony is just this ruthless resistance to allowing oneself to appear as a recognizable being. If one allows one's concepts or what one says to exceed one's point of view, then one can always remain other than, different from, or "above" the merely said. This is why Kierkegaard's *Concept of Irony* is "about" ways of saying and viewing as well as enacting a disjunction between voice and point of view. When Kierke-

166 POST-ROMANTICISM AND THE IRONIC POINT OF VIEW

gaard "speaks" in *The Concept of Irony*, he repeats the Socratic position, quotes various interpretations and descriptions of Socrates, and
allows the authorial point of view of the text to remain above and beyond the totality of its utterances.

Voice and History

For Hegel, a truly speculative philosophy frees itself from any voice or
viewpoint and does so through history: each voice in philosophy must
be recognized as an expression of the power of the concept. Hegel's history examines each philosophical position as an example of the manifestation of the concept, such that when we read philosophy it is not
Plato who is speaking so much as a certain level of understanding.
Whereas Kierkegaard insists on the singularity of the philosopher's existence, Hegel describes any single philosopher as nothing more than
a mouthpiece or vehicle for the revelation of an impersonal absolute:

> since Philosophy in its ultimate essence is one and the same, every
> succeeding philosopher will and must take up into his own, all philoso-
> phies that went before, and what falls specially to him is their further
> development. Philosophy is not a thing apart, like a work of art; though
> even in a work of art it is the skill which the artist learns from others
> that he puts into practice. What is original in the artist is his conception
> as a whole, and the intelligent use of the means already at his com-
> mand; these may occur to him in working in an endless variety of ideas
> and discoveries of his own. But Philosophy has one thought, one real-
> ity, as its foundation; and nothing can be put in the place of the true
> knowledge of this already attained; it must of necessity make itself ev-
> ident in later developments.[1]

For Kierkegaard, by contrast, the singular style of philosophy that
seems to articulate concepts is really the unfolding of personality or
existence. Indeed, the very concept of irony only opens, or becomes

possible, through the originally historical existence of Socrates, a historical existence that then inaugurates a possibility of exceeding history (*CI*, 9). Ironically, however, this existence is best expressed in its absence. When one becomes identified with some authorial point of view, one has been reduced to a character, as though one's existence were nothing more than a certain position. If what I say in a philosophical text is fully owned by me, then I present myself as adequately re-presented in the external work. If, however, one adopts a "voice" (as does Kierkegaard), one sustains the impersonality of existence, not reducible to a position within the world. When one displaces oneself through a persona, one's existence is sustained as different from, or other than, point of view. Irony, for Kierkegaard, is both the very heightening of one's existence and a hyperbolic impersonality.

If irony for the German Romantics was an intimation of soul or feeling beyond the limits of rhetoric or voice, then we might see this movement as a rather untidy uptake of Kantian critique. Acknowledging the limits of experience, Kant insisted, ought to prevent us from speculation regarding the unlimited. By positing a soul that exceeded the limits of any given knowledge or concept, the Romantics would have missed the point of the Kantian limit. And many, including Hegel and Heidegger, have criticized Romanticism for returning Kant to some postulation of a hidden soul.[2] The self or soul is not some metaphysical foundation that precedes all thought, speech, and synthesis. Against Romanticism's intensification of the absolute and unlimited there has been a "modern" and antimetaphysical reading of Kant that stresses an antifoundationalism in which reason does not *precede* or ground articulation but is given only through the event of articulation.[3] Reason is purely procedural and formal: not a set of rules or a self that we are given but the process we follow in the absence of rules. Because no soul can be known or given, we are committed to autonomy or the ongoing process of justification. Autonomy is

not the expression of a self but the awareness that selves and positions
are constituted through dialogue. The modern reading of Kant, which
asserts that the soul is nothing other than an effect of the limit, would
ostensibly provide a proper, and therefore antipsychologist, reading of
Kant's critical enterprise.[4] Against a Romanticism that stresses Kant's
noumenal soul, contemporary Kantianism insists that the soul is an
(illegitimate) effect of a perceived finitude.

Kierkegaard moves between these two possibilities with his insistence on irony and personality. It may make no sense to posit a soul beyond the limit of language, but this is not because we cannot think beyond language; on the contrary, it is because the idea of the soul is still
far too human and inauthentic, still too much like a substance rather
than a subject. Kierkegaard saw irony, rather than the soul, as absolute
infinite negativity—a power to be other than a self, soul, mood, or
sentiment. Whereas German Romantic irony used irony and literature to intimate the soul, Kierkegaard regarded the soul "itself" as
ironic. The soul just "is" this gap, distance, or difference between the
idea and existence. Irony is neither a higher position nor an intimation of a soul beyond all position, it is negativity—not an elevated position but *a movement of continual elevation*. The "split" irony of Socrates indicates a self beyond any presented content: "He was not like a
philosopher delivering his opinions in such a way that just the lecture
itself is the presence of the idea, but what Socrates said meant something different. The outer was not at all in harmony with the inner
but was rather its opposite, and only under this angle of refraction is
he to be comprehended" (*CI*, 12).

Here, irony is the very production of interiority. From a displayed
disharmony we can posit the soul. Ironic distance is the only way in
which authentic subjectivity might recognize itself "as a refraction"
from the outer world. Indeed, it is the refractive nature of the Socratic
negativity that, for Kierkegaard, differentiates irony from the "Orien-

tal's" drive to overcome humanism altogether. The Eastern mystic's negation of bodily life is a striving for an animal nonlife. Rather than a return to the prehuman, Kierkegaard's ironist negates the human in order to achieve the soul in a higher form. The negation is positive: not a retreat from the self into unselfconscious animal passivity but an abstracted hyperactivity. This distinction between Eastern lethargy and Western activity is played out along a vertical axis, where the non-seeing mystic is contrasted with the elevated ironist who *sees nothing*. The "Western" sensibility marks out a site beyond the world, a liberation or negation of any geographical position:

> Therefore the Oriental may indeed wish to be liberated from the body and feel it as something burdensome, but this is really not in order to become more free but in order to become more bound, as if he wished for the vegetative life of the plant instead of locomotion. It is wishing for the foggy, drowsy wallowing that an opiate can procure rather than for the sky of thought, wishing for an illusory repose in a consummation connected with a *dolce far niente* [sweet idleness] rather than for the energy of action. But the Grecian sky is high and arched, not flat and burdensome; it rises ever higher, does not anxiously sink down; its air is light and transparent, not hazy and close. Therefore the longings to be found here tend to become lighter and lighter, to be concentrated in an ever more volatile sublimate, and tend not to evaporate in a deadening lethargy. Consciousness does not want to be soaked to softness in vague qualifications but to be stretched more and more. Thus the Oriental wants to go back behind consciousness, the Greek to go over and beyond the sequence of consciousness. But this sheer abstractness that it desires becomes ultimately the most abstract, the lightest of all—namely, nothing. (*CI*, 66)

Height and Negativity

Kierkegaard's association of negativity with a peculiarly Western consciousness—in contrast with an "Oriental" retreat from the split

of worldly existence—is utterly ambivalent. Like Rorty's irony, Kierkegaard's negativity would be parasitic, only known in its elevation
above inauthentic, worldly, or "Eastern" forms of mere life. At the
same time, whether such elevation could be said to be anything more
than an idea remains an open question: the West would not be a locale
as such but only the Idea of a view from nowhere, a hovering in non-
commitment. The Western sensibility of Socratic irony may have no
locus or being, "existing" only in its difference from life: "The more
Socrates tunneled under existence [*Existents*], the more deeply and
inevitably each single remark had to gravitate toward an ironic totality, a spiritual condition that was infinitely bottomless, invisible, and
indivisible" (*CI*, 19).

"Our" present would, then, not just be the time in which we recognized ourselves as ironic effects of speech. It would also be "our" spatial community, precisely to the extent that it was freed from any specific culture or place. Kierkegaard anticipates the problem of irony's
"liberal" atopia. In striving to free oneself from any specific concept or
figure of life one must hover above life. But there also remains the risk
that this hovering might produce one more dogmatically elevated
viewpoint that fails to recognize its own singularity. It is always possible that the intimated view from nowhere that lies beyond existence
will fall into the assertion of a specific and singularly Western style
of existence.

In undermining existence, irony *is not*. It is always other than, and
elevated above, any posited subject or being. After Kierkegaard, we
might argue, irony loses its soul. But this loss has always been irony's
very possibility, for the soul, as defined through Socratic irony, was always other than any positively defined sense of the human. For Kierkegaard, however, the power of irony is not that it takes us out of the
human to the soul's proper domain. Rather, the infinite negativity of

irony discloses the absence of a proper domain. And for this very reason two problems of irony come to the fore. In Kierkegaard irony is not in the service of truth; it does not hierarchically delimit a voice to posit truth elsewhere. Truth "is" the ironic delimitation of voice and nothing else. This is the difference, for Kierkegaard, between the ironic and speculative question: the latter seeks its desired content, while the ironic question "sucks out" any apparent content to reveal emptiness (*CI*, 26). This does not imply that irony is pure play; on the contrary, irony is the difficult recognition of the inauthenticity of everyday relativism, for one cannot but speak. In so doing we are always in a position: "Ordinary human life moves drowsily and vaguely between these two poles. Irony is a healthiness insofar as it rescues the soul from the snares of relativity; it is a sickness insofar as it cannot bear the absolute except in the form of nothing, but this sickness is an endemic disease that only a few individuals catch and from which fewer recover" (*CI*, 77–78).

Only the ironist has the strength to recognize that while there is an absolute beyond the everyday, it is never given in anything so existent or experienceable as the soul or feeling. This ironic recognition of everyday speaking as mere speaking, banality, or eloquence leads to a hierarchization. Kierkegaard's description of the ironist as "above" ordinary life reinforces a long-standing tradition of metaphors of ascent, elevation, and height that characterize the ironic viewpoint. Only with the height of irony does the happy relativity of everyday existence become perceived *as perspective*. The philosophical irony that recognizes the disjunction between speaking and the absolute is irony in its total striving; it is the irony of the ideal self that is "eternal unrest" and constantly engaged in the difference between speaking and what is (*CI*, 176). What sustains the true ironist is "a negativity which as yet has fashioned no positivity": "Thus his position in life was altogether predicateless" (*CI*, 180). Nevertheless, the risk of positing the negative as a positivity, of slipping into mythic or "Eastern" enthusiasm, is the ironist's perpetual tribulation. As a continual struggle against speculation irony is therefore not so much a philosophy of propositions as the performance of personality and standpoint that is set against banality. In fact, according to Kierkegaard, "Boredom is the only continuity the ironist has" (*CI*, 285). Defined against boredom and actuality, the ironist's subjectivity is the opposite of essence and existence such that "when everything else becomes vain, subjectivity becomes free." In being other than himself the ironist is also in a position to "look down" on the boredom of immediate understanding:

> If . . . what I said is not my meaning or the opposite of my meaning, then I am free in relation to others and to myself . . . .
>
> The ironic figure of speech has still another property that characterizes all irony, a certain superiority deriving from its not wanting to be understood, with the result that this figure looks down, as it were, on plain and simple talk that everyone can understand; it travels around, so to speak, in an exclusive incognito and looks down pitying from this high position on ordinary prosaic talk. In everyday affairs, the ironic figure of speech appears especially in the higher circles as a prerogative belonging to the same category as *bon ton* [good form] that requires smiling and innocence and looking upon virtue as narrow-mindedness, although one still believes in it up to a point. (*CI*, 247–48)

Kierkegaard criticizes the Romantics for believing that the recognition of our noncorporeal self can be experienced as some kind of moral soul. In so doing we merely describe the transcendental in terms of another worldly thing. The concept of poetic self-creation, on the other hand, sustains the distance between spirit and flesh. Poetic self-creation is the resignation to, rather than denial of, the gap between self and spirit. Poetic self-creation is not Schlegel's worldly "aesthetic stupefaction," not a lapsing back into "effeminate" unity, but "victory over the world." But while poetry can conquer the world, it still leaves the predicament of self and existence:

> If we ask what poetry is, we may say in general that it is victory over the world; it is through a negation of the imperfect actuality that poetry opens up a higher actuality, expands and transfigures the perfect into the imperfect and thereby assuages the deep pain that wants to make everything dark. To that extent, poetry is a kind of reconciliation, but it is not the true reconciliation, for it does not reconcile me with the actuality in which I am living; no transubstantiation of the given actuality takes place by virtue of this reconciliation, but it reconciles me with the given actuality by giving me another, a higher and more perfect actuality. The greater the contrast, the less perfect the actual reconciliation, so that when all is said and done there is often no reconciliation but rather an enmity. Therefore, only the religious is able to bring about the true reconciliation, because it infinitizes actuality for me. (*CI*, 297)

German Romantic irony had already opened the question of literature and philosophy, but the dispute was often seen as the difference between a truth that was felt and a truth that was cognitive or conceptually posited. The aesthetic was capable of achieving (through feeling) a higher truth beyond the limits of representation. The ironic limit was a form of intimation, if not revelation, of what lay beyond the limit of rhetoric. But in Kierkegaard the power of irony suggests not a surpassing of the limit but the vertiginous realization that the "nothingness" or abyss beyond the limit is only known as the limit itself. Furthermore, the infinite negativity of irony lies in the fact that this realization cannot be realized. Poetic self-creation is, therefore, a distance or difference from any representation that can, nevertheless, only be achieved through representation; the subject is only *ideal* in its ironic absence, in *not* meaning what he says. For Kierkegaard, poetry leads beyond its nothingness to a *lived* infinity: "It is no longer poetry's pantheistic infinity, but it is the finite subject, who applies the ironic lever in order to tip all existence out of its fixed consolidation" (*CI*, 302).

For Kierkegaard, there may no longer be a substantive soul, truth, ideal, or freedom beyond the limit of voice or tone. But art (more specifically, literature) as the tracing of the limit becomes the truth of voice or tone, which then leads to authentic existence. Kierkegaard's description of the poetic standpoint is strikingly similar to Goethe's "invisible point" and Flaubert's later famous description of the author: "an author in his book must be like God in the universe, present everywhere and visible nowhere." From the poetic standpoint, "Nothing becomes everything, and everything becomes nothing; everything is possible, even the impossible; everything is probable, even the improbable" (*CI*, 303). According to Kierkegaard, however, the "arbitrariness" of the poetic standpoint cannot remain at the level of the aesthetic, for the ideal striving of poetic self-creation always gestures to a negativity, an ideal striving or absolute beyond any description. Just as Socrates derives the truth of the soul from the fact that absolute realities exist, so Kierkegaard ultimately—at the end of a series of ironic speech acts—feels no less certain that there is an existence beyond the (limited) actual: "As certain as it is that there is much existence which is not actuality, and that there is something in personality which is at least momentarily incommensurable with actuality, so also it is certain that there resides a truth in irony" (*CI*, 270).

Existence is not any one thing or point; existence is not actuality but negativity. Kierkegaard's criticism of the Romantics was that they moved from the limits of irony to the existence of the soul, as though the soul preceded negativity. Kierkegaard's attempt to think existence and irony as not being any thing or positive actuality concludes with the certainty of existence as negativity. For this reason there is an essential and necessary incoherence in his work, at once insisting on the power or potential of negativity and nonexistence while also committed to a truth beyond truths and an existence beyond existing.

Authenticity and Possibility

This positing of the existence of infinite negativity, ideality, and the "truth" of irony is even less clear in modernist irony, and the difference is given most clearly not in statements about irony but in style. However difficult we may find it to read Kierkegaard, and however much Kierkegaard states that "irony in a strict sense can never set forth a thesis," his work is still a theory of irony and refers to the concept of irony. Kierkegaard brings us to the limits of irony, authenticity, and philosophy. His irony is ruthless, for while he insists on the limits of rhetoric, he also argues that the ironic position outside rhetoric cannot simply be another positive position. And the possibility of authenticity is no less difficult to grasp, for Kierkegaard insists on the need to form a worldly and existing personality alongside the negation of that personality. But it is the possibility of philosophy that truly meets its limits in the style of Kierkegaard's work. A truly philosophical position would, like Socrates, be other than rhetoric and other than a worldly point of view. But this can be achieved only through the rhetorical construction of personae. As an explicit mask or persona this implies that absolute and infinite negativity that exceeds personification.

Both Socrates and Kierkegaard's Socrates suggest a position beyond the limit of everyday speech. It is the existentialism of Kierkegaard—the idea that the viewpoint of theory that overlooks the world is produced through a way and style of life—that leads beyond philosophy to literature. In modernist irony we are not given one more literary position so much as a literature aware of itself as productive of positionality in general. The doubleness of sense that typifies irony, the elevated viewpoint or personality of the ironist, is not presented in Flaubert in any particular figure such as Socrates. For Flaubert, there is no longer a position other than eloquence. Irony, in Flaubert, is not the delimitation of everyday rhetoric in the service of a path to truth, and there is no ironic position of Socratic questioning, Schlegelian feeling, or Kierkegaardian negativity. Like Goethe's Shakespeare, Flaubert's artist is invisible, but this is no longer an invisibility of the universal ideal. Irony is performed entirely in the specificity and particularity of art and style. The artist is nothing other than a certain power of style. Only in the faithful repetition of the limits of bourgeois banality does the artist as such exist. The nothingness of Flaubertian irony is not a Kierkegaardian negativity; it is not a distance from positive things and everyday speech but the presentation of banality itself.

Flaubert's *Bouvard and Pécuchet* is the sustained, faithful, and minute presentation of an odyssey of bourgeois fact finding, classification, and knowledge. As does Foucault in *The Order of Things*, Flaubert traces the path of representationalism in the texts of Cuvier, Buffon, and the classicists. What is presented is an absurd belief in the correspondence between words and things with "man as its apotheosis."[5]

> "I should like to know how the universe came about."
>
> "It must be in Buffon," answered Bouvard, whose eyes were closing.
>
> "I can't go on anymore. I'm going to bed!"
>
> The *Natural Epochs* told them that a comet striking the sun had knocked off a piece, which became the earth. First the poles had cooled down. All the waters had covered the globe; they had withdrawn into hollows, then the continents divided off, animals and man appeared.
>
> The majesty of creation caused them an awe as infinite as itself.[6]

By presenting banality itself Flaubert institutes a mode of narration that surpasses any merely literary event, allowing for a whole new power of existing. The Flaubertian shift from irony to free-indirect style borders on but never achieves a realization that nothingness is impossible. Any intimation of a negativity other than style would possess its own style. In Flaubert's free-indirect style it is the everyday lack or absence of style that is rarefied into style itself, such that the author or narration is no longer outside the work. Flaubert's free-indirect narration is tied to a commitment to immanence. There is not a world that we then articulate through style or that we negate by speaking. Style itself is the very becoming of the world. Only free-indirect style, in which authorship immerses itself in the point of view of that which it describes, can apprehend and be at one with immanence. Unlike traditional irony, free-indirect style works *against* the implication or intimation of some point of view beyond style.

What this suggests is that there is an intimate link between style and position. Flaubert's practice of the inhabitation of voice without a clear delineation of authorial position fudges the limit or divide between the particularity of point of view and the transcendental genesis or subject from which point of view is posited. The Socratic soul that is no worldly thing, Schlegel's feeling that exceeds philosophical positing, or Kierkegaard's infinite negativity would still be, for Flaubert, further things, and still thoroughly human. Given the impossibility of ironic distance (for there may be no self outside stylistic manifestation), Flaubert will occupy or inhabit. Such inhabitation leaves the position of the artist *undecidable*. Whether there *is* a position or ideal self beyond the specificity of point of view is a constant question of free-indirect style, which challenges the ironic hierarchization of sense (or truth values). The positivity and immanence of Flaubertian style lies not in a clear difference between ordinary life and elevated distance but in the striving to *move through* or become other than the banal through banality. Flaubert's *Bouvard and Pécuchet* achieves and repeats the style of banality. In so doing, it is only other than banality itself through an act of stylization. What is ironized in Flaubert is not ordinary speech so much as the confident idea that one might be other than ordinary, other than a received style. For isn't a yearning to find a site of expression beyond the particularity of life the height of banality itself?

The following scene from the novel presents the world of everyday aesthetic judgment. It is the thoroughly bourgeois "professor" who affirms the possibility of a style that might free us from everyday banality, and it is Bouvard and Pécuchet who respond by seeing style as yet one more item to be learned and consumed:

> According to the professor a play's immediate fate proves nothing. *Misanthrope* and *Athalie* were failures. *Zaïre* is not understood anymore. Who talks to-day of Ducange and Picard? And he recalled all the great contemporary successes, from *Fanchon la Vielleuse* to *Gaspardo le Pêcheur,* deploring the decadence of our stage. The reason for it is contempt for literature, or rather style.
>
> Then they asked themselves what constitutes style, and thanks to authors indicated by Dumouchel they learned the secret of all its genres.[7]

Flaubert's *Bouvard and Pécuchet* has been explicitly lauded by a number of contemporary French writers working at the limit of philosophy, including Roland Barthes, Gilles Deleuze, and Michel Foucault.[8] Of course, there are a number of writers who for a long time now have been recognized as "important" for poststructuralism, including Nietzsche, Mallarmé, Freud, and Marx. But it is Flaubert's style rather than any offered problem or mode of theory that contributes to the very possibility of poststructuralism. Free-indirect style works by being and not being ironic. It delimits the limit of rhetoric but does not generate an unlimited. Not only does this description of free-indirect style recall some of the supposed "ideas" of poststructuralism, it also describes the style of much poststructuralist writing.

Poststructuralist Style

Roland Barthes was, in keeping with the tradition of irony, critical of the way in which language could circulate "mythically"—as so much noise divorced from any meaning, sense, or intention. Language becomes mythic, passive, or meaningless, according to Barthes, precisely when its meaning seems to be so self-evidently "ours." Mythic speech offers timeless, self-evident, and unquestioned truths. True speech, by contrast, is *historical*: engaging with the world, history, and existence. Myth, for Barthes, was a form of "frozen speech," evacuated of all historical content, appearing as immutable, without any sense of its genesis or becoming. His classic example, of a photo of a black soldier saluting the French flag in *Paris Match*, shows how certain signs seem to capture the "evidently true."[9] We do not *say*, actively, that the colonized embrace and accept their position, but myth continually *speaks* this message. The black soldier who salutes the flag is so natural, unquestionable, and recognizable that no one need actually state the meaning of this sign. Myth, for Barthes, is a specific register or mode of speech that has become divorced from active dialogue, performance, and subjects of enunciation. It circulates as self-evidently true and in *not* being spoken cannot be contested. The response to myth, however, is not the restoration of speech to speakers and history. Myth needs to be mythified—and it is here that Barthes appeals to Flaubert.[10]

There can no longer be an appeal to a proper and originating speech, for any such proper origin can itself be rendered into myth. (Barthes refers to the ways in which the avant-garde, in aiming to be *other than* the institution of "Art," itself became one more recognizable institution.) The belief in irony—that we might be in a position above the merely rhetorical circulation of speech—can itself become one more myth. The figure of the existential philosopher, the image of the poststructuralist rebel, the "radical" postmodern artist—all these types bear the quality of myth precisely because we believe them to be successfully other than the everyday. Since Barthes, there has been no shortage of "radical" movements—such as postmodernism, feminism, postcolonialism, punk, and anarchism—that become widely disseminated, recognized, and confirmed as our own. What these signifiers refer to, as myths, is no longer an *act* of transformation—say, a political claim—but the signifier itself, emptied of its force and power. We can wear punk as a style, use the devices of postmodern literature, adopt the appropriate nonsexist terminology, and affirm the rights of animals. But in so doing we are not so much *speaking* as comfortably reiterating a message that no longer *says* anything at all. This is exemplified in the contemporary problem of "political correctness." What begins as an attempt to transform language becomes a tic within language, no longer having any force or sense of engagement but functioning as so much automatic social noise. Barthes's "mythification" does not, therefore, strive to find an original and authentic voice that would lie outside the fall into mythic systems of signification. As in Barthes's *Mythologies*, mythification restates the everyday with a fidelity and closeness that disclose its specificity rather than its generality, exposing myth *as myth*.

Not surprisingly, when Barthes says that the only response to myth is not restoration but mythification, he cites Flaubert. It is in *Bouvard and Pécuchet* that Flaubert formulates a style that repeats just what seems to be factual, ordinary, and unremarkable. And to a certain extent this is the "method" not only of Barthes but of many of the French writers who follow in the poststructuralist tradition. We can think here of de Man's conditional. If point of view is necessary for meaningful speech, then we cannot but produce subject positions that speak. But any such posited subject is always an inauthentic effect of style. Authenticity would not be a posited self "behind" style and the speech act but a speech act that demystified and destroyed any such self. If it is impossible to find an authentic position outside style, and if style bears as its possibility an essential repetitiveness and inauthenticity, then the only writing strategy can be to write inauthenticity itself. Barthes's *Mythologies* faithfully repeats all the truisms and unremarkable significations of French culture. Michel Foucault will do the same for the history of ideas, not describing the past as an object but speaking through its own discourse, and Derrida will do the same for philosophy, not producing deconstruction as a "method" but inhabiting a text to the point of its own incoherence. Writing and play, far from being a freedom from philosophy and commitment, would stem from the impossibility of speaking from nowhere. If ironic distance is no longer possible, stylistic repetition will at least allow us to play with that writing from which all height and distance emerge.

In the repetition of banality Flaubert's free-indirect style occurs as a thoroughly immanent transcription of the human limit. This inhabitation of rhetoric is a recognition that any positing of an outside to rhetoric will always be another rhetorical effect. Flaubert's "irony" or free-indirect style does not lead us to truth (of the soul, the absolute, or Ideas), but it does produce a *sense* of banality. The artist is nothing other than this sense, achieved through the play and inhabitation of style. Literature, as the avowed use of tone, style, voice, and point of view, has a certain advantage over any position of knowledge that cannot but posit as real a certain view of the world. Style is a self-conscious repetition of the limit of any positive point of view. Style, in this sense, is nothing and everything, everywhere and nowhere. Flaubert is at once the culmination and end of irony. The artist as transcriber of everyday banality can, through repetition, be other than banality, but only through banality itself. Just as there is no more authentic style, whether of moral autonomy, feeling, or infinite negativity, that can be set against everyday speech, there is also no space, point of view, or position that would not itself be a certain style. Style, in its manifest particularity, is nothing and everything, all that there is, as well as being utterly inadequate to what is.

The Possibility of Contemporary Irony

If irony, with Socrates, occurred as a distancing from everyday speech in the service of a higher truth, it was also peculiarly worldly. The soul could still be known, lived through the philosophic life, and its noncorporeal status could be asserted with certainty. Kant, of course, precludes such knowledge but still allows the "vacant space" of the pure concept that will be located at the limit of experience. And it is the Romantic aesthetic that will allow that vacant space to be felt, if not known, in the work of art. But the mistake of the Romantics, as Kierkegaard maintained, lay in a far too human conception of what lay beyond actuality. The ideal self at irony's limit should not be an elevated version of the temporal ego but infinite negativity, totally other than any positive description.

Kierkegaard might stand, then, as typical of the transcendental move identified by Foucault in *The Order of Things*. With the increasing recognition of man's finitude in the human sciences and with the evaporation of man as a soul, man becomes a representational animal. As man increasingly becomes an object of study or an empirically determined thing, it is not surprising that he also, and in reaction to his increasing scientific objectification, regards himself as *other than a thing*. Man becomes other than merely human only by positing a transcendental horizon. Existential irony, also, is no longer a higher position or personality but is radically other than any posited point of view.

According to Foucault, the idea of man as *subject*—as that which posits itself in order to turn back and know itself—occurs from Kant to Freud as a refusal of man's *positivity.* On this picture, Kierkegaard might appear as one more instance of Foucault's "empirico-transcendental double." It is from the very limits of empirical being—man as an animal within the world—that a transcendental horizon of infinite becoming is presupposed: "the analysis of the *empirico-transcendental reduplication* shows how what is given in experience and what renders experience possible correspond to one another in endless oscillation."[11] In the nineteenth century man's transcendental origin is given in a number of different disciplines that set themselves alongside the study of empirical man: psychoanalysis, ethnography, and philosophies of the subject. Kierkegaard's "infinite negativity" could also be read as one more recuperation of the subject in the face of an ascending "anthropologism." Foucault aims to show that all those transcendental projects that resist the objectification of man still rely on some normalizing horizon from which empirical man is delimited. Even structuralism locates difference and becoming within a single plane of language that can be located, known, and recuperated. Foucault's own project might, therefore, be classified as anti-ironic. Indeed, his emphasis on positivity and the thoroughly corporeal production of the soul would seem to be evidence of a refusal of any infinite, absolute, or undifferentiated ground from which thought emerges.[12] The inner or ineffable subject that lies beyond our questions and definitions is in actual fact an effect of knowledge procedures. Against irony, and against a literature that would speak only to delimit itself from a hidden and infinite *said,* Foucault seems to celebrate a literature of *silence.* Such a literature does not *say* anything other than itself, thereby freeing itself from the inauthenticity of a supposedly natural prelinguistic standpoint: "Hence the necessity of converting reflexive language. It must be directed not toward any inner confirmation—not toward a kind of central, unshakable certitude—but toward an outer bound where it must continually contest itself. When language arrives at its own edge, what it finds is not a positivity that contradicts it, but the void that will efface it. Into that void it must go, consenting to come undone in the rumbling, in the immediate negation of what it says, in a silence that is not the intimacy of a secret but a pure outside where words endlessly unravel."[13]

Like Roland Barthes and Gilles Deleuze, Foucault regards Flaubert's *Bouvard and Pécuchet* as offering the possibility of freeing thought from its normalizing images. It is the positive presentation of *stupidity* that is crucial here. Stupidity is not error—a point where thinking has gone astray. Stupidity is a style of thought that is radically different from the recognized categories of good sense. Unlike error, stupidity cannot be tidied up, reformed, or corrected. Stupidity misconnects, misrecognizes, and stubbornly resists the elevation of good reason. And this is why the humor of *Bouvard and Pécuchet* lies as much in the optimistic educators, professors, and guides as it does in the simplicity of Bouvard and Pécuchet, for it is clearly *not* the case that *more* reading or expanded knowledge will bring the two to the height of reason.

How is it that from Socrates to Searle we have assumed the good will and sincerity of speaking subjects, such that once they are brought to the limits of the irrational they will recognize the force of reason? Stupidity is different from error precisely because it is incapable of recognizing the misuse of logical categories. Stupidity is a thought that is rigid, malevolent, and absurd in its very style. The phenomenon of stupidity shows the ways in which thought can be locked into the most dysfunctional and ridiculous modalities. It discloses the *singularity* and impersonality of thinking: that there is not some general reason that expresses who we are, but that "we" are nothing but a series of ad hoc, incoherent, and disconnected clichés.

The categories of thought are not necessary and transcendental but found, assumed, and limited. Flaubert's value lies, then, not so much in the delimiting power of irony but in the affirmation of the positivity of the stylistic limit.

The Order of Immanence

It is possible to read Foucault as *the* "philosopher" of brute immanence, such that any critical position that would judge life or knowledge is short-circuited by his rejection of transcendence. Western thought, he argued, has been *subjected* both to the truth of some "said" and to a transcendence or outside to which our knowledge ought to tend.[14] Against this subjection, Foucault's projects aimed to describe the ways in which various modalities of being were produced through the "foldings" that separate an inside from an outside.[15] How, then, might Foucault resist the eternal predicament of irony? As Kierkegaard had already suggested, there is always a risk that the elevation above personality reifies into one more personality. The refusal of human viewpoints becomes one more elevation of the human.

One possible approach is to rethink the very propositional style of philosophy. Foucault's writing does not so much offer a series of statements as repeat the very medium of knowledge. The style of *The Order of Things*, like *Bouvard and Pécuchet* and like so much contemporary French philosophy, takes the form of a free-indirect repetition of already established discourses of knowledge and classification. Compare the following two passages. The first is from *Bouvard and Pécuchet*:

> There had never been a complete global cataclysm, but a given species does not always last the same length of time, and becomes more quickly extinct in one place than another. Formations of the same age

contain different fossils, just as widely distant formations contain similar ones. Ferns of past times are identical with those of the present. Many contemporary zoophytes are to be found in the most ancient strata. In brief, present modifications explain previous upheavals. The same causes always operate, there are no jumps in nature, and periods, Brongniart asserts, are after all only abstractions.[16]

The following is from *The Order of Things*:

But what signature can the proportion itself bear in order to make itself recognizable? How is one to know that the lines of a hand or the furrows on a brow are tracing on a man's body the tendencies, accidents or obstacles present in the whole vast fabric of his life? How indeed, if not because we know that sympathy creates communication between our bodies and the heavens, and transmits the movements of the planets to the affairs of men. And if not, too, because the shortness of a line reflects the simple image of a short life, the intersection of two furrows an obstacle in one's path, the upward direction of a wrinkle a man's rise to success. Breadth is a sign of wealth and importance; continuity denotes good fortune, discontinuity ill fortune. The great analogy between body and destiny has its sign in the whole system of mirror and attractions. It is sympathies and emulations that indicate analogies.[17]

Both passages repeat the catalog of knowledge, the series of connections, and the assumptions that constitute the very medium within which thought takes place. Neither passage separates or implies a narratorial position "above" the catalog of facts. We might say, then, that Flaubert and those writers who take up the challenge of free-indirect style after him challenge the height and negativity of irony through the complete immanence of voice. There no longer appears to be a subject that speaks so much as an anonymous enunciation. It is the very generality or absence of stylistic flair that displays itself explicitly as the style of "universal man." Foucault's *Order of Things* strives to overcome "man," less by means of arguments than by tracing, repeating, and reinscribing those very styles of thought that have produced man as an absent "double" above and beyond any "said." Foucault's critique of nineteenth-century transcendentalism takes the form of a positive genealogy, looking at how certain questions and styles of knowledge produced "man" as an ever-receding limit. For it is by positing some horizon beyond the finite, empirical self—of consciousness, Being, history, or culture—that "man" is kept alive as a transcendental subject. The *being* of the subject depends upon a difference between man as a human thing within the world and the capacity or position that can recognize the human. This transcendental difference of the subject also depends upon locating the site of recognition in a region apart from the world. The subject that represents must be definitively other than representation. While the world is so much material to be named, defined, and ordered, the subject is an ordering power that resists order:

> Identity separated from itself by a distance which, in one sense, is interior to it, but, in another, constitutes it, and repetition which posits identity as a datum, but in the form of distance, are without doubt at the heart of that modern thought to which the discovery of time has so hastily been attributed. In fact, if we look a little more closely, we perceive that Classical thought related the possibility of spatializing things in a table to that property possessed by pure representative succession to recall itself on the basis of itself, and to constitute a simultaneity on the basis of a continuous time: time became the foundation of space. In modern thought, what is revealed at the foundation of the history of things and of the historicity proper to man is the distance creating a vacuum within the Same, it is the hiatus that disperses and regroups it at the two ends of itself. It is this profound spatiality that makes it possible for modern thought still to conceive of time—to know it as succession, to promise it to itself as fulfillment, origin or return.[18]

Foucault's intervention in the history of irony and subjectivism is a complex one and raises the possibility that "man" is not some uniquely indefinable horizon. If language is not the representation of the world for a subject but an anonymous "dispersion" that produces subject positions, then the constitutive gap or transcendental distinction between subject and world would be nothing more than a discursive effect. To avoid the positing of some original horizon, some archigenesis, or some transcendental field from which any particular position might be possible, Foucault, no less than Kierkegaard or Flaubert, presents his work as a problem of point of view. One of his earlier works, *The Archaeology of Knowledge*, concludes with a "dialogue" between two voices: a voice that accuses Foucault of a sustained complicity with the structuralism he criticizes and a voice of defense that insists that language is not an imposed structure but an immanent set of "positivities": "It is an attempt to reveal discursive practices in their complexity and *density*; to show that to speak is to do something—something *other than to express what one thinks; to translate what one knows,* and something other than to play with the structures of a language."[19]

"Man" according to Foucault, is the product of a particular discursive formation and the constitution of a certain "empiricity"—the effect of a certain style and grammar of questioning. He can be studied according to his political existence: his location within ideology, history, and culture. He becomes, therefore, an empiricotranscendental double: a being located within a general horizon of life. If man is an empirical substance within a transcendental and meaningful domain of life, he can be interpreted. As a thing to be "read," modern man is the site of endless interpretation, reflection, and hermeneutic labor. While Edmund Husserl's attack on the human sciences sought to define transcendental subjectivity as an irreducible and nonreifiable horizon beyond any concrete constitution of man as thing, Foucault's critique of modern anthropologism avoids this path. If man is not a specific substance, soul, or domain of interiority to be investigated in the manner of the natural sciences, he is no more legitimately posited as an infinite horizon that exceeds any positing.

To argue, as Foucault does, that the West has "refused" to think positivity suggests that any attention to a general "ground" for knowledge or Being or any positing of a *subject in general* will be yet one more compensatory illusion that will conceal the always located character of existence. It is only, therefore, in the "overcoming" of man that we will once again be able to think: "If the discovery of the return is indeed the end of philosophy, then the end of man, for its part, is the return of the beginning of philosophy. It is no longer possible to think in our day other than in the void left by man's disappearance. For this void does not create a deficiency; it does not constitute a lacuna that must be filled. It is nothing more, and nothing less, than the unfolding of a space in which it is once more possible to think."[20]

We might see Foucault's use of style as an attempt to overcome the predicament of structuralism identified by de Man. For de Man, we cannot authentically posit a subjectless metalanguage. Reading and speaking necessarily involve the assumption of those *who speak*. Foucault, however, follows in the tradition of free-indirect style and in doing so does not speak or say so much as repeat, delimit, and transcribe a history of speech acts. What is most telling, however, is Foucault's seeming departure from this strict immanence. The one occasion where Foucault does appear to be explicitly and positively endorsing the power of literature, he is actually speaking "through" Blanchot. In his work on Blanchot Foucault "argues" that literature can free itself from the commitment or subjection to transcendence or an outside. There can be a style that does not subordinate itself to truth or a "said."

Literature and Negativity

In his writing on Blanchot Foucault argues that literature reveals the limit of positivity (the brute fact of what is) and does so by way of revealing the "pure exteriority" of dispersion. This exteriority cannot be included *within* consciousness, subjectivity, or the human. As the possibility of presentation or point of view, literature's distribution is prerepresentational or prepersonal. Language is positive in that it is not secondary or representational (in the service of some other end such as truth). But it is also negative precisely because it reveals that any generality, identity, or givenness is the *effect* not of a general condition but of a specific dispersion. In his work on Blanchot and Roussel Foucault sets the space of literature against the temporal "interiority" of the philosophical subject as the self-present "I think":

> This neutral space is what characterizes contemporary Western fiction (which is why it is no longer mythology of rhetoric). The reason it is now so necessary to think through fiction—while in the past it was a matter of thinking the truth—is that "I speak" runs counter to "I think." "I think" led to the indubitable certainty of the "I" and its existence; "I speak," on the other hand, distances, disperses, effaces that existence and lets only its empty emplacement appear. Thought about thought, an entire tradition wider than philosophy, has taught us that thought leads us to the deepest interiority. Speech about speech leads us, by way of literature as well as perhaps by other paths, to the outside in which the speaking subject disappears. No doubt that is why Western thought took so long to think the being of language: as if it had a premonition of the danger that the naked experience of language poses for the self-evidence of "I think."[21]

The literary text gives us a radical incommensurability or noncoincidence of the "I speak." The "I" who utters is not given in the utterance. There is an event of saying that exceeds the said. But is *Foucault* speaking here? Those points where Foucault refers to what is other than the subjection to truth are also those points where Foucault is speaking *through* the voice of literature: speaking, as it were, from the position of Blanchot. The supposed freedom of literature from inauthenticity is given as a possibility through style. In repeating what Blanchot says, Foucault suggests that literature might offer us not a transcendent truth or self there to be read but a self or interiority produced through reading.

Paul de Man's ostensibly similar theory of irony argued that authentic subjectivity occurred with the recognition of the *difference* between presented point of view and the subject (or act) of presentation. This recognition could only occur by way of temporal reflection. After the event of narrative description, the subject recognizes itself (authentically) as other than any described self. Only in literature, de Man's work suggests, can the description of point of view and the *recognition* of point of view sustain the subject as above and beyond any given character. De Man's description of irony at once draws upon the traditional connections between irony and moral autonomy and radically reworks those connections in the tenor of post-Hegelian philosophy. Whereas Socratic irony had pointed back to a form of life and a care of one's soul, de Man's irony emphasizes a literary rather than a subjective "authenticity." The subject is most properly itself when it is not a thing, when it is nothing, and this subjective nothingness finds its recognition (and misrecognition) in literature. In the literary text, the description of the subject as a thing is seen *as description*. The literary trace presents itself in such a way that language is no longer a transparent representation but is seen in its *effective* dimension. The foregrounding of textuality is also a foregrounding of the subject's status as (the) nothing other than textuality.

De Man's description of irony, while still holding on to the function of the subject as that nothingness that exceeds point of view, also moves close to dissolving the subject into the general effect of writing.

What renders de Man's account both irreducibly subjective and ironic, however, is his emphasis on point of view. What both structuralism and philosophy of language fail to recognize in their positing of a subjectless metalanguage, he argues, is the necessary problem of the constitutive subject. In narrative we see subjective constitution as such taking place; narrative self-construction is a particular instance of the inevitable tension of intersubjectivity. In narrative the self is explicitly an object of construction and reflection that creates itself through the unfolding of narrative. But the "problems of the self that appear in narrative are not empirical" (*RCC*, 23). Literature makes manifest the disjunction between the constitutive subject and the represented self, as well as the gap between the world's meaning and the production of that meaning. Irony is the conscious foregrounding of this disjunction. There is an essential nothingness that separates the subject from its posited origin; indeed, the subject is produced only through this narrative distancing. It is in the narration or description of the self as *not* at one with itself that subjectivity is effected, produced through the fall into reification. Speaking of the *rien* in Romantic consciousness, de Man argues that "it refers among other things to the imaginary nature of the work that exists for us as a reflected source, beyond our grasp, lost in a past from which we are separated or away in a future that we cannot reach" (*RCC*, 48). The subject's constitutive narrative split is therefore inherently temporal and literary, depending upon narrative description only to both recognize and distance itself from any particular description.

For de Man, irony is nothing less than the movement of meaning as such. By referring to irony as "the permanent parabasis of the allegory of tropes," de Man defines irony as the condition for conceptuality, meaning, experience, and subjectivity.[22] We can only understand the world *as world* through meaning, through some positing of an existence beyond ourselves. Subjectivity opens in the difference between a world that is there to be viewed and spoken about and the domain of sense that refers to that world. There can only be a meaningful world if we posit a real that is other than our signs, perceptions, words, and concepts. This positing demands an originary differentiation between world and word, a gap between the literal and figural. This gap or "distance," according to de Man, is achieved through a certain irreducibly temporal narrative. To describe a difference between a metaphor and that to which it refers is to narrate and produce the world *as world*. Meaning, signification, and exteriority depend upon an originary *narrative of tropes*. The narrative of tropes produces, by describing or narrating, a gap between subject (meaning/the figural) and object (existence/the literal). It is in the self-conscious retracing of this narrative of tropes—the parabasis—that irony reminds us that we are effects rather than authors of our tropes. We cannot have a theory of narrative, for any theory depends upon the original narrative that produces the world of meaning as a correspondence with the "world in itself." Irony is essentially narrative in nature: it describes a gap or temporal distance between any origin and the words that necessarily belie that origin. But literary narrative is also essentially ironic, for in giving a description of the world, in producing a narrative temporal sequence, a gap is constituted between narrated past and narrative present, origin and figure, the authentic and the fallen.

So while irony is self-consciously literary and narratological, literal meaning remains at the level of allegory. Reference, literal meaning, and signification depend upon an allegory of tropes. That signs refer to a world is the result of a particular narrative of alignment. For de Man, the possibility of reference is effected through an implicit—and necessary—story about meaning. Irony is the disruption of this alignment, a stepping back from the allegory of tropes, a questioning of the coincidence between word and world: "irony is the permanent parabasis of tropes. The allegory of tropes has its own narrative coherence, its own systematicity, and it is that coherence, that systematicity, which irony interrupts, disrupts. So one could say that any theory of irony is the undoing, the necessary undoing, of any theory of narrative, and it is ironic, as we say, that irony always comes up in relation to theories of narrative, when irony is precisely what makes it impossible ever to achieve a theory of narrative that would be consistent."[23]

Literature is the privileged site of this parabasis. As ironic self-reflection, narrative is a *repetition* of the separation that constitutes us as such. Literature has a transcendental function and is an ironic reminder of the impossibility of any transcendental recognition. Further, the temporality of repetition and recognition, the description of irony as the arche-narrative of subjective authenticity, depends *essentially* upon point of view. The recognition of the described point of view is achieved by that higher point of view of the authorial subject that remains forever (and necessarily) absent. This temporality of irony is, from Socrates to de Man, nothing other than the possibility of the transcendental shift or disjunction between the closed description of position and the point of view that delineates that position. Irony, for de Man, is like Derrida's *différance*: a radically anterior condition of conceptuality that itself is "not a concept."[24] Writing on Flaubert's conception of the ironic novelistic imagination, de Man argues: "it defines the self of the author as disinterested, as a self that, in the fiction, has renounced his empirical status in the world for an altogether different project."[25] This "altogether different project" of irony is the classic (and once philosophical) move of anti-anthropologism. Any empirical self will always raise the question of the subjective condition of that self.

What makes Paul de Man's theory of irony so challenging today is that it sustains itself both as a theory and as a process of deconstruction. The theoretical stress in de Man's work lies in his insistence on the ethics of subjectivity: any structuralist-style attempt to dissolve the self into language refuses the inevitable predicament of *theōria*: language inevitably produces the point of view of one *who speaks*. At the same time, this production of the subject as origin of language can only be effected through the narrative function of language: there will necessarily have been one who preceded the event of enunciation. Irony, for de Man, is still a subjectivism. The rejection of the worldly or anthropological self opens the space for a subject as *other than thing*. But the oscillation between anthropologism and subjectivism can only be an oscillation, never an achievement or recognition of authenticity. For the *subjective* condition of man, once posited *as condition*, becomes yet one more recognition, one more repetition of the human. Philosophy as the categorical intellectual imperative to ask the question of the condition meets its limit and fulfillment in irony. In irony we recognize the limit of any anthropologism and psychologism, but the recognition will also be—*as recognition*—a repetition of anthropologism and a fall into the human.

Ironic Misrecognition

What all this suggests is that if we were to set ourselves the task of moving beyond ironic oscillation in order to think the condition of the empirical self *as other than a higher form of the self*, we would also have to move beyond the temporality of recognition. We would have to rework the style of point of view. A literature that sought to overcome the subjectivism of this temporal oscillation of point of view would need to challenge point of view as such. It is perhaps not surprising, therefore, that Foucault not only praises the style of the "new novel" (as absence of psychological point of view) but also begins his own archaeological project with an attempted style of "anonymous dispersion." It is in his reaction against transcendentalism and its constitutive "retreat" from any positive point of view that we can locate

Foucault's own style. And it is here, also, that we can notice an irreducible connection between style and metaphysics. Flaubert's authorial absence strives to avoid *positing* a subject that would transcend any given style. To do so would locate the author as some thing that exceeded any specific articulation. The style of Foucaultian archaeology is, similarly, an anonymous and silent inhabitation or repetition of discourse, a faithful description that avoids commentary or interpretation. It is in the presentation or repetition of a discourse that discourse itself becomes visible. The Foucaultian move within and against philosophy is, in this sense, postironic, working at the limit of meaning but in order to avoid rather than reveal a subjectivity that surpasses any given meaning. Against the *temporal reflection* on point of view, which enables subjective authenticity, Foucault's antisubjectivism or immanence describes itself as *spatial dispersion*.

In this regard irony—an understanding other than everyday meaning—is both deployed and destroyed. Everyday meaning is presented, but in being presented in all its banality and prolixity it is shown as inert and positive and not as a negation of some depth or meaning. The limit of everyday sense is not to be surpassed or overcome in order to move to a higher meaning or a sense of the concept "to come." Rather, everyday sense is repeated and presented as a particular and effective folding or event. Foucault's project of immanence—thinking what is in terms of itself and not some other thing—is at once an anti-anthropologism and an antihermeneutics. There is no content, meaning, or intention that is then expressed. Expression is an event itself. In order to avoid the primacy of mental content, subjectivity, concepts, or ideas, both Foucault and Deleuze regard interiority as one effect among others, a particular type of folding within a univocal field. Against the existential irony that turns back from the world in order to reflect upon the knower of that world, Foucault sets the spatial notions of fold and order: "between the use of what one might call the ordering codes and reflexions upon order itself, there is the pure experience of order and its modes of being."[26] It is only *after* "what is" has been disclosed, ordered, or folded that we can distinguish the one who looks from what is viewed. A spatial analysis will examine the "middle region": neither subject nor object but that which distributes one from the other. In order for the subject to apprehend a world, in order for the look and temporality of point of view to occur, there must have been an impersonal ordering or folding that allows us to think: "Between the already 'encoded' eye and reflexive knowledge there is a middle region which liberates order itself ... This middle region, then, in so far as it makes manifest the modes of being of order, can be posited as the most fundamental of all: anterior to words, perceptions and gestures, which are taken to be exact, more or less happy, expressions of it (which is why this experience of order, in its pure primary state always plays a critical role)."[27] This middle region does not exist, and it is not an extended space perceived *from* point of view. Rather, there is a spatial dispersion *from which* we then think in terms of point of view. Foucault's emphasis on the historical positivity of this middle region is insistently immanent. It is not that there is some being or ground that is then ordered or expressed. There are positive modes of ordering such as the knowledges of the human sciences, the disciplinary practices of prisons, or the self-interpretation of sexuality, and from this ordering or "encoding" of the eye there is produced a "general space of knowledge." Foucault's history of the "Same" is just this insistence on the continual redistribution of order within which thought and its other are continually realigned.[28]

Literature is important for Foucault not because it brings us back to the genesis of our point of view but because it can *exist* or *speak* without saying or meaning—without effecting a point of view. Nineteenth-century literature, according to Foucault, is poised at the very limit of modernity. Whereas de Man regarded the problem of literary point of view as transcendental, as producing the very possibility of meaning and subjectivity, Foucault cites post-Romantic literature as a form of dispersion beyond point of view and self-narration. Literature is language without speech; it is silent. For Foucault, literature offers a way of thinking the impersonality and inhumanity of the fold and the visible. Literature in its radical form undoes the fold that constitutes interior from exterior. The speech of literature does not effect a point of view. Literature is language freed from voice and temporality; language is dispersed, spatialized, and silenced. Unlike ironic literature, which exacerbates the gap between what we say and what we must mean, such that a voice speaks through our use of concepts, Foucault sees the force of literature as radically impersonal. It is not that we always mean more than we say, for literature can say *without meaning*. Here we are brought up against the unthought, not the transcendental subject that precedes all thinking but the singular, accidental, and technological differences within which we move.

This goes some of the way toward explaining Foucault's own style of genealogy. If the soul is the effect of a certain grammar or propositional structure, then freeing thought from its subjection to "man" will require the production of a different style. One of the common criticisms of Foucault is that his concept of power and modernity is so all-encompassing as to preclude all possibility of agency or an outside.[29] But it is just this subordination to an outside or truth that Foucault's analysis of the production of exteriority has as its target. The aim of *The Order of Things* was to write a history of the various modes of exteriority such that thought does not have an outside. Subject and object, viewer and viewed, knower and known, and man and being are effected through historically specific and singular foldings. It is the inability to think the difference of these foldings that has marked Western thought. The outside has always been thought of as simply there to be viewed, as though the look were a passive re-presentation of a grounding presence. By focusing on the history of "foldings" that allow us to think the middle region between interiority and exteriority, Foucault exposes both the limits of man and the limits of speech. It is only when we move from the political—the recognized relations between speaking subjects—to the micropolitical—all those inhuman movements and differences that disperse speaking positions—that we will really be able to think power and think differently. Far from speaking outside power, Foucault's own style retraces its operations and divisions. If the radical force of literature lies in its capacity to disperse language beyond speech, the similar force of Foucault's own style will be to retrace knowledge's own limits. In many ways his own writings are themselves instances of free-indirect style. Consider, for example, the third paragraph of the first volume of *The History of Sexuality*, where the narrating voice is not Foucault's but the inflated tone of modern, enlightened sexual liberation: "But twilight soon fell upon this bright day, followed by the monotonous nights of the Victorian bourgeoisie. Sexuality was carefully confined; it moved into the home. The conjugal family took custody of it and absorbed it into the serious function of reproduction. On the subject of sex, silence became the rule."[30]

Part of Foucault's endeavor in *The History of Sexuality* is to challenge the self-evidence of the repressive hypothesis, or the idea that sexual repression is the consequence of a Victorian dark age. But he does not just counter the hypothesis of repression with another proposition. First, as in *The Order of Things*, a certain way of knowing and thinking is repeated. In the paragraph above, we are presented with the speech of the post-Victorian sexually liberated individual. It is as though what Foucault is attacking could not be presented in the form of propositions so much as in a manner of speaking. And when Foucault's own voice does speak it is always hesitant about a position of judgment. There is *not yet* a space or position of enunciation outside the point of view of sexuality or man. We can begin to give some "room for thought" only after a genealogical repetition of knowledge's very medium.

On the one hand, then, Foucault's use of free-indirect style works against the notion of some ironic philosophical elevation. The metaphors he uses to describe his own method, like the metaphors he uses to embrace literary language, work against the image of a vertical axis. His work is an "archaeology" that focuses on "dispersions," "distributions," "strata," the "planes" or "tables" of knowledge and all its "diagrams." And this would seem to suggest not only that critique will always be implicated in the style of thought from which it distances itself but also that the transformation of thinking will proceed by mutation rather than a radical disruption. On the other hand, while resisting the notion of philosophy or judgment as a metaposition or heightened viewpoint, Foucault's style and writing testify to a necessity to confront the limits of language. By transcribing where "we" are we might be forced to confront those unthought dimensions of knowledge. We might *see* language not as the pure medium for expression but as an event in its own right, with its own force and intensity.

Like Foucault, Gilles Deleuze also refers to the language of literature through a spatial metaphorics, and, again like Foucault, he also regards the elevation of language to a transcendental subjective power as the culmination of a slavish history of metaphysics. If we think language spatially rather than temporally, then we do much to disrupt the rigid logic of point of view. As Paul de Man had argued, the transcendental status of the subject is tied to linguistic point of view. It is after the event of speech or narration that we must presuppose a subject as having been, a transcendental or authentic subject that will always recede behind any of its speech acts. Both Deleuze and Foucault will argue that this retroactive temporality of the statement is the effect of a spatial dispersion. A subject speaks through a system of marks and inscriptions. Whereas structuralism had placed this system in a single space of *langue*, Foucault shows a spatial dispersion of system: different strata, series, mutations, and foldings of discourse. Foucault's method is to provide a genealogy of statements that refers to all those nondiscursive distributions and forces that intersect with discourse. Far from language issuing from the single point of temporal becoming, language is dispersed across a field that no single point can govern, comprehend, or express. Foucault's analysis of discourse is not so much the production of an outside or higher point. Indeed, it is just this idea of a language that can grasp the very genesis and structure of language that Foucault's *Order of Things* aims to delimit. What literature offers is language in its positivity—neither the ground nor being nor the expression of a subject. Literature has no truth, ground, or justification outside itself. Far from being the expression of a look, Foucault describes literary language as bearing its own "shining" and luminosity.[31] If a certain way of speaking has produced man as the soul of discourse, then it is not so much another argument as another style that will open thinking again.

Style and Immanence

Gilles Deleuze makes two telling comments with regard to the difference between his own (and Guattari's) project and that of Foucault. In *Foucault* Deleuze argues that Foucault refuses to "cross the line" to the outside and that this refusal is connected to a residual Kantianism (and therefore a dualism) in his work.[32] We only see power in its effects, in Foucault's works, *after* the event of distributions and dispersions. This suggests that there "is" a power known only in its singular articulations. In *A Thousand Plateaus* Deleuze and Guattari explain the difference between their use of the term *desire* and Foucault's notion of power. Power is given through its effects and events. Desire, however, is the intensity of life itself.[33] The task of thinking, for Deleuze and Guattari, is the confrontation with intensity, not the critical engagement with effects. In many ways both Deleuze's and Foucault's projects are similar and raise similar problems for the question of irony and point of view. From Socratic irony to Rortyan irony, irony has been defined as a recognition of personal viewpoint. The question then follows as to whether one can transcend personality through philosophy, or whether philosophy can be nothing more than a recognition of viewpoint and persona. After structuralism, however, the very existence of distinct points or positions has been seen to depend upon some prepersonal process of systemic differentiation. The *post*structuralism of Deleuze and Foucault is critical of any attempt to explain meaning either from a position (of consciousness, the subject, or man) or from a structure in general. Both Deleuze and Foucault are critical of a structuralism or phenomenology that would locate difference within a single plane such as language or the subject, and they are also critical of a heightened position or genesis "outside" any structure. But it is perhaps the question of style and irony that most separates the two. Foucault's project remained critical and experimental, working within the archive to effect mutations, disruptions, and transformations. In this regard he is both within and beyond the tradition of irony. He was aware that no discourse could saturate its field and that genealogy would always be to some extent a critical inhabitation. But he also seemed to be resigned to the unavoidable effects of point of view; a self would always be formed through discursive procedures. The most we can hope for is a self freed from the normalizing grammar of the subject: not a self that precedes enunciation but a self effected through enunciation. The later volumes of *The History of Sexuality* explore practices of self-formation: neither relying on some image of the self nor imagining that thought could be freed from all images of selfhood. Like Socratic irony, Foucault's genealogies refuse any given definition of life, not by presenting a positive image of the soul but by displaying the soul in its power of becoming, as other than any of its inscribed forms. But this power of becoming would also disrupt any complacent pragmatism that would reduce irony to an acceptance of finitude. Once we recognize our singularity and specificity we are also confronted with what resists recognition: the process of force and becoming that allows that any event might be otherwise. Power becomes for Foucault not some anonymous system to which all life is subjected but just that which gives distinct and singular differences, never exhausted in any perceived or actual difference.

Deleuze's stated difference from Foucault implies that power, unlike desire, is reminiscent of the absence, negativity, and distance that have marked the history of Western thought. We never perceive power itself, and so Foucault's project would remain critical, always delimiting any given instance of power but never speaking with the voice of power. For Deleuze, by contrast, *being itself speaks*. There is no gap or distance between life and its perceived expressions. Life is never given in any one expression, but it is also nothing other than its eternally different events of expression. This issues in a style of desire, a style in which that which speaks (the enunciation) and what is spoken (the enounced) are coterminous. The "planes" of *A Thousand Plateaus*, for example, describe various strata of life, with desire being just this power of life itself to become different. There is, then, an insistent *literalism* in Deleuze and Guattari's work. Only the reactive intellect feels that it is imprisoned within images of life; active and affirmative philosophy strives to speak life itself, to become with and through life. *A Thousand Plateaus* does not hesitate to predicate life, from descriptions such as "God is a lobster" and explanations of the emergence of the eye through to remarks about life as such.[34] To say that "desire is a machine" is *not*, they insist, a metaphor. Indeed, Deleuze and Guattari insist that desire is the real itself and that this real is nothing other than its processes of expression or "writing":

> The recordings and transmissions that have come from the internal codes, from the outside world, from one region to another of the organism, all intersect, following the endlessly ramified paths of the great disjunctive synthesis. If this constitutes a system of writing, it is a writing inscribed in the very surface of the Real: a strangely polyvocal kind of writing, never a biunivocalized, linearized one; a transcursive system of writing, never a discursive one; a writing that constitutes the entire domain of the "real inorganization" of the passive syntheses, where we would search in vain for something that might be labeled the Signifier—writing that ceaselessly composes and decomposes the chains into signs that have nothing that impels them to become signifying. The one vocation of the sign is to produce desire, engineering it in every direction.[35]

Such statements are not propositions added on to life but expressions of life. This commitment in *Anti-Oedipus* to desire as the writing and expression of life itself is followed more faithfully in *A Thousand Plateaus*, which speaks the many voices of desire: through genetics, history, linguistics, music, anthropology, and microbiology. *A Thousand Plateaus* is not a "book" that would provide a series of ordered arguments so much as one more strand of life's creative power.[36] Foucault's style of power, by contrast, presents any voice and position as other than that which gives or effects position. Whereas Deleuze and Guattari multiply and expand the styles and voices of life, Foucault uses free-indirect style to indicate the limit or finitude of any style. If *The Order of Things* was written in the styles of knowledge that it sought to illuminate, this did not allow for a truer voice of power itself. Unlike Deleuze and Guattari's "desire," Foucault's "power" is always other than any of its effected terms. *Discipline and Punish*, for example, opens with a narration, a fragment of voice from the archive. It is neither Foucault nor the author who is speaking. The torture of Damiens the regicide is not so much an objectified document from a unified historical plane as it is a way of seeing and speaking, a style of punishment that is at once a style of speech.

If Foucault is difficult to read it is precisely because the line between critical repetition and Foucault's own voice is never clearly drawn. His texts are not propositions about the Western archive; they repeat and reconfigure that archive. And this is why, perhaps, so many have attributed theses to Foucault that are ostensibly contrary to what he *wanted to say*: the idea that history is a transcendental horizon (Habermas); that modernity has no outside (Taylor); that our redemption lies in ancient Greece, or that Foucault is a structuralist for whom everything is "discourse" (Macdonell).[37] All these are possible readings of Foucault precisely because many of his writings repeat the very statements—without quotation or attribution—that he is trying to delimit. In fact, this is just what a "statement," for Foucault, is. It is not what someone *actually says*. It is just that assumed discursive plane within which "we" speak.

This is also, of course, the art of free-indirect style. When James Joyce wrote *Dubliners* he did not "quote" modern Ireland, and Flaubert's *Madame Bovary* did not "quote" the provincial moralism of late-nineteenth-century France. Free-indirect style gives voice to an everyday discourse that is so unremarkable that it need not be spoken, the jejune truisms that are all the louder for never having been said. The unsaid or the unthought is not some absolute or unconscious that exceeds the limits of speech. Free-indirect style discloses the unthought as thoroughly immanent. The question, then, between Deleuze and Foucault is both a question of style and the question of our epoch. Can we, as Deleuze suggests, liberate ourselves from a history of irony and transcendence, a history in which the Real has always been posited as a point beyond what we see and say? Would it be possible to become-animal, become-imperceptible, or become-woman: become with and through life, rather than being a point of speech or judgment set over against life? Or is the outside always beyond the thought and perception of the outside?

Inhuman Irony and the Event
of the Postmodern

If philosophy were to be knowledge, if it were to have a content or offer a set of propositions, it would have to have an object. But a philosophy that claims to have an object or that claims to represent some thing— mind, humanity, the soul, virtue, meaning—is not, for Deleuze, philosophy proper. Philosophy is not the adequate recognition of either the world or the thinking subject. Philosophy does not judge life; it is an event of life itself. Philosophy creates concepts and in so doing gives "consistency" to the plane of immanence.[1] In line with the history of irony, Deleuze defines his project against the ready-made rigidity and complacency of common sense. Common sense works with already given terms and imagines the world as so many already formed and extended units of time and space. By confronting the plane of immanence, philosophy steps back from common sense to intensity, prior to the systematization or actualization of the world. Here, difference is not the difference *between* things or extended beings; difference is intensity itself, that from which relative differences emerge. Unlike Foucault, who saw the project of immanence as primarily critical, refusing the height and elevation of the philosopher, Deleuze describes his transcendental empiricism as a "superior irony." Deleuze's critique of Foucault—that he refuses to cross the line and think power directly—is not just a quibble within philosophy; it concerns the very style of philosophy.[2] Although Deleuze and Guattari praised free-indirect style and high modernism, the two volumes of *Capitalism and Schizophrenia* move well beyond the immanence of modernism. They do not just offer a critique of philosophy so far or work within already given ways of speaking. They create an entirely new lexicon and an entirely new mode of predication. Their aim for a truly immanent philosophy does not accept any pregiven image of thought, nor does it substitute yet one more image. The creation of concepts, which is philosophy's essential task, will issue in forms of writing that are neither expressions nor descriptions of a subject.

Philosophy, as thought, is other than any already given sense. Like literature, philosophy is the creation of sense. But the event of sense is achieved in philosophy through the concept. The concept does not name what is already given, nor is the concept a form that the subject bestows on being. Deleuze and Guattari's philosophical concepts, like Hegel's Concept, are dynamic. Concepts are the very difference and violence of thinking. Like Hegel, Deleuze refuses to see the world as an undifferentiated Absolute that is then differentiated through concepts. Life is difference itself. But this difference, in contrast with Hegel, is positive. Rather than a life that negates itself through concepts and then realizes itself as nothing other than this power of negation, Deleuze's "life" is a power of difference, with the concept being an event of difference and not the origin of difference. This means that

there is not a single medium of differentiation—such as the Concept—but divergent series of difference (*DR*, 123). The concept is one
series of difference alongside others, and each concept differs differently according to the intersections it makes with other series. A
philosophical concept creates difference differently from the everyday
concepts of common sense. Deleuze's own philosophy leaps across divergent series, confronting the sensible encounters of art, the functions of various sciences, and the diverse forms of life and becoming
within the single plane of immanence. A great philosopher is not,
therefore, someone who merely creates a new lexicon, for a philosophical concept does not just rename, it re-encounters (*DR*, 145). For Deleuze, this constitutes a superior irony. We do not just reach the limits
of our concepts. We write in such a way that the very form of the concept, its fold between inside and outside, is created anew. Philosophical concepts are not tokens within a language; they reconfigure the
very modality of language.

Take the concept of the subject. When Descartes created this concept he provided a way for thinking conceptuality in general; the subject is not one more being within the world, it is the point from which
all being can be conceptualized. The concept of the subject in Descartes changes the very "plane" of conceptuality. The creation of the
Cartesian *cogito* emerges from a drama and playing out of problems:
this is the concept's *sense*, or the very field across which it is drawn.
Concepts also come with personae and norms for thinking.[3] In the
case of the *cogito* there is the "doubting Descartes" and the norm of
clear and distinct ideas. A new philosophy creates its concepts not in
order to rename old problems but in order to confront new problems
(*DR*, 159). *The* problem of philosophy, and the ironic philosophy of
Hegel in particular, is that concepts have always been subordinated to
the demands of representation and recognition. Hegel's dialectic
aligns difference with negation and the concept, such that difference

is identified and generalized (*DR*, 50). Hegel's concept negates what is other than itself only to recognize that negated content as itself an effect of the concept. Difference is seen to derive from and depend upon the movement of the concept, a movement toward recognition. Deleuze's notion of difference, by contrast, insists that each event of difference is itself different. Linguistic differences are different from genetic differences, which are different from differences in tone, color, or number. And all these differences express the power of difference as such, which is "Life": the potential *to differ*. There is no difference in general. Only if we grasp each event of difference in its singularity will difference be positive. Hegel had already criticized the undifferentiated Romantic absolute, which was then differentiated by concepts; but Hegel still elevated absolute difference to the level of *the* concept. But for Deleuze, what philosophy shows us is that each concept also differentiates differently. Difference is positive precisely because each of its instances insists with its own force and has its own way of becoming. This positive difference then gives us Life in its differing intensity, never reducible to any of its already differentiated terms. A superior irony assesses the force of each event of difference and responds to each difference through style. Deleuze's "transcendental empiricism" or superior irony will create new concepts that transform the very nature of conceptuality. This means moving with and beyond irony and free-indirect style.

The Subject of Irony

Traditional irony is essentially tied to a subjectivism. The subject, as that which precedes or underlies all predications, provides irony with a logic that will oscillate between the limited and the unlimited, the subject and its predicates, or the ground and its effects. Whether the unlimited is always belied by the concept or whether the unlimited is effected after the conceptual limit, irony has always operated around thought, speech, and its own limits. Whether the soul is an effect of irony or whether the soul is the ground of irony, the soul has also been tied to human speech. Deleuze moves beyond the idea that it is human speech and thought that is the privileged site for difference and de-limitation, and he does so by theorizing an inhuman irony. Souls and contemplations are neither subjective nor human; all life is contem-plation, and all life is ensouled: "These contemplative souls must be assigned even to the rat in the labyrinth and to each muscle of the rat" (*DR*, 75):

> A soul must be attributed to the heart, to the muscles, nerves and cells, but a contemplative soul whose entire function is to contract a habit. This is no mystical or barbarous hypothesis. On the contrary, habit here manifests its full generality: it concerns not only the sensory motor habits that we have (psychologically), but also, before these, the primary habits that we are; the thousands of passive syntheses of which we are organically composed. It is simultaneously through con-traction that we are habits, but through contemplation that we con-tract. We are contemplations, we are imaginations, we are generali-ties, claims and satisfactions. . . . We do not contemplate ourselves, but we exist only in contemplating—that is to say, in contracting that from which we come. (*DR*, 74)

The human speaker is an event within an eternal repetition of be-coming. Language, far from being *the* delimiting condition of being, is merely one event of difference among others. More importantly, language is not the opening of point of view. Each point of difference within the universe is a point of view opening out to the infinite. The smallest particle or atom *is* only insofar as it becomes toward what is not itself. The human point of view is merely an extension of a look-ing, perception, or imaging that typifies life in general: "That there are molecular perceptions no less than molecular reactions can be

seen in the economy of the cell and the property of the regulatory
agents to 'recognize' only one or two kinds of chemicals in a very diverse milieu of exteriority."[4]

Hegel had criticized irony for remaining within the limits of the
concept, and he had also stressed the speculative possibility—through
the concept—of looking at the very genesis of point of view. Hegel's
"concept of the concept" does not generalize about particulars within
the world. By thinking the concept *as such* we can also think the very
positing of the world. The sublation of irony, for Hegel, could only be
achieved with the elevation and extension of concepts. If our concepts
appear to be limited, this is only because we have not fully conceptualized or rationalized what exceeds our point of view. Overcoming irony,
for Hegel, is achieved through a heightened subjectivism or idealism.
What appears as other than the concept, or other than our limited
viewpoint, needs to be recognized as effected from the difference of
conceptuality and viewpoints; we need to extend the range of the concept. For this reason, Deleuze refers to Hegel's philosophy as an expansion of representation to the "infinitely large" (*DR*, 45). But Deleuze
argues that we need to take irony in the opposite direction, not elevating the power of concepts but affirming all the contemplations, looks,
and imagings from which human life emerges. On the one hand,
then, Deleuze extends the history of irony by arguing that we have
been far too complacent in accepting the ready-made character of our
concepts and grammar. We need to assess the force and strategy har-
bored in our ways of speaking.[5] To this end, Deleuze and Guattari
affirm a number of literary strategies, including free-indirect style:
"My direct discourse is still the free indirect discourse running
through me, coming from other worlds or other planets."[6] Moving beyond the critical inhabitation of style, Deleuze's "superior" irony goes
on to argue explicitly for descent rather than elevation (*DR*, 234). A
philosophy of immanence or transcendental empiricism refuses to see

concepts as the limit of the given. Indeed, the challenge of philosophy is the creation of concepts that do violence to common sense and good sense. The task of the philosopher is not to tell us what we already are or already mean. Philosophy is not recognition or definition. The philosopher creates concepts that inaugurate inhuman viewpoints. Deleuze and Guattari's own concepts—of the rhizome, the schizo, nomadology, or desiring-machines—are attempts to think the very becoming of existence itself.

Molecular Irony

It is only from the vantage point of late capitalism and subjectivism that the genealogy of human speech is possible. It is only after the event of speech and concepts that we can write the inhuman origins of sense. Both volumes of Deleuze and Guattari's *Capitalism and Schizophrenia* write a history of the viewpoint of the subject. And both refer to the emergence of persons from a certain coding of body parts. Speech is only possible through a "deterritorialization" of the mouth, and signification is only possible with the elevation of a certain look. In the beginning, we might speculate, the world is all intensity—a pure continuum of differentiating difference with no outside or inside. "Territorialization" sees the formation from this intensity of extended divisions. The pure flow of desire is coded. Tribal societies emerge with extended systems of exchange, such that one flux of genetic material is inscribed as opposing another. There are not yet persons at this stage, only territories. And the exchange from one tribe to another is only possible because of an inscription or marking that divides one tribe from another. Differentiation, then, is not the division of an amorphous mass. In the beginning difference is intense and singular. From a far greater range of differences—the intense flow of life—tribes are collected or assembled by the production of territo-

ries. The flow of life is organized into extended units such as tribes and
eventually the state (as an overarching unit or law to which difference
is subjected). Persons (or egos) and speech only emerge with deterritorialization. It is only when the inscriptive system that cuts into the
pure flow of desire is centered on what Deleuze and Guattari refer to
as the "despotic signifier" that speech and subjects become possible.
Here, inscriptions are taken to be the bearers of sense, and the mouth
is deterritorialized as the bearer of speech. The mouth is no longer
located on the body but becomes the locus of a language that flows
through all bodies.[7] The idea of law—the condition of any speaking
system—emerges only with the "eye" that subjects all instances of inscription to the point of view of sense. We can only speak and expect
meaning and recognition if we assume some shared code. What "we"
say and what "we" see can only form a collective point of view through
the "look" or point of view of the law, the "despotic signifier": that
which signifies for "us" all. The project of Deleuze and Guattari's
"universal history" of sense is to describe the emergence of this point
of recognition. The subject of modernity, capitalism, and psychoanalysis is only possible after the pure flows of desire are territorialized
into units, deterritorialized into signifiers, and then overcoded by the
idea of the human point of view.

The question is, of course, whether it makes sense to write a history
of sense. Is it possible to step outside the self-recognition of the subject,
to write the origin of the human point of view? All this depends on
how we see the task of philosophy and the limits of style and irony. A
superior irony, according to Deleuze, plunges into the depths of sense,
reversing the elevation of the concept. It may make *no sense* to write
the origin of sense. In so doing we will be moving into wild speculation, never fully outside concepts and the human. The chaos and
depth that we wish to confront will always be marked by the point
from which we are writing. To remain at the level of irony would be to

sustain philosophical rigor; what lies beyond the concept and sense
can only be grasped by concepts. But such rigor would be timid and reactive, a refusal to confront the unthought, the violence, and the necessity of a life well beyond human conceptuality. From his earliest
work in *Difference and Repetition* Deleuze makes two interventions
into the relation between irony and concepts. First, we need to recognize the differential force of life beyond the recognition of concepts:
the perceptions and souls well beyond the range of the human viewpoint. Second, we need to think concepts differently: not as ways in
which we generalize and order our world but as events that happen to
us. Experience is not grounded in a subject; subjects are effects of experience. Concepts, considered positively, are just one of the ways in
which different events of life—thought and chaos—confront and
affirm each other. The concept gives consistency to chaos, not by being
"applied" or spoken by a subject but by *creating* a persona or viewpoint. It is the concept that connects certain intensive differences and
thereby opens a view or perception of the world.

The history of the concept and the speaking subject in *A Thousand
Plateaus* is an attempt to write the chaotic and inhuman genesis of
meaning. Such a history is in keeping with Deleuze's earlier aim of a
"superior irony" and a "radical empiricism." If traditional irony views
what is other than the concept only from the limits of the concept, it
will remain, as Deleuze suggests in *Difference and Repetition*, connected to height and elevation, always viewing the world from a point
of view that sees beyond the concept. Deleuze's superior irony and the
later historical project with Guattari are committed to depth rather
than height. The history of *A Thousand Plateaus* seeks to explain the
very emergence of sense, how the mouth as an organ of eating becomes
an organ of speech, how the face moves from being a body part to becoming the sign of subjectivity. Such a history may be possible only after the event of meaning and sense, but this is just why philosophy and

literature are *other* than the accepted limits of common sense. Philosophy is not about accepting the limits of the concepts and conventions
that we have. Both philosophy and literature, in different ways, need to
create concepts and events that allow us to think and confront the very
emergence of life. For Deleuze and Guattari, this is just where the
challenge of a whole new style of philosophy comes in. The philosophy
of a "people to come" will no longer be recognized in the form of a "we"
and will no longer speak from the point of view of a subject.[8]

Deleuze's philosophy of immanence and Foucault's project of
"thinking otherwise" might be defined as extensions of the philosophical departure from everyday sense that characterized Socratic
irony. The path of Socratic irony is the repetition of everyday sense in
order to reveal its limit; but this is done both in the name of a higher
truth and as a critique of any positive definition. Traditional irony, we
might say, is the constitution of a point of view, an elevated perspectivism. Such a point of view recognizes the inherent finitude of seeing
but also recognizes this recognition. Once we acknowledge that we
view the world from some perspective, it is always possible to think
just what those perspectives are perspectives *of.* This would give us a
way of thinking that general field or context within which any distinct point of view is located. This is what allows Searle to refer to context, Rorty to refer to vocabularies, and a whole history of ironists to
refer to the absolute or infinite. Any acknowledgment of a finite point
or perspective leads to the question of the context, field, or plane
within which such points would be located and generated. Ironic style
would then be a way of signaling what lay beyond all style and perspective. The immanence of Deleuze and Foucault's style is, by contrast, a recognition of *the stylistic production of point of view.* It is style
that creates the illusion of a prestylistic transcendence or outside. For
this reason, we should try to live up to the challenge of a style that
would not create a point outside itself. Style would not be the expres-

sion *of* point of view, for point of view itself is the effect of style. There are only singular points and events of difference, with each point or perspective imagining or effecting its own general field or plane. Each style creates its own origin. There is no context or plane in general. (This is how Deleuze and Guattari use the notion of a "body without organs": life is the constant production of different bodies, with each body producing the image of that general field from which it emerges. From organized bodies we retroactively imagine a Body Without Organs.)[9] This means that *style* or difference does not punctuate an already given plane. It is from the singular events of style that any plane, ground, or surface is effected. There are three implications from this strict commitment to immanence. First, no point can stand outside and explain the field. The genesis of point of view cannot be explained from or included within any position. Second, and more importantly for the history of irony, style needs to be understood well beyond its human manifestations. Third, we can think a "nonoptical" eye, an eye that does not see and judge but that is an intense and engaged organ of feeling. It is this notion of a point of view flush with the real—a real that is nothing more than its events of difference—that also opens the possibility for a new aesthetic:

First, "close-range" vision, as distinguished from long-distance vision; second, "tactile," or rather "haptic" space, as distinguished from optical space. "Haptic" is a better word than "tactile" since it does not establish an opposition between two sense organs but rather invites the assumption that the eye itself may fulfil this nonoptical function . . . .

There is no visual model for points of reference that would make them interchangeable and unite them in an inertial class assignable to an immobile outside observer. On the contrary, they are tied to any number of observers, who may be qualified as "monads" but are instead *nomads* entertaining tactile relations among themselves.[10]

Deleuze (and Deleuze and Guattari) present a literature that does not *speak* so much as "stutter," an animal or "machinic" becoming that tears writing away from subjects of enunciation. Whereas the proposition produces the effect of a subject *that* judges, forms of "minor literature" and free-indirect style allow language to function as a machine.[11] Speech needs to be freed from the human soul, and the soul needs to be extended beyond one who speaks. A style that enables speech without subjects of enunciation will be the first step to a truly transcendental empiricism. For Deleuze, the univocity, innocence, and immanence of existence are given in the affirmation of the infinitive: not that which differs but life as the power *to differ*. Rather than a subject/predicate proposition that would attach any attribute or event to some prior, undifferentiated, and neutral substance, the infinitive expresses the unity of the event. There is, to recall Nietzsche, no separation between the doer and the deed. There is not a subject who then thinks or the separate substance of thought but merely "To think."

> We must conceive of an infinitive which is not yet caught up in the play of grammatical determinations—an infinitive independent not only of all persons but of all time, of every mood and every voice (active, passive, or reflective). This would be a neutral infinitive for the pure event. . . . From this pure and undetermined infinitive, voices, moods, tenses, and persons will be engendered. . . . the verb goes from a pure infinitive, opened onto a question as such, to a present indicative closed onto a designation of a state of affairs or a solution case. The former opens and unfolds the ring of the proposition, the latter closes it up, and between the two, all the vocalizations, modalizations, temporalizations, and personalizations are deployed, together with the transformations proper to each case according to a generalized grammatical "perspectivism." (*LS*, 214–15)

Deleuze's valorization of the infinitive also draws upon Spinoza's theory of modes (*LS*, 214.–15). Here, there is not some prior or transcendental genetic power that then expresses itself. Rather than this temporal and active genesis, there is the concurrent and "static genesis" or "passive synthesis of a single field of distribution." Like Flaubert's "infinite impassivity," Deleuze's "static genesis" is set against the *act*: there is no subject, agent, or ground of expression. There is expression. There is not one *who acts*; there is impassivity or a static genesis that has no point of origin outside itself. The static nature of this genesis frees us from a temporal logic of point of view. For it is only from the restriction to one point in the whole of time that one event follows another. If we think *eternally*, then no point is privileged over any other, and there is no hierarchization of subject and action, ground and effect. No point of becoming can ground or explain any other. "No series enjoys a privilege over others" (*DR*, 278). We could also refer to this idea of static genesis through Nietzsche's "eternal return," eternal precisely because there is no prior condition or future fulfillment, only the perpetual innocence of time as a whole beyond any single present. Rather than the fall, reflection, and *felix culpa* of narrative temporality, literature is conceived by Deleuze as a prehuman becoming, a nomadic distribution. It is not a self-creating organism but an anonymous proliferation, a machine or rhizome.

Irony, if understood affirmatively, is not, for Deleuze, the enemy of thought or philosophy. It is neither an elevation above life and common sense nor a negation of life. As long as irony remains above life in a position of negativity and judgment, it has not really found its power. Irony begins with equivocation of voice, a saying distinct from a said. It is connected with height and a play that constitutes an *order* of surfaces (*LS*, 247). But the height of irony and its explicit constitution of surfaces are also what enable irony to be "vanquished on its own terrain" (*LS*, 247). It is from the *equivocity* of voice, height, and point of view that irony undoes itself and becomes the event of surfaces in *uni-*

vocity. Once we see voice and style, as we do in literature, as the creation of viewpoint, then we also see that the distinction in points (equivocity) emerges from a single field (univocity):

> There is therefore an excessive equivocation from the point of view of the voice and in relation to voice: an equivocation which ends equivocity and makes language ripe for something else. This something else is that which comes from the *other*, desexualized and metaphysical surface, when we finally go from speech to the verb, or when we compose a unique verb in the pure infinitive—along with the assembled words. This something else is the relation of the univocal, the advent of Univocity—that is, the Event which communicates the univocity of being to language.
>
> The univocity of sense grasps language in its complete system, as the total expresser of a unique expressed—the event. The values of humor are distinguished from those of irony: *humor* is the art of surfaces and of the complex relation between the two surfaces. (*LS*, 248)

In the move from irony to humor the equivocity of voice moves from the question of "Who Speaks?" to the pure infinitive, from point of view to an anonymous murmur, from a single series of time as recognition to a multiplication of paths and lines. It would be well to bear in mind Henri Bergson's understanding of laughter: we laugh when human agency and intent break down, when the body appears machinelike or inhuman and no longer governed by its own chosen ends.[12] However, as in traditional irony, this literary liberation from the human through style always risks returning to banality; style can always be recognized and *interpreted* as a sign of some underlying subject: "What can the work of art do but follow again that path which goes from noise to voice, from voice to speech, and from speech to the verb, constructing this *Musik für ein Haus*, in order always to recover the independence of sounds and to fix the thunderbolt of the univocal. The event is, of course, quickly covered over by every-day banality or, on the contrary, by the sufferings of madness" (*LS,* 249).

The Postmodern Epoch

The two senses in which "point of view" can be used to explain irony resonate throughout Deleuze's work. Philosophy, he argues, has long been governed by a certain sentence form—the proposition uttered by a first person—and a certain mode of looking—the "optics" of good sense that recognizes and determines a stable object. According to Deleuze, the privilege of the first person proposition and the look of the impartial subject that determines an object need to be seen as *effects* of an indirect speech and an impersonal optics. (Deleuze draws on a history of philosophy that tears the eye away from its lived and bodily intensity in order to produce the look or viewpoint of "man" in general.) Voice begins as effective incantation before it becomes recognized signification. Speech is, therefore, essentially deterritorialized, always a voice from elsewhere, never owned by a single body. Speech is not originally in the first person but begins indirectly in the third person. Everyday, banal, and unquestioning speech takes the form of an "It is said that . . ." For Deleuze the first-person point of view—both existentially and grammatically—is derivative of the indirect speech act or the "collective assemblage" of prepersonal perspectives. Deleuze insists that there have always been two directions in philosophy, the height of irony and the descent of humor. Both directions are tied to an expansion of point of view beyond the first person or subject.

If, as Deleuze has argued, irony has always operated on a vertical axis of depth and height, it has also been tied to a certain modality of time, history, and the dialectic. Paul de Man described this most acutely, tying irony to temporality and point of view. In the act of speech the subject will be constituted as *having been*, as the point of view from which sense emerges. Only after the tense logic of the sentence can the transcendental subject be seen as having fallen into the representation of time. The ironic or authentic subject, however, realizes itself as nothing other than this fallenness. In this regard, irony is *epochal*. It works at the very limits of the thought of temporality and historicity. In irony there is an abyssal awareness that temporality is only effected through the spatial inscription of language but that language only gives the *sense* of this temporality after *having been*. Neither the horizontal axis of time nor the hierarchizing vertical axis of the subject's depth and point of view is originary, and neither can fully account for the other. Irony oscillates from one epochal limit to the other: depth and height, interiority and exteriority, time and space. Viewing where we are—or self-recognition—will always require some virtual apparatus that allows us to think the very "image of thought." What ties traditional irony to temporality and dialectic has been its commitment to metaphors of height and elevation, such that the temporality of irony has been thought through at the expense of its spatiality and its optics. What Deleuze offers in the history of irony and its various delimitations of human speech is an attention to the spatialization and visuality that governs our conceptions of sense and point of view. The very idea of *history* is only possible with the distribution of a surface and a look: the construction of a single temporal plane and the point of view of "man" that can overlook that plane. Indeed, the very idea of the *post*modern—that point in time when we realize that the ground of being is really an effect of all its surface simulations—still relies on a progressive history viewed from a single point within the grand epoch of the West.

Deleuze and Guattari wrote their own philosophy in an attempt to capture divergent series and temporalities, such that the idea of a

viewpoint that theorizes what is—the point of view of the subject—
could be seen as the effect of a certain way of speaking. Overcoming
the temporality of irony would be at one with Deleuze's utopian project of achieving thought without an image. No longer a subject who
precedes or becomes through speech that is always *other than* the subject, Deleuze will insist on an immanent plane of molecular perceptions with no point privileged over any other. Writing and philosophy
can be eternally new, affirmative, and inhuman, only with a liberation from a puerile sense of history that would merely see one work of
writing following another and one act of thought adding to another.
If we accept the radical nature of Deleuze's monadology,[13] each point
of the universe opens out onto eternity in its own way, producing its
own duration. Each work of philosophy rewrites the whole corpus of
philosophy; each work of art rereads the entire canon; and each event
of thought transforms the very image of what it is to think. If the act
of speech effects a depth and a height (a subject who views and a world
viewed), and if this also effects a linear temporality (a subject who
spoke), then *new*—or eternal—writing will have to free text from the
speaking mouth and free the look from the eye. A truly postmodern
irony will not just displace the modern by repeating received styles *as
received*. It will displace the unified temporal and spatial axes that
condition the very idea of the modern epoch. Time will no longer be
viewed from *a* present, with one past and one future, but will occur as
a multiplicity of durations. Space will no longer be "a" transcendental
horizon within which we view the world but the opening of a multiplicity of planes, plateaus, or spatializations. Such multiplicities can be
achieved, if at all, only through a pulverization of point of view—
thinking a time that becomes through divergent series and a space
that is viewed all at once, as a virtual and open whole, over and over
again, and each time anew.

   What Deleuze takes from Nietzsche is not just an attempt to free thought from the burden of the past but a striving for a form of the new that will be self-renewing, eternally dislocating itself not only from its own time but from time in general. What is new, Deleuze argues, is not just what supersedes the old; the truly new is eternally new, tearing itself away from all narratives of historical recuperation. Nietzsche's "untimely" philosophy would be exemplary of this mode: write in such a way that the very figures of time can no longer be recognized within a coherent history. From as early as *The Birth of Tragedy* Nietzsche took the style of nineteenth-century philology and created a way of writing that disrupted complacent historicism. Picture the Greeks, Nietzsche urged, as a culture strong enough to invent their own origins, capable of creating gods and divine births. When we turn back to the Greeks we should not be viewing our origin, passively enslaving ourselves to a timeless moment of the past. We should view the Greeks the way the Greeks viewed the gods, as invented origins that ennoble our sense of the present.[14] Here, the style that describes the past also demands the production of new styles. The past is created as that which challenges us to invent a future. Nietzsche's narrations use the very style of philology and historicism to produce ideas that exceed all history: the idea of eternal return, as that ever-renewing force that *gives* history but that cannot be enclosed or comprehended within history; or the idea of a radical perspectivism or "overman," a point of view or personality that refuses recognition of self, subject, or location. Just as Nietzsche challenged the notion of a continuous history within which "we" are located, he also challenged the notion of an actual world that is then viewed from perspectives. Overcoming the human demands overcoming the privilege attached to "a" located viewpoint and the primacy accorded to "a" human time. History is not a unity from which we can discern disparate moments, and life is not a ground within which we are located as perceivers. In the beginning is chaos or disparity, and it is from these disparate points that various continuous histories and viewpoints are then imagined. In the beginning is the active event or the moment, to which the momentous order of history is a reaction. Similarly, in the beginning is the look or point of view, from which we (reactively) assume some present world that was there *to be seen* (some "x," as Nietzsche put it, that lies behind our appearances).[15]

Both eternal return and perspective in Deleuze and Nietzsche begin as temporal concepts but then go on to short-circuit the very logic of time. The eternal return is just that power that affirms the events that constitute time, but it is also a power that radically exceeds any temporal order or sequence. The eternal is not just the extension of temporal points ad infinitum. To think the "eternal" adequately is to think it beyond the point of any present. Eternity is not the collection of all presents or viewpoints; eternity is not some given whole, for as eternal it remains forever in becoming and potential. There is, therefore, no already given whole of which each point would be a partial perspective; eternity is the possible infinity of points and perspectives. Perspective or point of view traditionally suggests some undifferentiated continuity within which each point of experience is located; but for both Nietzsche and Deleuze there is only the eternal genesis of "singularities." This means that we need to rethink point of view beyond its location within history, within experience, or within the world. It is not that there is a world that we only grasp through perspectives or points of view. Nor is it that there is no world or reality— this would be nihilism. Rather, each point of view is the affirmation of its own infinite world: not a point within the real but the real itself.

If it is impossible to adopt a God-like view from nowhere, then we can at least write from a perspective that displays the very paradox of perspective and point of view. No matter how much we assert the relativity of our perspectives or viewpoints, the very idea of perspective or viewpoint entails a position within some field. Just what are our relative viewpoints relative to? We can either remain within a happy and complacent relativity (and this is one of the ways that Nietzsche has been read, as a philosopher of personal styles and perspectives),[16] or we can play up the impossibility of this relativity: the very thought of relativism is itself historically relative, and the very immanence of point of view is itself always articulated from point of view (*LS*, 260). It is this second path from Nietzsche—of a perpetually decentered perspectivism—that Deleuze pursues (*LS*, 174). The first path is an irony generated from a sense of history and a sense of the concept, an irony that could always be accused of remaining other than life, aware of its temporal finitude. The second path is described by Deleuze as a "superior irony" (*DR*, 182). This is an irony that attempts to create a style that is not just historically new but that troubles all sense of temporality. This is an irony that does more than work from the limits of a particular concept or epoch; it is an attempt to think the eternally recurrent emergence of concepts in general. There are some styles that manage to open their epoch.

The irony of eternal return is just such a style. If a style can be created that exposes itself *as style*, then style is no longer the ornamental overlay of a timeless concept. The concept is affirmed in its full temporal becoming. Such an irony would be aligned with the project outlined in *What Is Philosophy?*: not only must we avoid locating our concepts within some transcendent plane (such as God, Being, or the Subject), we must also attempt to think "*the* plane of immanence" as such.[17] Style can work in just this way: not as the style of some prior expressing subject or being but as the fullness of expression itself.

To think this way would reverse Edmund Husserl's description of the relation between style and epoch. According to Husserl, the concept of the transcendental subject enables us to think of a being that is not within this or that historical moment; the subject is that point from which all history emerges.[18] The subject might be described from within the style of a certain philosophy, but this style then enables the thought of the origin of all philosophy and all style. The concept of the subject enables us to think the ground of all concepts. Deleuze and Nietzsche's eternal return, by contrast, affirms a style that would preclude any concept from operating as a ground. What is willed in eternal return is not this or that style or this or that concept but the very force that over and over again constructs new styles and concepts (*DR*, 7–8).

Postmodern Style

This gives us two ways of thinking about style, either as the particular way in which concepts are articulated or as a force that disrupts the generality of concepts. This also gives us two ways for thinking of postmodernity and postmodern irony. The first would be to see postmodernism as a movement that "quotes," "mentions," or repeats styles but without any sense of a proper or privileged style and with a sense that one set of concepts is no more "proper" or grounded than another.[19] Here, one would, as Rorty suggests, remain within the contingency and finitude of one's style, aiming for maximized stylistic invention from within. The second form of irony would do more than accept the provisional status of our concepts or language games; it would think the very emergence or birth of sense. Such a birth would be *monstrous*: not concepts that emerge from a thinking subject or language game but the chaotic production of sounds, nonsense, and voices that subsequently become recognized as forms of sense or concepts.

The first form of irony would include all those modes of "postmodern" literature and interpretation that repeat our language games in an empty, provisional, or pastichelike manner, such that "we" would now recognize our position as particular and located. There is a dominant and recognized idea of the postmodern: an epoch that abandons all truth claims, metanarratives, and historical transcendence. Reading the postmodern in this way would allow us to encounter texts as "metafictions," as nothing more than reflections on the signs that "we" are and that produce our time. Thomas Pynchon's *The Crying of Lot 49*, for example, employs all the devices of a detective novel but with clues that lead nowhere, signs that remain uncoded, and a conclusion that maximizes, rather than dissolves, mystery.[20] The novel is written in first person from the point of view of a character with a located history and political background. What we are given is not a world but a fiction aware of itself *as fiction*, a fiction that demonstrates the stylistic production of history.[21] The second form of postmodern irony would preclude recognition, such that the postmodern would be more than the shock of the new and more than the retracing of the present. It would problematize not just a specific style, genre, or meaning of the present but the problem of meaning or sense in general. When we "read" Pynchon's *Mason & Dixon* it is this second or "superior" form of irony that we encounter. The "style" of the novel is not that of a character or person; it is the style of a typeface or form of newsprint. The novel opens with the capital letters and punctuation of the broadsheets of its time, but the syntax is not that of newspaper reporting. Written in present tense but disrupted by noun phrases in the past tense and with a use of the passive voice, there is an absence of narrating and narrated subject. Instead, we are given actions and objects not located within a viewing consciousness so much as "listed." These events are described through a combination of idiomatic phrases set alongside tongue-twister epic epithets that resist being spoken at all ("a stocking'd foot Descent"; "a long scarr'd sawbuck table"). What is being described is the very opening of the narrative scene, the home from which the story of Mason and Dixon will be narrated. It is as though the voice of the novel emerges from a collec-

tion of found objects, objects that already impersonate or interpret another style ("some Second-Street Chippendale, including an interpretation of the fam'd Chinese Sofa"):

> Snow-Balls have flown their Arcs, starr'd the Sides of Outbuildings, as
> of Cousins, carried Hats away into the Wind off Delaware,—the Sleds
> are brought in and their Runners carefully dried and greased. Shoes
> deposited in the back Hall, a stocking'd foot Descent made upon the
> great Kitchen, in a purposeful Dither since Morning, punctuated by
> the ringing Lids of various Boilers and Stewing-Pots, fragrant with
> Pie-Spices, peel'd Fruits, Suet, heated Sugar,—the Children, having all
> upon the Fly, among rhythmic slaps of Batter and Spoon, coax'd and
> stolen what they might, proceed as upon each afternoon all this snowy
> Advent, to a comfortable Room at the rear of the House, years since
> given over to their carefree Assaults. Here have come to rest a long
> scarr'd sawbuck table, with two mismatch'd side-benches, from the
> Lancaster County branch of the family,—some Second-Street Chip-
> pendale, including an interpretation of the fam'd Chinese Sofa, with a
> high canopy of yards of purple Stuff that might be drawn all 'round to
> make a snug, dim tent,—a few odd Chairs sent from England before
> the war,—mostly Pine and Cherry about, nor much Mahogany, except-
> ing a sinister and wonderful Card Table which exhibits the cheaper
> Wave-like Grain known in the Trade as Wand'ring Heart, causing an il-
> lusion of Depth.[22]

While Pynchon's novel is an historical epic, it is narrated neither
from the point of view of a character of the past nor from a present
recollecting narrator. If we ask "Who speaks?" of this novel we are not
only given a number of voices, including a talking dog, we are also
given a language beyond speech. Unlike the first "recognizing" form
of postmodern metafiction that exposes where we are as a style or way
of speaking, *Mason & Dixon*'s "irony" can no longer be recuperated as
the parody of a genre, voice, or epoch. It is the inhumanity of this

style—its refusal of genre, parody, or recognition—that makes a definitive but not final break with the modernist project of thinking the
limits of "the West" or "man" in general. Whereas Joyce's *Ulysses* had
already incorporated newspaper headlines into the stream of consciousness of Leopold Bloom or the voices of Dublin, Pynchon's language resists even this insecure location. The disembodied voices of
high modernism were still *voices*: local dialects, quotations, stream of
consciousness, and recorded lyrics. The language of *Mason & Dixon* is
not the language of a genre, a character, or a locale. As the novel proceeds, the language pulverizes into a chaotic overlay of impersonal,
unfamiliar, and near-surreal ways of writing (rather than ways of
speaking or ways of seeing). We are taken from the readable to the unreadable; it is not just this or that concept, this or that style that is disrupted but the very conditions of style and meaning.

It is possible, then, to see postmodernity as a consequence of the
failure of modernism. The panoramic impersonality that culminates
in *Finnegans Wake* or *The Cantos* is articulated as the voice of the
West in general. After these epic projects to locate the very emergence,
limit, or origin of sense in consciousness or culture, postmodernity
"returns" to those local, limited, particular projects of character or
sensibility. This has been described by Fredric Jameson as a retreat
from the sublime to the beautiful, from the limits of the concept to the
"aesthetic" or the "sensible." But Jameson also offers a dialectical way
of reading this historical "transition," and he does so through the notion of "epochality." This demands seeing the postmodern as more
than an empty repetition or pastiche of past styles.[23] Indeed, we might
see the *sensibility* of postmodern art and literature as a confrontation
with the very force that gives history style and meaning. To use Deleuze's terminology: rather than thinking the sensibility *of being*, as
though the sensible were a mere sign or indicator of some ultimate
real, we might think the *being of the sensible* (*DR*, 140). This would be

a sensibility experienced in all its difference and immanence, not a sensibility that was given through concepts but a sensibility from which concepts and sense emerged. We normally think of the sensibility *of being* as though the sensible were always the sign of some underlying presence; to think the being of the sensible reverses this series. It is the sensible itself and not some (limit) meaning or intention that is the very medium of the postmodern. Pynchon's *Mason & Dixon* presents the intensity of style itself: not a voice *that speaks* but a speaking "machine," a sound and literal marking from which time and humanity are effected.

Rather than see the postmodern, then, as one more literary period, we might regard it as a challenge to the very sense of periodicity. Modernity is often defined as a project of coming to oneself, of reducing alienation, of recognition, transparency, and universalizability.[24] Postmodernity, on the other hand, is both an inscription of the very limits of "our" epoch (through quotation, pastiche, and repetition) and the impossibility of a sense of ownness (taking us to the impersonal or eternal force that gives repetition in the very sound and materiality of art and literature).

Reversing Hegel/Reversing Modernity

While Deleuze has described his project as a reversal of Platonism (turning the series of "being plus representation" into a series of "image plus image plus image . . ."), his work on irony can also be read as a reversal of Hegelianism. Hegel regarded irony as a precursor to recognition and modernity. It is when we overcome the ironic distance between our concepts and the world that subject and substance will coincide; the world will be the medium of subjective recognition, and the subject will be the medium through which world history recognizes itself. For Deleuze, by contrast, it is only when we no longer treat our concepts as mirrors or reflections of things but as positive creations or events that we will really be doing philosophy and really affirming style.

In *The Logic of Sense* Deleuze describes philosophy as traditionally occupying one of two forms: either metaphysics or transcendental philosophy; either a gesture to some transcendental field outside the "I" (a formless ground, absolute, abyss) or the location of all sense within the subject (*LS*, 106). Interestingly, Deleuze defines this "fundamental problem" of philosophy as the question of "who speaks?" (*LS*, 107), and it is this question that Deleuze's own philosophy seeks to surpass, and through a more profound transcendentalism. The problem with all previous transcendentalisms is that they have been metaphysical: they refer experience or the given back to some prior ground or origin. Transcendental *empiricism*, however, does not seek the genesis of the given. The given—the real or desire—is becoming and genesis itself. There is no being or substance that then becomes or is given; there is just givenness and becoming. Neither thought, nor the subject, nor being can provide a point from which genesis or synthesis emerges. All metaphysical philosophies have offered a single point of genesis and a single series of synthesis and becoming. According to Deleuze, the supposed shift in point of view or perspective (from God to the subject) that occurs with Kant is no shift at all, precisely because we still remain within a *problem of point of view*.[25] This problem, coupled with the question of "who speaks?" is only overcome, Deleuze argues, with Nietzsche's discovery of "a world of impersonal and pre-individual singularities." What this suggests is that a sense of the philosophical epoch is intimately connected to style. If philosophy has always been generated by the attribution of what is said to a voice that speaks, then new thought might demand a style or grammar that dislocates point of view and enunciative position. Point of view locates speech or language as the speech *of* some speaker (or as the literature *of* some epoch). Deleuze and Guattari, on the other hand, will argue that speech is in the first instance a "collective assemblage," not located within a subject but a movement from which subject positions are derived.

Deleuze therefore sees Hegelian irony as going only so far in its critique of the rigidity of concepts. Hegel's resolution of the ironic gap between what we say and what we mean was achieved by generating both the subject and the object, or concept and meaning, from the negating force of the concept in general. This is why the exemplary style of the Hegelian dialectic is the chiasmus: "the real is rational and the rational is real."[26] Here, there is no privilege of subject over predicate; what something *is* is just how it expresses itself. For Hegel, then, the voice of the proposition is more than a vehicle for the articulation of concepts. It is through the voice of philosophy that reason speaks itself and recognizes itself (and all that "is") as effected through this saying: "The *proposition* should express *what* the True is; but essentially the True is Subject. As such it is merely the dialectical movement, this course that generates itself, going forth from, and returning to, itself" (*PS*, preface, sec. 65, 40). Deleuze, however, takes voice in the opposite direction. Voice is not an elevation to a self-present concept, such that the tone, style, or materiality of voice would be nothing more than a passage to recognition. For Deleuze, voice is at first noise and nonsense. Indeed, it is only the "depressive" position that recognizes voice as a superego coming from "on high"—imposing a meaning or law. For Deleuze's valorized "schizo," by contrast, "speaking will be fashioned out of eating and shitting" (*LS*, 193). And there are forms of literature that affirm this event of sense: where concepts are not elevated forms expressed *through* voice but vocalizations that subsequently take on an incorporeal dimension. Lewis Carroll's nonsense words, for example, explicitly imbricate noise and sense. But all language has passed through this event, from the corporeal to the metaphysical surface, from eating to speaking. *The Logic of Sense* draws on Carroll

to reaffirm the event of sense as it emerges from the mouth; in so doing, literature retraces the very opening of style: "We have seen this
struggle for the independence of sounds go on, ever since the excre-
mental and alimentary noises which occupied the mouth-anus in
depth; we followed it to the disengagement of a voice high above; and
finally we traced it to the primary formation of surfaces and words.
Speaking, in the complete sense of the word, presupposes the verb
and passes through the verb, which projects the mouth onto the metaphysical surface, filling it with the ideal events of this surface" (*LS*,
240–41).

The pre-Socratic philosophers, according to Deleuze, also possessed
this "schizophrenic" art of the surface; and it is from this surface of
sound that a distinction between depth and height is subsequently inaugurated in Platonism (*LS*, 191). The Platonic distinction between
depth and height *interprets* noise and the mouth as both the expression of some underlying subject and as the articulation of a universal
meaning (*LS*, 182). Socratic dialogue allowed the voices to gather
around the meaning of the concept, and this created a clear hierarchy:
between the Sophists, who felt that their worldly definitions captured
the concept, and the Socratic questions that allowed the concept to exceed the given definition (*LS*, 256). This created a clear distinction
between voice and sense, or the saying and the said, between the use
of the word "justice" and its higher meaning, a meaning that tran-
scended any worldly use (*LS*, 259).

Like Hegel, Deleuze is critical of beginning philosophy from the
simple terms of the understanding. For Hegel, reason ought to be dynamic, speculative, and differential, recognizing its own power in the
conceptualization of the world and the concept's power in the possibility of speculation. But, against Hegel, Deleuze refuses to include all
finite points within the general self-regard of the concept. There is

not some higher speculative point that could encompass the look in general; looking is not located within point of view. For Deleuze, from a series of impersonal looks, imagings, reflections, and repetitions something like a point of view can be effected. This means that we have to take seriously Deleuze's emphasis on viewing apparatuses and molecular perception along with his emphasis on style.[27] We cannot subordinate looking, receptivity, or the givenness of the world to the site of the subject, as though the world were located *within* point of view. Before the representing power of the subject there is an infinite series of looks or "contemplations." Genetic codings, reflective surfaces, the passive responses of bodies, cells, life, and animality are all, to use Henri Bergson's terminology, forms of "perception."[28] What makes this (nonhuman) perception pure is its immediate relay. When one point of life responds to another it does so immediately and is thus a pure instance of perception. When there is a delay in response, when the human mind considers how to act in relation to a perception, then the subjective or representational point of view is formed. This means, strictly, that there is not a subject *that then comes to perceive the world*. There is pure perception. From a "contraction" of this perception a subject is formed. The subject does not reach the world by looking. From a field of looks something like subject and object are contracted: "Perhaps it is irony to say that everything is contemplation, even rocks and woods, animals and men, even Actaeon and the stag, Narcissus and the flower, even our actions and our needs. But irony in turn is still a contemplation, nothing but a contemplation" (*DR*, 75).

It would be an extreme reactivism, on this Deleuzean model, to see point of view as the origin of images. This is the error of representation, an error that has dogged philosophy and impeded its power. If we accept the affirmation of eternal return, then we accept a single and univocal field of images, not the image *of* some real, not the giving *of* some given, but a giving, imaging, or perpetual difference *from which* identity and the given are effected. Imaging and giving cannot be contained within or subordinated to some privileged image, for the subject is itself an image among other images. Despite this original multiplicity of points, both philosophy and its concomitant style have produced the subject not as an image among others but as the ground or origin of all images. This is where the question of style intervenes. Like Hegel, Deleuze will insist that it is not that there is a subject that is then expressed through propositions. It is the style of the proposition that unfolds the subject. For Hegel, the proper grammar that would extend the subject beyond its finite location would be the speculative proposition. Here the "is" would not assume a ground (or subject) that then has certain attributes (or predicates). For Hegel, the difference between subject and predicate is achieved through the "is" of the proposition. It is through the proposition that the subject unfolds itself as being what it is. For Deleuze, philosophy will also have its proper style, not a Hegelian speculative proposition but a collective assemblage that creates a "we" or "people" forever in becoming. This style will be properly philosophical only in its refusal of any propriety.

Both Deleuze and Hegel therefore work against a tradition of irony that had subordinated thought to the "elevation," distance, or negativity of the concept. For Hegel, the subject is nothing other than the concept, and it requires a certain style of philosophy to realize their identity. For Deleuze, both subject and concept are effects of style. But style for Deleuze is not just the external expression of what is, as though style were a way of capturing a certain perspective or point of view. On the contrary, perspective and point of view are enabled by style. Style is not the expression of the human point of view; the human is an effect of a certain style. If style were extended faithfully *as style*, then it would take us beyond point of view.

Humor and Irony

In his references to irony Deleuze describes irony as ascent—a movement tied to the infinitely large (and aligned with the infinite representation of Hegelian dialectic). In contrast, humor is descent—a movement progressing to the infinitely small (and aligned both with finite representation and with the thought of Leibniz) (*DR*, 11). Now there are two broad responses that Deleuze makes to his distinction. The first is a preference for Leibniz over Hegel, for descent over ascent, for a voice from the depths as opposed to a voice from on high, humor over irony, the infinitely small over the infinitely large (*DR*, 51). We can see the crude reification of this debate in the "opposition" today between Deleuze and Derrida. Derrida will ask the question of a concept and demonstrate the concept's force or elevation above and beyond any context or voice, such that all speech is a "becoming theological."[29] Deleuze, by contrast, describes the creation of concepts from the very depths of being: all the ways in which voices emerge from sounds and the pulsations of the body, such that philosophy of the future would be a "becoming animal" or "becoming machine," an affirmation of the inhuman. But Deleuze does not just opt for the movement of humor over irony. Deleuze's second response is the retrieval of dialectic and irony in a *superior form*: beyond Hegel and Leibniz, beyond representation, and beyond the good voice of reason (*DR*, 268–69). Such retrieval will demand a new style of philosophy—no longer a style that proceeds from the movement of concepts grounded in good sense.

Realism, Representation, and Common Sense

The Western project of representation, Deleuze argues, has been tied to two moral commitments: good sense and common sense. Good sense contains all thought within a grounding subject, while common sense directs all thought to an object of recognition. Both good sense and common sense establish a clear and unambiguous representational point of view. The subject is the ground of good sense: that point from which thinking proceeds. The object is that toward which all thought is directed. What is assumed is that there is a general point of view that characterizes thinking in general and that there is a world of recognition that corresponds to this viewpoint of good sense. This is, of course, most easily recognized in the style of high realism and omniscient narration. Here, the point of view comes from "nowhere" and can pass from character to character, as though there were a general human thinking, given particular form in each of its psychological viewpoints. Good sense is given in the very possibility of this style, a style that captures each character's way of seeing by attributing attitudes, values, and propositions and by locating all these different positions within a single style of description—as though style were the mere vehicle for a thought that preceded stylistic particularity. Consider the following passage from Anthony Trollope's *The Warden*:

> There is living at Barchester, a young man, a surgeon, named John Bold, and both Mr. Harding and Dr. Grantly are well aware that to him is owing the pestilent rebellious feeling which has shown itself in the hospital; yes, and the renewal, too, of that disagreeable talk about Hiram's estates which is now again prevalent in Barchester. Nevertheless, Mr. Harding and Mr. Bold are acquainted with each other; we may say, are friends, considering the great disparity in their years. Dr. Grantly, however, has a holy horror of the impious demagogue, as on one occasion he called Bold, when speaking of him to the precentor; and being a more prudent far-seeing man than Mr. Harding, and possessed of a stronger head, he already perceives that this John Bold will work great trouble in Barchester. He considers that he is to be regarded as an enemy, and thinks that he should not be admitted into

the camp on anything like friendly terms. As John Bold will occupy much of our attention, we must endeavour to explain who he is, and why he takes the part of John Hiram's bedesmen.[30]

On the one hand, the voice passes from character to character, as though psychological states were open for viewing: "Mr. Harding and Dr. Grantly are well aware that to him is owing the pestilent rebellious feeling which has shown itself in the hospital." At the same time, the voice is also that of everyday opinion or town gossip, referring to "that disagreeable talk" and using the frequent point of view of "we" and our obviously unanimous concerns. It has long been noted that omniscient narration harbors an implicit politics: as though there were a subject in general that preceded any stylistic variants or voices.[31] Irony can be considered both as an extension and as a disruption of this grounding voice of common sense. In the forms already discussed, irony shares with omniscient narration the *possibility* of a view from nowhere or a God's-eye view. In omniscient narration this higher point of view is actualized as the very subject of the narrating voice. The style speaks from the ground of good sense. In irony, most frequently, this higher viewpoint does not itself speak but is implicit or virtual and is generated from the limited viewpoint of the speaking voice.

In Jonathan Swift's *A Modest Proposal*, for example, the speaking voice uses all the discourse of a strict and calculating rationalism. The proposal—to solve the problems of poverty and hunger by consuming the poor—is ostensibly the very height of reason, but the discourse—by extending reason as mere calculation to its extreme version—generates a critique of that reason, for reason *cannot mean* simple calculation and interest. Swift's irony takes the concept of reason as it is used—for calculation and rationalization—in order to question whether this is really reason. The proposal begins with an invocation of shared voice or common sense: "It is a melancholy object . . ."; "I think it is agreed that . . ."[32] However, the "we" that is invoked here is disrupted in the extension of our common concepts. "Our" language of reason, calculation, and utilitarian charity is spoken so faithfully that it yields the most absurd outcomes. "We" can no longer share this voice, and yet no other voice is articulated: "I have already computed the charge of nursing a beggar's child (in which list I reckon all *cottagers, labourers*, and four fifths of the *farmers*) to be about two shillings *per annum*, rags included, and I believe no gentleman would repine to give ten shillings for the *carcass of a good fat child*, which, as I have said, will make four dishes of excellent nutritive meat, when he hath only some particular friend, or his own family to dine with him. Thus the Squire will learn to be a good landlord, and grow popular among his tenants, the mother will have eight shillings net profit, and be fit for work until she produces another child."[33]

Swift also presents a classic example of Deleuze's distinction between irony as elevation and humor as descent. In irony the speaking voice continually limits itself and thus generates a higher but absent point beyond that limit. *A Modest Proposal* speaks through a reason that is mechanical and arithmetical and entirely devoid of any more subtle considerations. The reader is thereby able to see above the point of view of the speaker: reason *cannot mean* that it is rational to consume one's children. But there is also a point at which the proposal also "descends" into humor, and this is when a duplicity of voice enters: "I have reckoned upon a medium, that a child just born will weigh 12 pounds, and in a solar year if tolerably nursed increaseth to 28 pounds. I grant this food will be somewhat dear, and therefore very *proper for landlords*, who as they have already devoured most of the parents, seem to have the best title to the children."[34]

There is a joke here in the Freudian sense. The word "devoured" is being used literally, for the proposal suggests the consumption of flesh;

but it also deploys the figural meaning of the devouring landlord. It is as though the elevated voice betrays itself by falling into the body. In this slip into humor the irony descends. We are given more than the single point of view of the rationalist and his limited computational way of seeing. The play on words allows the everyday voice of humor to erupt. Irony generates a higher point of view by delimiting a way of seeing; but humor returns any supposedly elevated viewpoint to the depths: in the case of Swift, the proposal is reduced to a position not of social concern but of literal consumption. What makes this a "descent" of humor is that the "other" voice is actually articulated. Humor criticizes the devouring landlord, whereas irony generates a higher point that sustains itself above and beyond any articulation.

Irony in its traditional form, as deployed by Swift, extends the demands of representation. *A Modest Proposal* delimits a way of viewing the world, such that the irony then demands ascent to a higher viewpoint. In humor, by contrast, a putative elevation into concepts and high reason is dragged back down into its worldly interests. (Think of how Samuel Beckett's humor draws the questions and concepts of existence and meaning down to the level of machines, bodies, and stray objects. Or how Henry Fielding shows the concepts of "virtue," "honor," and "character" to be rhetorical ploys for characters' interests.) Both irony and humor play off the gap between concepts and world. In irony our world is inadequate to the lofty strivings of our concepts. In humor these elevated concepts are shown to be masks or veils for the uses and desires of our world.

Against this separation of representational logic in humor and irony Deleuze puts forward the possibility of a logic of *immanence*: the event of the given is nothing other than itself and not the givenness *of* some grounding presence. This means that rather than finding propositions that unify subjects with predicates (Hegel) or concepts that transcend their articulation (irony), Deleuze demonstrates the emergence of concepts from life or modes of style. If style is not the expression *of* what is, if style is not the becoming *of* some subject, it is because for Deleuze style is not an overlay. It is not that there is a being that then differentiates itself through style. There is just stylistic differentiation: life as style. Certain styles—such as the proposition—lead us to think that style is the style of some voice. Other styles show voice to be the effect of style itself. This logic of immanence insists that there are not points of view that then mark themselves with a certain style; rather, point of view is effected from style.

Free-indirect style, to take one example favored by Deleuze and Guattari, is not a picture, proposition, or representation of what is; it is a way of being in itself.[35] Deleuze's appeal to style, then, is not "aesthetic." It refuses to think of writing as the effective laid over the actual. If actuality is nothing other than its effects, then *style will itself be a mode of being.*[36]

We might distinguish free-indirect style's distance of voice from within by defining it against irony. Irony estranges or alienates voice in order to set the particularity of voice against a transcendent Idea that resists all articulation or determination. While irony shows the limits of voice, it does so by showing the ways in which speakers *mean more than they say.* When Plato's Thrasymachus says that justice is the advantage of the powerful, the *concept* of justice already undercuts Thrasymachus's attempt at moral relativism.[37] What makes free-indirect style different from irony is the peculiar ontological commitment of irony. In irony a way of speaking is identified as limited from within. And irony is not only, as Deleuze argued, the style that has always tied philosophy to the question of *who speaks*; it is also a style tied to establishing height and recognition (*LS*, 248; *DR*, 5). When John Milton's Satan says, "Evil, be thou my good," *we* can see Satan ironically undercutting himself. Satan has to use the very concept of good

in his embrace of evil and in so doing refutes his own project of embracing evil.[38] We cannot say that we no longer value the good; insofar
as we utter the concept, "good" already instates a certain value. Irony
is a style that relies on the *sustained force of concepts*, so that a speaker
can say one thing and be understood to mean another. Satan wants to
say that he embraces evil, but we who hear him understand him
differently, for to take evil as one's good is to recognize it as a good and
therefore to remain within some unavoidable law of the good. Irony
is inherently tied to this work of the concept and recognition. A concept has a form or force beyond its individual utterance, and it was
this transindividual or grounding force of concepts that drove Plato's
ironic dialogues and the moral projects of German Romanticism:
irony is that collective form of a concept that "comes from above" and
situates speaking subjects within some more general logic (*LS*, 230).

Free-indirect style, on the other hand, is beyond good and evil.
In free-indirect style it is not as though there are concepts that can
be recognized as the voice of law. In free-indirect style we are given
highly particular, located, idiosyncratic ways of speaking that are,
as Deleuze and Guattari describe them, "collective assemblages."[39]
Whereas irony plays on the difference between the universal force of a
concept and its individual utterance, free-indirect style traces the very
becoming of concepts as highly particular events. In free-indirect
style it is not as though there is a general concept that is then situated
in a point of view—as in irony. Free-indirect style effects a located
logic and concepts, demonstrating that concepts are always forms of
speaking, that styles are ways of being, and—most importantly—that
styles are the expressions of places or "collective assemblages" and
not subjects.

Consider the following paragraph that concludes Franz Kafka's
Metamorphosis. We have just read how Gregor Samsa has been trans-

formed into an insect, how his most passionate concerns are that he might be late for work and lose his position, and, finally, that his home life and stability might be threatened by this annoyance. There is humor in this story. The Samsas go on living as though human-to-insect metamorphosis were a worldly inconvenience. The human loses its naturalness and fluidity to become awkward, cumbersome, and rigidly fixed to the body. There is an absurdity in the juxtaposition of daily human norms—going to work, feeding the family, and fulfilling one's duty—with the incongruous animal body. We can think of this as humor in Henri Bergson's sense. We laugh when the daily fluidity and humanness of our bodies break down; our seemingly effortless mastery of life is confronted by the bizarre *in*humanity of the body. But the conclusion of the story moves beyond humor and irony to free-indirect style. The story concludes with the style and tone of a "happy ending" and resolution. It is as though Gregor's being as an insect has merely formed a minor interruption in the family's humanity, a humanity that reveals itself as a certain style of speech. What makes the opening of the story so humorous is the maintenance of linguistic conventions and niceties in the face of Gregor's tragedy. When Gregor first becomes an insect he speaks with all the same conventions, insisting to his employer that "one can be temporarily incapacitated, but that's just the moment for remembering former services and bearing in mind that later on, when the incapacity has been got over, one will certainly work with all the more industry and concentration."[40] As the story progresses Gregor loses his capacity to be heard as human, and he is drawn strangely to the power of music as his sister plays the violin. It is only after Gregor's death and the return to "normality" that the narrative takes on a voice of bourgeois convention and expectation, speaking of "prospects for the future" and "improvement in their condition." It is as though the return to humanity is also a return to an unquestioned and shared vocabulary and genre:

Then they all three left the apartment together, which was more than they had done for months, and went by tram into the open country outside of the town. The tram, in which they were the only passengers, was filled with warm sunshine. Leaning comfortably back in their seats they canvassed their prospects for the future, and it appeared on closer inspection that these were not bad at all, for the jobs they had got, which so far they had never really discussed with each other, were all three admirable and likely to lead to better things later on. The greatest immediate improvement in their condition would of course arise from moving to another house; they wanted to take a smaller and cheaper but also better situated and more easily run apartment than the one they had, which Gregor had selected. While they were thus conversing, it struck both Mr. and Mrs. Samsa, almost at the same moment, as they became aware of their daughter's increasing vivacity, that in spite of all the sorrow of recent times, which had made her cheeks pale, she had bloomed into a pretty girl with a good figure. They grew quieter and half unconsciously exchanged glances of complete agreement, having come to the conclusion that it would soon be time to find a good husband for her. And it was like a confirmation of their new dreams and excellent intentions that at the end of their journey their daughter sprang to her feet first and stretched her young body.[41]

By presenting the very style of humanism *as a style* we no longer recognize the human as the already given ground of our being. We become capable of thinking the becoming of the human through style and also becoming other than human or becoming-animal.

Deleuze's attention to style is an affirmation rather than a critique. Rather than arguing that any point of view will raise the question of the ground from which a point of view emerges, Deleuze aims to think a style that troubles the attributive and critical force of point of view. What is so difficult in free-indirect style is not just the answer to the question of who is speaking but also the very possibility of this question. Free-indirect speech does not, like irony, "come from on

high." It is the very wandering or "nomadics" of style, dislocated from
a speaking subject, producing a multiplicity of positions, a collage of
voices, or an assemblage. It is not as though there is a law or logic that
is then belied by the particular utterance of the speech act (as in
irony). In free-indirect style law or logic is the reaction or interpretation that comes after the event of voice, speech, tracing, or wandering.
It is only after having spoken that we recognize the human as one who
speaks and intends. And if *meaning* and subjects are just the reactive
effects of certain ways of speaking, then we will only overcome our
reactive submission to meaning and the law if we regard speaking not
as the vehicle of sense but as a movement or event alongside other
events. There just are events of speech, and from them certain regularities, such as located speakers, are effected. It is this event that is
affirmed in free-indirect style.

But what do other styles do? How can Deleuze account for the over-
whelming Western corpus of literature and philosophy that deploys a
representational grammar? If "what is" is *not* a presence there to be
represented, how did we come to think and speak in this way? Deleuze
and Guattari's reading of Kafka offers some answer to this problem.
Even those great texts of the Law and the father can be *activated*.
What their reading of Kafka's text does is not ask what it *means*, for
this is the work of irony, showing how utterances have a meaning beyond the speaker's intention. Instead they ask how texts *work*: how
laws are effected, subject positions carved out, desires instituted, and
ideas of presence and ground produced through textual events and
questions. There is, then, a twofold tactic. First, we need to affirm a
style that is adequate to life. Free-indirect style is not the style *of* some
being; it is existence or language *speaking itself*, a way of being
effected through style. Second, we need to read in such a way that all
those texts of Law are not taken as representations of law but as ways

of speaking, moving, and writing that then effect a law they supposedly represent: "A Kafka-machine is thus constituted by contents and
expressions that have been formalized to diverse degrees by unformed
materials that enter into it, and leave by passing through all possible
states. To enter or leave the machine, to be in the machine, to walk
around it, to approach it—these are all still components of the machine itself: these are the states of desire, free of all interpretation."[42]

Postmodernism/Post-Deleuzism

Since its earliest definitions irony has worked upon, and generated, a
distinction between the saying and the said. This is what ties irony to
the concept and what ties Western thought to the "concept of the concept"—the idea that what we say is the faithful repetition of some
higher meaning or "said." The saying is the material word, the actual
utterance, the corporeal movement of sound, while the said is the
meaning expressed by that singular articulation. When Thrasymachus utters the word "justice" there is a certain meaning that surpasses his "saying," and this is what allows Socrates to insist that Thrasymachus means or says more than he is saying. It is this notion of the
said that, according to Michel Foucault, opens the Western "will to
truth" and coincides with the routing of the Sophists. It is with Plato,
according to Foucault, that attention was henceforward directed not to
what discourse did or was but to what it said, and it is this production
of a "said" that inaugurates an "ethic of knowledge."[43] With the idea
of a "said" or meaning that lies above and beyond the force of an utterance we are able to subordinate discourse to some general meaning.
The "said" that supposedly exceeds our singular statements provides
thought with a foundation or ideal and thereby disavows the constitutive event of thinking or the production of the incorporeal meaning

from corporeal force.[44] In Deleuze's terms, we reactively subordinate the activity of thinking to some pregiven and recognizable ground, rather than affirming thought as the very event of difference.

Against this "ethics of knowledge" we might consider Deleuze's ethics of *amor fati*, an ethics that resides in the transcendental movement of freeing the saying from the said and undoing the conceptual subjection of irony (*LS*, 149). What Deleuze will insist upon is not the ironic difference between saying and said, the corporeal and the incorporeal, but the passage or movement from one to the other. It is literature that gives us this passage of sense, this event of the incorporeal. By not reducing sound (or the saying) to its meaning (or said), literature replays the emergence of concepts from style. Literature is most forceful, then, when it adopts a style beyond the human: not a voice that subordinates itself to the concept but a voice that moves preconceptually, nomadically, or at the level of nonsense.

If free-indirect style shows the human to be an effect of a certain style, another possibility is to free voice from the human. In so much literature of the twentieth century voice was shown to extend beyond the human: not located in the higher point of the concept or idea but in the depths of noise, machines, and the "buzz" or anonymous murmur of discourse. The high modernism that is so often invoked by Deleuze can be characterized as a genealogy of speech that disclosed the way language created, rather than expressed, human positions. Modernism is littered with speech that emanates from machines and objects, looks that extend from cameras and viewing apparatuses, and quotations that are repeated like so many found objects. T. S. Eliot's *The Waste Land* and Joyce's *Ulysses* repeat phrases of popular tunes, voices from radios, advertising slogans, and newspaper headlines—all in voices no longer located within a point of view. Thomas Mann's *Death in Venice* concludes with the "look" of a camera left idle on the beach as the high Romantic artist, Aschenbach, wanders to his death

in the ocean. F. Scott Fitzgerald's *The Great Gatsby* is dominated by
the image of an advertising billboard for an ocularist—the two giant
and manufactured eyes staring out at the landscape of moving vehicles. Irony traditionally demonstrated the limits of the concept by
generating a higher point of view—an imagined God's-eye viewpoint
of the idea or the infinite. Modernism shifts the inhuman point of
view, not to a point of higher meaning but to an inhuman machine,
where the look is reduced to a lens or camera and the "voice" is reduced to a recording, quotation, or slogan. The extension of this modernist gesture is the postmodern disembodied voice, not the voice of a
subject but a voice from which subjects and concepts are interpreted.
We can make sense of this through Fredric Jameson's distinction between parody and pastiche.[45] The parodic voice of modernism gathers
quotations and disembodied voices behind which the high point of
authorship remains—like God—above and beyond his handiwork.
Postmodern pastiche, by contrast, is a fragmentation without grounding unity—not a voice that has alienated itself from the human but a
voice from which the human might be derived. As an instance we can
think of Deleuze's (and Deleuze and Guattari's) idiosyncratic readings of high modernism: rather than a voice that has fallen away from
its ground, Deleuze reads Lawrence, Woolf, Joyce, and Kafka as the
movement of a voice that is pure becoming. Modernism is reread as a
challenge to the present, as part of a more profound power of life to exceed the epoch and time of man. Alongside their invocations of modernism are all those inhuman forms of semiosis described in *A Thousand Plateaus* (the striations of space, the codings of genetics, the
geological movements and animal burrowings that form the "mechanosphere"). What is at stake in Deleuze's superior irony is the very
limit of the human. Could we have a dialectic that allowed the concept to move beyond the said? Is it possible to articulate a style of the
inhuman—a style of style and not a style that would be the style of

some subject? If a machine could speak, could we avoid humanizing or understanding "him"?

Both Foucault and Deleuze were insistent that power or desire could not be reduced to the human. And both insisted that certain literary styles could take us back to the inhuman buzzing of discourse, to a white noise that plunges us from the heights of meaning to the depths of materiality. Foucault celebrated the "silence" of Blanchot—a style that managed to speak without saying—and the sounds of Roussel and Mallarmé. Deleuze also proffered Roussel and a plethora of voices from Melville, Beckett, Lawrence, and Woolf: authors who could revive voice in its event of becoming rather than its genesis from a speaking subject. It is this movement in literature that takes us from the inhuman voices of high modernism—the voices of gramophones, quotations, newspaper headlines, and received phrases—to those postmodern moments when objects themselves adopt a point of view. Two of the most famous works of postmodern literature open with the image of a television screen. Thomas Pynchon's *The Crying of Lot 49* opens with a point of view that moves from its central character to the viewing screen that is within her hotel room. William Gibson's *Neuromancer* opens with a sky likened to a tuned-out television screen. Both of these examples are indicative of a strong thematic strain in postmodern literature that depicts points of view that exceed the human. These are texts about machines rather than styles that have become "machinic." Deleuze and Guattari had already drawn attention to Beckett's alignment of Molloy with his bicycle and Kafka's description of animal burrowings. Here, the subject or content is the inhuman, but this is achieved by having the inhuman "speak" or "look." Is it possible that there might be a new style of the inhuman and not just the description of the inhuman from the viewpoint of a speaking subject? Is it possible that beyond first-person, third-person, and free-indirect narration, machines might transform our grammar or give us what Deleuze refers to as the "fourth person" (*LS*, 103)? The problem is this: if we extend voice beyond the human, this can have two effects. The first would be to dehumanize voice; the second would be to humanize the inhuman. This might explain why postmodern literature can seem to be something like a "retreat" after the radical anonymity of high modernism. After *Finnegans Wake* most literature has been written within point of view, not in a sustained free-indirect style or stream of consciousness but in what seems to be a return to the human.

Once modernist free-indirect style demonstrated that the human was the effect of a certain style, and once postmodernism then extended this style beyond the human, it was always possible that this very dehumanization or posthumanism would become one more site of recognition. Consider the controversial style of Brett Easton Ellis. *Glamorama* is composed from a series of brand-names, popular song lyrics, celebrity names, and ephemeral and fashionable references. But far from dissolving point of view, all these references become the very hallmark of the narrating character—a character who is not even the effect of a singular style so much as the simulation of received style. What is open to question here is the status of this form of postmodernism in relation to Deleuze's ethics of *amor fati*. According to Deleuze, style is inextricably intertwined with affirmation and ethics. If we think of style as the style *of* some subject, ground, or concept, then we subordinate the event of style to one of its effects. We proceed as though our actions (of speech, thought, or movement) were reactions to some determining ground. If we affirm style *as style*, however, we have no foundation upon which our events are grounded. We would be confronted with the groundlessness of events. And if no event could be given privilege or ground over any other event, then there could never be a *proper* style (a style that was adequate or accurate). Rather, the challenge would be to affirm the difference of style eternally. If style were taken to be the style *of* some point of view, it would lose its force as style. How, then, might we think of a postmodernism that has ostensibly fallen back into point of view, once again raising the question of who speaks?

The Glamour of the Postmodern

What Ellis's *Glamorama* illustrates is one of the movements long ago identified in the theory of irony. As Kierkegaard argued, once voice has been freed from the security of the self, it is always possible that this very impersonality might be taken as one more form of positive selfhood (*CI*, 166). Isn't this just what happens in the tradition of freeing voice from point of view that culminates in *Glamorama*? Machinic repetition, quotation, simulation—all those devices once used to disrupt the human become one more recognizable style, one more banal form of humanity. There is an irony here. We could regard *Glamorama* as the ironic extension of Deleuze. Those theories of the inhuman and the machinic voice that seemed so radical in *A Thousand Plateaus* become, when cashed out, yet one more consumable, assimilable mode of the human. But to argue in this way would be to accept Deleuze as the prescription of a certain style—a style that could have its day and its moment of shock. But as Deleuze himself pointed out, the truly new is eternally new (*DR*, 136). What Deleuze affirmed was not a certain style—the free-indirect style of modernism—but the event of style. We need to confront style as that which produces, rather than expresses, thought. This means that instead of repeating Deleuze's celebrations of modernism we need to face the event of the postmodern. In the case of Ellis we have to ask not what this style means or says but how it works and what it does. This brings us back to irony and the eternal challenge of Deleuze's superior irony. What happens when the inhuman, the machinic, the disembodied, and the cybernetic become our ground of recognition?

What *Glamorama* demonstrates is not the awful moral consequence of postmodern irony and antihumanism. Indeed, it is the resistance to irony, the failure to generate a higher viewpoint above all the vignettes of the novel, that makes this work truly postmodern. We might say that Ellis achieves a Rortyan universe in which we are nothing more than our vocabularies and in which we have given up trying to "eff" the ineffable. *Glamorama* presents a world in which all the once disjunctive claims of postmodern antihumanism—that we are nothing more than social constructions—have become the very model of the human. We can no longer ask the elevated question of whether this is a book that celebrates or mourns postmodern consumer culture, for such a question would require a viewpoint above and beyond the positions of the novel. There are moments in all Ellis's writing that do seem to be set outside the plethora of voices, noises, and labels in his texts, moments when the central character expresses his emptiness and loss. But such moments are undermined by virtue of the fact that such "sincerity" can be read as yet one more received ersatz human affectation. Lamenting the fact that your world is empty and meaningless is just what it means to be a postmodern individual. Rather than *Glamorama* being a novel that delimits or thematizes the horrors of consumer culture, and rather than being a celebration of the posthuman, *Glamorama* creates a style of misrecognition. On the one hand, all the simulacra of postmodernity are reduced to utter banality, spoken from the point of view of a character who is nothing more than the labels he wears and the styles he identifies. On the other hand, while the radical antifoundationalism of postmodernism is reduced to a human point of view, we are not given some higher critical viewpoint. Any voice of lament or critique appears as one more style, one more act of feigned sincerity.

Deleuze's ethic of *amor fati*—that we live rather than judge life—
is not so much the affirmation of a certain style, such as the style of
postmodernism, as it is an insistence that no single style should be
read as authoritative and grounding. If there is an ethics of *amor fati*,
it cannot be reduced to a position, an argument that, say, the indeterminacy of postmodern style is necessarily a resistance to conservatism,
dogma, or quiescence. An ethics of eternal repetition cannot find its
end in *a* style or epoch. If there is a link between style and ethics, it is
perhaps this: because style is difference itself and not the style of some
ground, then we have to ask of each stylistic event what its force is and
what positions it produces. Whereas free-indirect style had repeated
the human to disclose all those points where the concepts of the human *mean nothing*, where humanity appears as so much received banality, postmodern antihumanism demonstrates that the stylistic repetition of the meaningless can suffice to produce one more form of the
human. Ellis's sentences are frequently not propositions and are often
more like lists of brand-names and celebrities, or noun-phrases without any subject or predicate. Unlike high modernist stream of consciousness, in which the string of words was generated from the system of language, thereby critically producing a genealogy of the West
and suggesting some ultimate synthesis of consciousness in general,
Glamorama's language is devoid of semantic, etymological, or even
punning modes of connection. We can contrast a passage from Joyce's
Ulysses with *Glamorama* to see the extent to which, for Joyce, there is
still some human system or ground that speaks through characters. In
the following section from the "Hades" section of *Ulysses* there is an
equivocation of voice, but all the phrases are linked through a connection with death and burial. It is as though the stream of phrases is indeed a stream *of consciousness*, even if that consciousness is already in-

vaded by voices from elsewhere and passing through collections of objects: "Mr Bloom walked unheeded along his grove by saddened angels, crosses, broken pillars, family vaults, stone hopes praying with upcast eyes, old Ireland's hearts and hands. More sensible to spend the money on some charity for the living. Pray for the repose of the soul of. Does anybody really? Plant him and have done with him. Like down a coal-shoot. Then lump them together and save time. All souls' day. Twenty-seventh I'll be at his grave. Ten shillings for the gardener. He keeps it free of weeds. Old man himself. Bent down double with his shears clipping. Near death's door. Who passed away. Who departed this life. As if they did it of their own accord."[46]

The narrative voice opens in third person, describing Bloom, and then moves to phrases from Bloom's point of view ("More sensible to spend the money on some charity for the living"). But the voice shifts again to phrases that come from nowhere, phrases that wander through Bloom's stream of consciousness ("Pray for the repose of the soul of"). The voice then seems to become more like an errand list ("Ten shillings for the gardener"; "Twenty-seventh I'll be at his grave") or an advertisement ("He keeps it free of weeds"). And then the voice turns back to idly repeated phrases ("Who passed away") set alongside Bloom's reflection on those clichés ("As if they did it of their own accord").

Glamorama, by contrast, has an entirely different mode of construction. Phrases are not linked by their meaning, their sound, or their etymological connection, nor do they flow through a consciousness that provides a unifying character. *Glamorama*'s central character is nothing more than the names he repeats, the objects he finds, and the songs he quotes. And these phrases are merely found, often repeated in empty lists without a verb or subject, or with a subject occurring late in the sentence, well after a list of objects. (It is as though we have finally achieved Emerson's "gigantic eye-ball": a look that is pure look, freed from intent, location, or organizing center.) The following "sentence" opens section 28:

> Stills from Chloe's loft in a space that looks like it was designed by Dan Flavin: two Toshiyuki Kita hop sofas, an expanse of white maple floor, six Baccarat Tastevin wineglasses—a gift from Bruce and Nan Weber—dozens of white French tulips, a StairMaster and a free-weight set, photography books—Matthew Rolston, Annie Leibovitz, Herb Ritts—all signed, a Fabergé Imperial egg—a gift from Bruce Willis (pre-Demi)—a large plain portrait of Chloe walking seminude through the lobby of the Malperisa in Milan while nobody notices, a large William Wegman and giant posters for the movies *Butterfield 8*, *The Bachelor Party* with Carolyn Jones, Audrey Hepburn in *Breakfast at Tiffany's*.[47]

There is a complete absence of psychology; there is no report of mental states or interior depth—just the repetition of surface effects. Often, the passive voice is used, as though there are just actions and objects with no grounding subject: "Speedos after Bermudas, baseball caps are positioned backwards, lollipops are handed out, Urge Overkill is played, Didier hides the Polaroid, then sells it to the highest bidder lurking in the shadows, who writes a check for it with a quill pen. One of the boys has an anxiety attack and another drinks too much Taittinger and admits he's from Appalacjia, which causes someone to call for a Klonopin."[48]

We might believe that there is a style or grammar of becoming and that whatever managed to free itself from the labor of irony would take us beyond ourselves and recognition to the "chaosmos" or the "mechanosphere." But wouldn't this be to belie the very style of style? We would then feel that "we" had found the proper style for "our" epoch, disavowing style's power to open epochs. Style is style, not so much in its expressive dimension (as the style *of* a certain position) but in its production of positions. Confronting style's effective dimension is the challenge of Deleuze's thought. If we do not know what thinking is, if there is no good subject that might determine in advance what it is to speak, then we need to engage with literature in terms of the connections it makes and the problems it carves out. The upshot of this is that we are now presented with an ironic challenge *beyond irony*.

Postmodernism has often been celebrated as the playful repetition of phrases with no ground—and therefore as essentially libratory.[49] And postmodernism has also been denounced as a naive loss of critique, reason, and political force.[50] An ironic position would play between the two: any attempt to pulverize identity can fall back into one more identity, but any assertion of identity also relies on those pre-identical forces that it must negate. Deleuze, however, suggests moving beyond this oscillation between identity and nonidentity and beyond the accompanying moral rhetoric of liberation and transgression.

This is why I have chosen Ellis as an "example," for if we are truly to assert the style of postmodernity, there can be no example. Rather, style would be the continual affirmation of singularity in the face of the threat of exemplarity. We might say that postmodernity is that epoch that refuses epochality: refuses the idea of some grounding or identifying genre. And we might say that postmodern style works against the very concept of style, against the idea that there are ideas or content that are then rendered aesthetically. To move beyond style is to reject the *concept* of style, or the concept of the concept. It is the very thought of the concept—that there is a sense to what we say— that allows the distinction between content, on the one hand, and the form or style that allows us to think and communicate that content, on the other. Whereas irony points beyond itself to a moral height, the banality of *Glamorama* takes all the moral rhetoric of postmodernism—that of liberation through fragmentation—to its amoral exten-

sion. For some time now we have celebrated (or berated) postmodernism as a moral conclusion, as though the dissolution of voice, the
collapse of truth, and the death of the subject might free us from the
burden of the question or the problem. *Glamorama* presents us with
the glamorous truth about nontruth: it is no answer at all. The
achievement of a Rortyan world of speech without metaphysics or
commitment is not a liberation we can call our own or a delimitable
loss we might overcome. *Glamorama*, in this sense, moves beyond
ownness and loss to what Deleuze refers to as superior irony: "Instead
of the enormous opposition between the one and the many, there is
only the variety of multiplicity—in other words, difference. It is, perhaps, ironic to say that everything is multiplicity, even the one, even
the many. However, irony itself is a multiplicity—or rather, the art of
multiplicities: the art of grasping the Ideas and the problems they in-
carnate in things, and of grasping things as incarnations, as cases of solution for the problems of Ideas" (*DR*, 182).

We have arrived at that point in the twenty-first century where Deleuze might seem to herald an ethics that would take us beyond recognition to affirmation. And so we might rest easily, celebrate the voices
of high modernism, and recognize ourselves as having achieved the
posthuman. Alternatively, we might remind ourselves—through the
postmodern—that it is just when we think we have freed ourselves
from subjectivism and recognition that we have fallen back into banality. Deleuze's superior irony is not a style to be found, a position to
be lived, but a challenge to our relation to style. Once a style is "ours" it
is no longer *style*. Perhaps all those texts of postmodernity—texts that
wander through machines, simulacra, phrases, and voices—are best
read not as the voice of the inhuman but as instances of the eternal
challenge of style. The inhuman, then, is not a style we can discover
or achieve so much as the perpetual (and eternal) challenge of writing anew.

The risk of irony, as Kierkegaard insisted, is that the ironic existence, which hovers above the world, might fall back into being yet one more posited self. In this regard Deleuze's superior irony needs to be articulated through eternal return (*DR*, 7). The descent of voice away from meaning is not a position that can be attained once and for all but needs to be affirmed again and again with each new movement of style. Postmodern literature is at one and the same time a movement beyond recognition to voice, sound, and the inhuman *and* a diagnosis of the continual recuperation of the human. The question that needs to be asked in relation to Deleuze's work takes us back to the problem of irony and recognition. On the one hand, there is a long tradition of Socratic irony that would insist that our use of concepts will always lead us out of this world to some sense or idea anticipated or intended by those concepts. In such a case it is through the human event of speech that we are led to what lies beyond the merely human. On the other hand, writers like Rorty have affirmed a more postmodern irony, where the limits of human language do not lead us beyond the human so much as they force us to recognize the contingency and finitude of the human. Deleuze moves beyond irony by insisting that what is other than human is neither some higher supersensible idea nor a merely immanent vocabulary, context, or language game. It may be that all we have is this world here in all its immanence, but it is possible to see this immanent world as productive of infinite, eternal, inhuman, and monstrous inventions. But a question remains as to the possibility of this superior irony of immanence. Can we refuse all recognition and achieve the very becoming of style? How might we avoid seeing the overcoming of human elevation as "our" destiny? Is it possible to remain, or sustain, the projected anticipation of a "people to come," refusing the rigidity and inauthenticity of a "we"?

Conclusion

What is at stake in irony and its metaphors of height and depth? Is Deleuze's overturning of Hegel toward a philosophy of surfaces a metaphysical or a political issue? These questions turn on the force and being of the concept. Today, no philosopher has been more insistent on the power of the concept than Jacques Derrida, who stresses both the rigors of the concept and the imperative to think beyond concepts. Indeed, it is Derrida's insistence on the limits of the concept that, according to Searle, leads to the absurd question of a meaning beyond concepts. Derrida has failed to realize, Searle insists, that we no longer think of meanings or ideas as things that transcend social use.[1] Derrida, however, regards this thought of the idea or concept that cannot be reduced to context as the very promise (and violence) of philosophy. On the one hand, concepts such as justice, democracy, and freedom

bear a promise; they open a sense or intention that can never be exhausted or determined within this world. On the other hand, such
concepts are also effected through what cannot be conceptualized: a
process of emergence or *différance* that precedes all meaning and intent and all notions of precedent. If we follow Kant, Hegel, and Derrida, we accept the *practical* force of height and conceptual elevation—the radically unnamable and anterior "being" that will always
be other than or in a relation of negation to what we say.[2] Our relation
to what is not named allows us to think beyond any intraworldly, empirical, or contextual finitude.[3] The history of philosophy and theology demonstrates that we have an idea or concept of the absolute. If
this is so, we can *think* what lies beyond our finitude. For Derrida, this
"mad," demonic, or Cartesian project, which questions the totality of
"what is," enables philosophy to be other than "a violence of a totalitarian and historicist style which eludes meaning and the origin of
meaning."[4] To reduce the meaning of a concept to its use would be a
violent decision, a refusal to allow the concept of justice, for example,
to challenge what we say. At the same time, there is also a violence
opened by the question of the concept, a violence in adopting a point
of view above and beyond any given voice or judgment. But for Derrida, not to ask this question or not set oneself above this world would
be to fall into a "worse violence."

Derrida extends a line of Kantian philosophy explicitly avoided by
Deleuze. If there are concepts of what lies beyond experience, then it
is possible to think what is other than the given: an absence and negativity that also allow thought to think what is *not*. For Kant, this capacity of ours to think what is *not given* presents us with evidence of the
moral destiny of our soul: "the moral law reveals a life independent of
all animality" (*PR*, conclusion, 169). The very *Idea* of that which lies
beyond our finite, sensual, and determined being allows us to imagine
ourselves as beings not of this world, as members of a higher ideal of

humanity. Derrida follows Kant in insisting on the ethical opening of the concept: any attempt to explain the emergence of concepts or meaning from some closed context closes off the possibility of *the question*, the question of what our concepts might do or might mean. For Derrida, philosophy has always testified to the possibility of conceptual opening and futurity: we might refuse to recognize any of the already given uses of our concepts and ask what our concepts mean in general.[5] Philosophy is an *anti*-empiricism in refusing to recognize any determined, given, or present instance as the ground of what we say:

> But empiricism always has been determined by philosophy, from Plato to Husserl, as *nonphilosophy*: as the philosophical pretension to non-philosophy, the inability to justify oneself, to come to one's own aid as speech. But this incapacitation, when resolutely assumed, contests the resolution and coherence of the logos (philosophy) at its root, instead of letting itself be questioned by the logos. Therefore, nothing can so profoundly *solicit* the Greek logos—philosophy—than this irruption of the totally other; and nothing can to such an extent reawaken the logos to its origin as to its mortality, its other.[6]

Derrida is both within and beyond this anti-empiricism.[7] He insists on the violence of philosophy's hierarchical or hyperbolic assertion of the *logos* but also affirms the capacity of the *logos* of philosophy to open any context. It may be true that the metaphysical elevation of the question, the *logos*, and the concept emerge from a graphic disorder, "assemblage,"[8] or depth that can never be comprehended, but it is for this reason that the question and the concept (and deconstruction) are also *impossible*, never finalized. Any concept that offers a promised or anticipated sense is also the outcome of a violent genesis: it is never fully open to the future but always in some way bears some force, decision, and limitation. Because such a decision or opening of the concept is never fully conscious and intended, there is always a force and a pos-

sibility in concepts that ramify our responsibility, a responsibility beyond knowledge, autonomy, and humanity.

The challenge Deleuze presents to this philosophy of height and
depth and of the elevation of concepts is to think from an eternal point
of view. If we traditionally tend to think of a being *before* its becoming, we do so because of a linear temporality that places one moment
before the next, from a single point of view that can only grasp time
as a series of "nows." And this linear grasp of time also requires an axis
of height and depth (a determined optics, a subject that views the
world). The origin or "being" is the ground upon which or from which
the concept, height, or point of view is suspended. It matters little, for
Deleuze, whether one is Heideggerean (affirming grounds, dwelling,
unveiling, earth, and abyss) or Kantian/Hegelian (affirming speculation, elevation, and the height of law). Both metaphors are enabled by
each other, and both ways of thinking are enabled by metaphor: a literal, sensible ground that is then spoken, imaged, figured, or illu-
mined. Metaphor has an imaginary geography as part of its possibility: a mouth that elevates itself through speech, an inert being that
mirrors itself in a projection, representation, or figure.[9] Both Derrida
and Deleuze argue that metaphor is not a device or an idea *within* philosophy; metaphor is the imaginary that has propelled the thinking *of*
being. Only with the idea of metaphor, or a being that is then figured,
can there be speech, metaphysics, or philosophy. For both Deleuze and
Derrida, another logic and politics are possible only at the limit (Derrida) or beyond (Deleuze) of metaphor.

By what right have we determined human speech, the concept, or
logos as the necessary condition for being? How is it that the silence,
presence, inertia, and ground of being have required the look of theory or the voice of the *logos*? For Hegel, this is because being in itself
does not say itself; only with the concept can being *be*. And only with
the concept of the absolute, recognized through philosophy, can being

be without contradiction. To counter Hegel and the necessary elevation of the concept, we might have to think a being that does *say itself.*
Such a saying or writing would be inhuman, aconceptual, and other
than metaphor. We might have to consider speech not as a negation of
what is (a becoming rational, ideal, or supersensible) but as imbri-
cated within a real that already "virtualizes" itself, a real that does not
go through becoming but "is" becoming "itself." Such a real would
not be a full actuality that is *then* imaged virtually, nor would it be an
actuality that *then* bears certain possibilities. The real itself would be
potential and becoming, with the "actual" being a secondary reification of this self-virtualizing life. The virtual would not be enclosed
within the voice of the human; we would need to acknowledge becomings, images, looks, contemplations, traces, and semioses beyond
the human mouth. If we do not separate being from its (logical) becoming, then we can think what is and becoming as coterminous: neither elevated above the other, neither one before the other. A surface
philosophy. An assemblage. A multiplicity. Not being and its concept.
Not sensible ground and the negation and height of speech. From an
eternal point of view each point represents and speaks its other (and
the whole) as much as it is spoken and represented by another point on
the whole. This is why, for Deleuze and Guattari, overcoming dualism
and locating saying and writing as immanent to "what is" is at one
and the same time a monism and a pluralism.[10]

For Derrida it is *différance*—neither sensible nor intelligible—
that allows for the spatial and temporal distributions that enable metaphor, light, and the thought of being. This means that *logos,* the
concept, and the supersensible always bear the trace of a radically
"untamed genesis." But *différance* cannot be said or named; it is a non-
concept. For this reason, and in line with a tradition in which neither
being nor text can be said to speak themselves, deconstruction cannot
be anything at all.[11] Part of deconstruction lies in tracing the force of

a concept through its unspoken dimensions. There is an inhuman, animal, or machinic dimension in our thinking. Thought cannot be pure decision. This is nowhere better demonstrated than in *Of Spirit*, a text that tracks Heidegger's "use" of the word *Geist* and the ways in which the concept remains tied to a metaphysics Heidegger seeks to avoid. If, following Heidegger, we sought to eliminate all those elements in our philosophy that tied us to a rigid metaphysics or that were unthinkingly received, we would do so in the name of an ethics of authenticity or ownness. Against an "idle chatter," or *Gerede*, that merely reiterates the voice of the "they," we should leave no aspect of our thought as unreflected, undecided, or unintended. Heidegger's *Destruktion* of philosophy returns to our language and grammar and the ways in which grammar determines our thinking; the future is only possible in this project of destruction, retrieval, and *Selbstbehautung*. A purely active thinking that said only what it intended to say would require a rigorous exclusion of accidental, inherited, unnecessary, or vague marks and concepts. To do this, however, to *not* allow thought to passively prop itself onto ready-made markers, would require a ruthless destruction of the very medium of speech:

> Pause for a moment: to dream of what the Heideggerian corpus would look like the day when, with all the application and consistency required, the operations prescribed by him at one moment or another would indeed have been carried out: "avoid" the word "spirit," at the very least place it in quotation marks, then cross through all the names referring to the world whenever one is speaking of something which, like the animal, has no *Dasein*, and therefore no or only a little world, then place the word "Being" everywhere under a cross, and finally cross through without a cross all the question marks when it's a question of language, i.e., indirectly, of everything, etc. One can imagine the surface of a text given over to the gnawing, ruminant, and silent voracity of such an animal-machine and its implacable "logic." This would not only be simply "without spirit," but a figure of evil.[12]

If such a pure activity of speech is impossible, it is because there is necessarily always a machinic passivity at the heart of what it is to think.
Perhaps an inhuman politics would have to face this "evil." Beyond
the decision, right, and law there is always the textual errancy that
allows for both height and depth, subject and act, origin and event.
Thinking this through would require moving beyond a modernist
aesthetics, not plunging into the depths, genesis, and origins of sense
but tracing the contiguous machine of thinking. What is unthought is
not some *condition* that temporally precedes thought's present or some
lost past at the limit of thought. The unthought is within and alongside thinking. From this point of view we can see Derrida's own work
as poised between a modernist and postmodern aesthetic. Many of his
texts do, in modernist fashion, trace the genesis or emergence of the
Western *logos*, its determined figures, and its limits, such as the classic
"philosophemes" of light, metaphor, and voice. And these works tend
to be written in free-indirect style, adopting philosophy's own images
and ways of speaking and extending them to what the text did not
want to say. But in addition to retracing the conditions and emergence
of sense and to the ways in which we *cannot but* remain within the
conditions of sense, Derrida's writings also evidence a more "machinic" style, where what is said is the effect of ad hoc, accidental, spu-
rious, and "found" assemblages. His work on Antonin Artaud plays on
the word "subjectile," not because it is one of the determining concepts of the Western logos, not because of its capacity to commit us to
what we *must mean*, but precisely because of its demonic "noisiness"
and its capacity to disturb the meaningful axis of height and depth:[13]

> About the subjectile we would have to—yes—write what is untranslat-
> able. To write according to the new phrasing, but discretely, for resis-
> tance to translation when it is deliberate, noisy, spectacular, we al-
> ready know it has been repatriated. In truth its secret should only be
> shared with the translator.

> A subjectile appears untranslatable, that is axiomatic, it sets up the struggle with Artaud. This can mean at least two things. First, the word "subjectile" is not to be translated. With all its semantic or formal kinship, from the subjective to the tactile, of support, succubus or fiends with a projectile, etc., it will never cross the border of the French language. Besides, a subjectile, that is to say the support, the surface or the material, the unique body of the work in its first event, *at its moment of birth*, which cannot be repeated, which is as distinct from the form as from the meaning and the representation, here again defies translation.[14]

This text, in modernist fashion, still speaks *through Artaud*, but it also presents the ideal of an art practice that is neither visible nor sayable, not at the limit or conditions of sense but itself an event of sensibility. This is a sensibility that can be perceived *as sensible* only after the event of sense: "This spatial work would be first of all a corporeal struggle with the question of language—and at the limit, of music."[15] For Derrida, deconstruction is still a limit practice. It is because being does not say itself that voice also does not say itself. There is always an invasion, contamination, or spread of *différance* within the same. Voice does not give the law to itself. The *logos* is not the voice of being; it emerges from an anarchic or untamed genesis that is not its own. Tracing the convulsions, projections, and timbres of voice constitutes deconstruction's double method: the necessary opening of the concept alongside its unthought, given, and structural genesis. Derrida's "method," which is not a method in its refusal of any proper or given path to being, resists any *final* overcoming of the concept. It is only through what is not and cannot be present or given that there can be any room for thought.

For Deleuze, by contrast, the challenge to irony and height lies in the avowal of the eternal point of view. Deleuze does not present local incursions into the motifs of philosophy in order to intimate a process of difference that is necessarily absent. The eternal point of view affirms the possibility of living, perceiving, and confronting the very life of difference itself, over and over again, in all its voices. This demands moving beyond the *limit* of thought and speech through the tradition of empiricism. Being does indeed say itself. Only with this positive affirmation can there be a philosophy of surfaces. Voice, machine, animal-becomings, geological strata, silicon, and genetics—so many ways in which one point opens to another. And all these becomings can traverse their own series. Viruses can leap from one form of life to another. Animal life becomes in its own way but does so in response to the becomings of other forms of matter. This is what Bergson refers to as a *creative* evolution, with each point in the whole of life capable of transforming the becoming of the whole through the affirmation of its own tendency.[16] Philosophy can also confront differential movements that lie outside its own becoming, differences not drawn from speech or concepts. Philosophy is not literature and it is not science, but it can create its concepts by confronting all form of events. When Deleuze and Guattari "draw" upon mathematics, physics, genetics, or biology they do not subordinate their writing to some superior science, and it is a category mistake to accuse them of "misreading" the findings of science. The difference between science and philosophy is a difference *in kind*; philosophers create concepts in order to enable new ways of thinking, so that we do not rest easy with an "image of thought." Scientists organize states of affairs, allowing us to think in terms of extended objects. Philosophical concepts move in the opposite direction from science, not organizing experience into extended actualities but expanding the point of view in order to think the virtual whole of experience, the intensive difference that gives "life."[17] Deleuze's philosophy of the future is an "antigenealogy" precisely because it sustains a utopian belief that philosophy is not a retracing of its own emergence, it is the creation of new and open differences.

This is why, perhaps, the universal history that Deleuze and Guattari present in *A Thousand Plateaus* moves beyond a genealogy of human sense to consider geological, chemical, genetic, and literary temporalities: all those histories that become through their own intensities. *A Thousand Plateaus* claims to disrupt the single temporal point of view of history precisely in its own manner of composition— written rhizomatically, in overlapping plateaus and voices, with no privileged starting point. This fulfils and overturns the tradition of irony. On the one hand, there is a "postmodern" recognition that it makes no sense to posit some ground for life beyond life. This is an irony in tune with Rorty's notion of recognition and the end of metaphysics: no term or point can justify or provide a foundation for the contingency of life. On the other hand, there is an affirmative anti-irony, and this is where Deleuze lies closer to Derrida and the refusal of a supposed "postmodern" resignation to life. We cannot just remain within our vocabularies and already given contexts. For Derrida, this is because beyond irony—beyond the sense and intention of our concepts—there is a force of *différance* at work in what we say, a force that demands a new responsibility and a new vigilance. For Deleuze, difference is also beyond human life, human recognition, and human contexts. However, far from difference being an ever-receding absence that solicits life from beyond, difference is the very force of life itself that we can affirm through a superior irony. Such an irony does not work at the limits of concepts or speech; it confronts all the perceptions and contemplations of the inhuman. If Deleuze and Derrida are "postmodern," this is not in the sense of abandoning the modern project of moving beyond any given thought to its foundation. Their work refuses the idea that we can be *post*modern, that we can simply *not* think about what lies beyond thought and the human. Even more importantly, they both refuse the temporality that informs the work of Rorty and Searle, both of whom assume that we should "now" realize that it no longer makes sense to ask Socratic questions because we have come of age when we desist from asking unanswerable questions. For Deleuze and Derrida the question of life is not something that occurs at a certain point within history. Life itself "is" the very possibility of the question. Life just "is" that which has the force or potential to not be at one with itself. A *post*modern ethics and aesthetic take us beyond irony and beyond the very notion of the "post." Both Derrida and Deleuze take us beyond the idea that the past is something behind us from which we emerge, for the "past," our "origin," remains within thought as its forever unassimilated force.

For both Deleuze and Derrida, it is the figure of the human subject—speaking man—that has inhibited us from thinking difference. Their projects differ quite radically as to how difference might be liberated from voice, and they also give difference a different character. Deleuze argued that there was a tradition of affirmative philosophy capable of thinking a full and positive being, a being that produces "itself" differently. The task of present philosophy is therefore a re-creation of an eternal difference through the construction of concepts. Derrida, by contrast, has argued that the play of *différance*—at least for philosophy—will necessarily be determined and belied by one of its effects and can therefore only remain as an opening or possibility. Deleuze and Guattari affirmed that it was possible to "kill metaphor" and think in terms of a proliferation of connections,[18] whereas Derrida has argued for a necessary hierarchization or metaphorization within the project of meaning and philosophy. Thought will always be propped on one of its determined figures; there will always be one metaphor *less*—one figure that thought cannot comprehend precisely because thought works through this figure.[19] Despite these and other differences, the limit of Western reason, for both Deleuze and Derrida, is the limit of the voice: a voice that a philosophy of becoming-

animal can surpass (Deleuze), or a voice that deconstruction can speak
through and destabilize (Derrida).

It is possible to argue that the recent philosophical project that
glimpses the limit of the West at the very borders of human speech is
both doubled and problematized in a postironic aesthetic. The very
idea of a limit of "the West" is a profoundly modernist notion. So
much high modernist literature was epic in its attempt to retrieve the
very emergence of voice. Apart from Ezra Pound's *Cantos*, Joyce's
Ulysses, and Eliot's *The Waste Land*, which were manifestly presented
as attempts to confront the chaos and contingency from which a culture of history, universality, subjectivity, and law emerge, the postmodern aesthetic project of achieving nonmeaning also assumed that
the task that confronts thought is the liberation from the rigidity of
sense. This project is, to use the words of Artaud, "to be done with
judgment." Only if we free thought from any of its pregiven images
can we confront a radical responsibility. The greatness of Brett Easton
Ellis's work displays the failure and disappointment of such a project.
As Roland Barthes had argued many years earlier in *Mythologies*,
there is nothing to stop the most transgressive of aesthetic projects
from reifying into one more myth. Surrealism, feminism, environ-
mentalism, and anarchism can all provide wonderful slogans. It is not
just that the shockingly new becomes old or that time passes. What
happens in the process of myth and recognition is that an *event* of
speech—an active formation of a context—becomes a seemingly natural, recognized, and self-evident system, no longer spoken so much as
repeated, confirmed, and humanized. When avant-garde art becomes
"myth" it becomes like Rorty's irony: nothing more than a sign alongside other signs. Irony, in its non-Rortyan and traditional sense, had
always tried to restore temporality to language, and Barthes's critique
of myth (with his appeal to Flaubert) is no exception. Speech begins

as active world formation, a contingent activity that produces, rather than referring to, foundations. What Barthes calls myth, or what ironists have presented as "ordinary language," mistakes and reverses this temporal sequence. Mythic or ordinary language presents itself as natural, immutable, and unremarkable, as a faithful reflection of the way things are, or who we are. In order to arouse temporality, irony does not give speech another foundation or context; it reverses the relation between speech and context. Irony displays the force or power of speech to exceed contexts. Each speech act is productive and transformative of context. What appears to be the ground or cause of our speech—the world or context of human life—is actually effected through speech. Art and literature recall the world-constitutive function of language. In so doing they elevate the human above human*ism*. Human life is effected through speech; the subject is not some being that then speaks. Subjectivity is speech and is irreducibly temporal. The subject emerges as one *who has spoken* only through the lateness of speech. Irony is required when one of the effects of speech (the subject, context, and humanity) is misrecognized as a ground from which speech emerges.

Against this temporal genealogy that would return transcendental synthesis to the active voice, both Derrida and Deleuze have drawn attention to "assemblages" that exceed the temporal and autonomous genesis of human becoming. Speech is not the only mode of synthesis or world constitution. The significance of writing in general for Derrida is just this necessity or errancy of what is *not life*. The time of speech—a word that refers back to one who speaks and forward to a sense intended—relies on a never temporally continuous or present system of traces. In order to think presence, there must have already been a radical absence, a tracing or difference, that allows presence to be thought or to be. Life must be structured by nonlife—the word freed from all voice and intent—in order for life to *be*. This mourning or death within life is required because life does not speak itself; there must be a dehiscence, gap, or abeyance that is not merely negative. The difference between negation and positivity can only be thought after the event of a *différance* that does not emerge from the point of view of speech but that allows any such point to be punctuated. This *différance* needs to be approached through a more complex temporality than that of irony.

Postirony

If the task for contemporary philosophy is realizing a postsubjectivism that never arrives (because we are always falling back on one more "plane of transcendence"), perhaps the task for contemporary aesthetics is thinking the postironic. If we take an *eternal* point of view, a view in which time is not a line passing from origin to effect, then the actual and virtual are within the real, neither privileged over the other. The traditional point of view of the subject subordinates this univocal plane to a linear temporal ordering: the actual world is doubled by a pale world of representation and recognition. Sense and the virtual become passive copies of some prior ground. The eternal point of view undoes this subordination: virtuality or simulation is not an event subsequent to the real. According to Deleuze, the real itself is eternal and infinite simulation: "Everything, animal or being assumes the status of simulacrum" (*DR*, 67). It is the height of human reactivism to locate the virtual and sense within thought. Thought is possible only through the event of sense, and this becoming of sense emerges from nonsense and the mouth (*DR*, 155). Sense is not, as in irony, an elevated meaning that our propositions never grasp but an inhuman production—an Idea—that is not meaningful. Sense is a transcendental and incorporeal distribution that is also empirical (thoroughly within life). Before we can say a proposition is true or false it must make *sense*; and it will do so according to the problem that thought *is*. Sense is not a negation of life and this world; it is just the distribution of a problem, the creation of a difference, orientation, or possibility for thinking:

> The failure to see that sense or the problem is extra-propositional, that it differs in kind from every proposition, leads us to miss the essential: the genesis of the act of thought, the operation of the faculties . . . .
>
> The problem of sense is at once both the site of an originary truth and the genesis of a derived truth. The notions of nonsense, false sense and misconstrual [*contresens*] must be related to problems themselves (there are problems which are false through indetermination, others through overdetermination, while stupidity, finally, is the faculty of false problems; it is evidence of an inability to constitute, comprehend or determine a problem a such). Philosophers and savants dream of applying the test of truth and falsity to problems: this is the aim of dialectics as a superior calculus or combinatory. However, as long as the transcendental consequences are not explicitly drawn and the dogmatic image of thought subsists in principle, this dream also functions as no more than a "repentance." (*DR*, 157, 159)

In order to speak or make sense there must be some presupposed distribution of differences, the plane of a problem or question. "We" do not form or intend these problems; we are effects of the problems sense presents to us. Philosophy, Deleuze argues, needs to destroy the plane of transcendence (of the subject) that allows *logos* or speaking to be located within the voice of man:

> It is as though there were two "Logoi," differing in nature but intermingled with one another: the logos of Species, the logos of what we think and say, which rests upon the condition of the identity or univocity of concepts in general taken as genera; and the logos of Genera, the logos of what is thought and said through us, which is free of that condition and operates both in the equivocity of Being and in the diversity

of the most general concepts. When we speak the univocal, is it not
still the equivocal which speaks within us? Must we not recognize here
a kind of fracture introduced into thought, one which will not cease to
widen in another atmosphere (non-Aristotelian)? But above all, is this
not already a new chance for the philosophy of difference? Will it not
lead towards an absolute concept, once liberated from the condition
which made difference an entirely relative maximum? (*DR*, 33)

A Truly Depthless Irony

It is possible to argue that something like the destruction of a "voice
from on high" also accounts for a peculiarly "postironic" aesthetic that
characterizes some postmodern fiction—a postmodernism that is
quite different from Hutcheon's or Rorty's depthless irony in which
we no longer believe what we say. If *the* problem of philosophy is transcendence or presence, then perhaps the problem of literature is irony.
How can we really *speak*? Is all we say only readable insofar as it is
structured from the already said? Is there an essential monotony or
banality at the heart of speech, leaving all speech soulless, empty, and
trivially ironic? (A trivial irony is the predicament we are left in if we
accept Rorty's "textualism": we can only speak, but we can never really mean or *say* anything.) Today more than ever, alongside a sense of
emptiness, speech is also taking on a profound seriousness, most notably in the politics of voice, in hate speech, and in political correctness.
It is the latter that discloses, most of all, the sustained problem of
irony. We recognize, pragmatically, that speaking is often *not* just saying what we mean precisely because speech is part of a system of
overarching power. I might not *mean* to be racist or sexist, but my lexicon—referring to "Negroes," "fags," or "mankind"—somehow organizes my thinking and does so beyond any conscious politics. So in the
name of thinking otherwise we may alter our lexicon; we decide to
speak differently in order to think differently. Political correctness os-

tensibly reorders the very ideology of speech. It is not "we" who speak, such that speech is the expression or externalization of what we mean. Political correctness aims at a new "we" through a new mode of speech. But who or what reconfigures the lexicon? One—optimistic—answer is that the lexicon is modified from within, such that "we" are nothing other than this constant, ever-renewing linguistic innovation. Our speech would not be an expression of our becoming; speech and becoming would be in *eternal* transformation: no "we" behind speech, and no speech that is *the* consummation of good speaking. This comes close to Jürgen Habermas's ideal speech situation, governed neither by normative notions of human subjectivity nor by any single discourse. The only ideal is that of remaining ideal, never falling into a position, dogma, or standpoint. And perhaps this is the ideal of political correctness, of a "proper" speech that will not determine me or you *as* this or that, that will not ossify into stereotypes, hierarchies, or the reification of values.

It might seem that Deleuze and Derrida's criticisms of metaphysics would lead to this perpetual openness of speech. But an eternal openness is not a perpetual openness. Part of the challenge of eternity lies in rethinking totality over and over again but without the assumption that this renewal is *self*-renewal, located within some privileged and unique point of speech. It is no accident that political correctness is— alongside a critique of language's rigidity—also the most laughably rigid of positions. It is the transcendence or "we" of the position of political correctness that is crucial for its diagnosis. And it is important to free this diagnosis from a temporal dialectic. It is not that we shake up our language and use new terms—"personkind," "gay," "African American"—only then to find that the revivified language becomes one more dogma (and one that needs to be renewed in turn). The problem is not temporal but coterminous. All speech acts are at once personal and machinic. Traditional irony plays on this oscillation between the subject that speaks and the voice or "we" that speaks through us. Literature after the advent of political correctness needs to rethink this oscillation. The play between rigidity and authenticity that had always characterized irony today takes place in a political *landscape* rather than a hierarchy within voice. We could therefore say that we no longer have the homely arena of Socratic dialogue or the recognizing "contexts" of ordinary language; we are now in a world where voices cannot be regulated through communication, use, interaction, or exchange. Any speech or text is immediately subjected to a circulation and production well beyond its intended force. But this contamination or destruction of contexts is not a postmodern political event or an accident that has befallen voice and context. Irony has always been postsubjective and postpolitical, for irony is just the recognition that the force of what we say cannot be contained within the intent of the subject or the recognition of the *polis*.

Today, the use of the word "political" in "political correctness" is evidence of this eternal irony. The political is, supposedly, an arena of decisions, forces, rights, and obligations. But when we refer to what is "politically correct" we accuse it of being *merely* political: having nothing to do with rightness, having only to do with the maintenance of a system. To refer to a phrase, decision, or action as politically correct is to accuse it of merely repeating what is advantageous or recognized as good, not what we really intend or believe to be good. To say that a way of speaking is politically correct is to say that it is the way "they" are telling us to speak. Denouncing political correctness is an ethical accusation against moralism. Such criticisms imply a "they" no less than a "we." Political correctness is what "they" want "us" to say. Who is this "they"? It depends on the context. But this just shows that context is essentially produced through diverging lines of recognition, asymmetrical speech acts, and conflicts.[20] Just what counts as politically correct is not only decided by who we are and how we would like to speak but also how we imagine the tyrannical other who is attempting to impose moral restrictions on our voice. Accusing a statement of political correctness is an act of attribution: it's the gays, the Jews, the hard-line multiculturalists who are policing "our" speech. There has always been a political correctness—a policing of what "we" say—*and* a repudiation of the merely "correct" in the name of the good. The rigidity of political correctness is not an accident that befalls ethics but is the very essence of the ethical. Speaking properly, deciding on being ethical, is necessarily in tension with a speech act that would be nothing other than transformation, mutual recognition, and self-renewal. The ideal of *not* falling into the banality of moralism—of avoiding being merely "correct"—is the essentially irresolvable ethical and aesthetic problem of the present. Why does this problem engage both ethics and aesthetics? Because speaking well or speaking authentically is a problem of style as much as a problem of content. If there is something absurdly machinic or inhuman in political correctness (its capacity to manufacture a "we" that is not one of us and yet to which we are all subjected), this is because something like the problem of irony remains.

Consider Philip Roth's novel *Sabbath's Theater*. The main character speaks as the very personification of life—a vibrant sexuality that lampoons middle-class and received notions of propriety. But this celebrated "life" is also utterly particular. The narrative is a litany of Mickey Sabbath's highly obscure, diverse, and numerous sexual encounters. The novel opens in the third person by recalling a command that is delivered to the promiscuous Sabbath by his now-dead lover. The novel begins with a forthright maxim, only then to disclose that position as one of a series of moralisms and prohibitions—including those offered by life and death itself—against which Sabbath will battle:

Either forswear fucking others or the affair is over.

This was the ultimatum, the maddeningly improbable, wholly un-
foreseen ultimatum, that the mistress of fifty-two delivered in tears to
her lover of sixty-four on the anniversary of an attachment that had
persisted with an amazing licentiousness—and that, no less amaz-
ingly, had stayed their secret—for thirteen years. But now with hor-
monal infusions ebbing, with the prostate enlarging, with probably no
more than another few years of semi-dependable potency still his—
with perhaps not that much more life remaining—here at the approach
of the end of everything, he was being charged, on pain of losing her,
to turn himself inside out. (*ST,* 3)

Roth's novel speaks through and affirms the very pathos of Mickey
Sabbath, but the narrative's force lies in the character's comic
smallness. He is neither a great artist, nor a great mind, nor a great
embodiment of sexuality; his loves are passionate but limited,
haunted, obscure, and contrived. He masturbates over Drenka's grave
and over his friend's daughter's underwear. The novel's affirmation of
sexuality lies in just this realism: life itself is sufficient, even a life that
embraces death, decay, corruption, and absurdity. Like many traditional figures of ironic elevation, Sabbath's character is typified by his
refusal of the resignation and ordinary "values" of the other characters: "For some people this is the best thing to be said for death: finally
out of the marriage. And without having to wind up in a hotel. Without having to live through those miserable Sundays alone in a hotel.
It's the Sundays that keep these couples together. As if Sundays alone
could be any worse" (*ST,* 305).

We could read Roth's novel as an ironic critique of moralizing middle America, but to do so would be to privilege the point of view of
Sabbath. Far from doing so, the very style of the novel refuses to be
either inside or above the voices it traces. The true pathos and near-
irony occur in what is at once the most readable and most unreadable

section of the novel. As a teacher, Sabbath has had an affair with a student and has been accused of sexual misconduct. An action group (Women Against Sexual Abuse, Belittlement, Battering, and Telephone Harassment, or SABBATH) sets up a phone-in line that replays the incriminating conversation. The "tape" runs as a footnote across twenty pages:

> *What follows is an uncensored transcription of the entire conversation as it was secretly taped by Kathy Goolsbee (and by Sabbath) and played by SABBATH for whoever dialed 722-2284 and took the thirty-minutes to listen. In just the twenty-four hours, over a hundred callers stayed on the line to hear the harassment from beginning to end. It wasn't long before tapes reproduced from the original began to turn up for sale around the state and, according to the *Cumberland Sentinel*, "as far afield as Prince Edward Island, where the tape is being used as an audio teaching aid by the Charlottetown Project on the State of Canadian Women."
>
> What are you doing right now?
>
> I'm on my stomach. I'm masturbating. (*ST*, 214)

The initial irony, of course, is that the morally scandalized voice (SABBATH) that plays and distributes the tape actually provides salacious material for all those (like Sabbath) who refuse to hear the tone of morality. So confident is this "footnote" of the moral border between Sabbath and "us" that it can proclaim the widespread sale of the tape as a victory for the women's movement. The higher irony or postirony lies in the question of how "we" read this footnote. If we simply ironize the pious voice of the politically correct, then we fail to see or hear the force and the problem of this statement. The difficulty or unreadability lies in asking what this section *means*. Is this a parody of political correctness? The speaking voice is a tape recorder but also "no one"—the moralizing America that from Sabbath's point of view no one believes or affirms but that nevertheless enslaves us all. But reading this way—reading ironically—adopts Sabbath's viewpoint, which is possible but certainly not necessary. Indeed, the novel is typically postironic in that it is written in neither free-indirect style, nor unreliable or reliable first person, nor third-person omniscient. It is technically third person but spoken from the point of view of Sabbath. It differs from free-indirect style, however, with the use of language and diction that are highly *literary.* We read sentences that are spoken through Sabbath such as the following: "Anyone with brains understands that he is destined to lead a stupid life *because there is no other kind*" (*ST,* 204). These are set alongside another voice that is neither that of a judging narrator nor that of an implied author; the sentences become *textual* (descriptive, ornate, beautifully wrought): "So passeth Sabbath, seeing all the antipathies in collision, the villainous and the innocent, the genuine and the fraudulent, the loathsome and the laughable, a caricature of himself and entirely himself, embracing the truth and blind to the truth, self-haunted while barely what you would call a self" (*ST,* 198). This style is not pure immanence, where the text is nothing other than the voices of the characters through which it speaks. There is another voice, barely discernible, differentiated only by a manifest stylishness. This voice is not ironically elevated through concepts or morality, but it does resist Sabbath's own identification of himself with life itself. If Sabbath's entire personality is defined against a moralism that would contain life, it is the style and literariness of this other voice that allows—ever so problematically— a question or a problem to be posed to Sabbath's supposed positivity.

This is not a book "about" the political correctness that represses the fullness of sexual life, nor is it about a sexuality that by its very excessiveness exhausts its own limits. The "irony" is essential, eternal, and undecidable. Through Sabbath "we" read the miserly limits of antiracism, antisexism, and a series of other moralisms, but Sabbath's own embrace of life is no less haunted by loss, death, and its own strange form of conscience: "If he no longer gave a shit, why did he give a shit? On the other hand, if this limitless despair was only so much simulation, if he was not so steeped in hopelessness as he pretended to be, whom was he deceiving other than himself?" (*ST*, 205). Roth's affirmation of sexual life is explicitly *a* life, always this sexuality with its dubious, comic, and questionable investments but also driven and doubled by a nonironic conscience, a voice that is neither human nor life itself. The politically correct critique of life—in all its rigidity, judgment, and elevation—is an easily ironized supplement to life. Living without this voice is the problem of a postironic aesthetic. How can we ironize bourgeois morality and banality without falling into a blind and self-serving narcissism, without becoming what Hegel referred to as "unhappy consciousness": a life that merely exists only in its refusal of any presented values? The aesthetic of Roth's writing is disturbing. There is no voice elevated above life, no voice generated by disclosing what life itself must come to mean. The aesthetic of this literature is diagnostic and affirmative. We can be morally elevated by the machinic rigors of political correctness, believing that we might be other than the errancy of life and desire. But we can also fall into irony, believing that we might occupy a position above and beyond all the rigid and banal moralisms opposed to life. The futurity of this aesthetic lies in the copresence of machine and life, where speaking well is neither ironic elevation nor identification with the innocence of life itself. An ethics of the future cannot divorce itself from this aesthetics of style, where voice is neither flush with the real nor elevated above the real. It is no longer just a question of who speaks and from what position but how events of speech and machinic repetition produce the boundary between the truly spoken and the merely or mechanically correct.

Political correctness is both a new problem of irony and a departure from the temporal geography of irony. The elevated voice of traditional irony is produced through a recognition of the time of speech. Ordinary language speaks as though speaker and said could coincide in the act of enunciation. Irony bifurcates speaker's point of view through time. The idea that is spoken here and now is doubled by some higher sense that either must have been (Socratic irony) or that is forever more about to be (the concept's future sense). Irony oscillates within voice, between what we say and what we mean. The problem of political correctness forces us to address a distribution that exceeds voice and speech, and this for two reasons. First, the "other" voice or "voice from on high" is often not that of a speaker. Cameras, tapes, information technologies, and nonlinguistic codes all have a force or performative effect and yet cannot be traced back to the self-consciousness of a speaker's point of view. Second, even within human language, the other voice is not yet that higher sense of humanity within ourselves. Each problem of speaking well has its own political landscape, and politics here is not the relation between the voices of speakers but the spatial divisions within each event of speech.

Consider Ellis's *Glamorama*, which concludes with the multiplication of viewpoints and time lines. The text is more than self-reflexive, referring to its own fictive status; it also creates incommensurable levels of fiction. Various camera crews and terrorist organizations disrupt the narrative with the intervention of more "film-script." The boundary between terrorism and antiterrorism is not so much a boundary between good and evil as it is a boundary between who is merely reciting a script and who is really speaking. As the narrative progresses, the boundary is undecidable; violence and unreality contaminate both sides, as do the charges of propaganda and mere repetition. Eventually, all speech is derealized as the narrative point of view shifts to a camera. Section 32 begins with the noun phrase "A shot of Scorch tape being applied with rubber gloves to a white metal canister."[21] The action is increasingly undertaken not by human agents but by intersecting and proliferating machines (such as bomb devices triggered by stereos). Eventually, the sincerity of voice itself can only be gauged by the inhuman: "All the phones in the house analyze callers' voices for subaudible microtremors that occur when a speaker is stressed or lying, giving the listener constant LED readings."[22] Eventually, the point of view of the speaker is destabilized by the multiple time lines that run through the novel: "I deliver the line in such a way that it's impossible to tell whether I'm feigning innocence or acting hard."[23] The stratification of speech is overdetermined, moving from terrorism, to antiterrorism, to anti-antiterrorism, and so on. Each "voice" props onto and destroys the simulated moralism of the other. And isn't this the very problem of terrorism? "Terrorism" is the irrational and unthought commitment and repetition of slogans, whereas "politics" is reflective and engaged. But who can speak politically without a tone of terror, without some received and decided style?

Each problem within speech bears its own time of difference, whether the "other" voice refers to a future (the utopia of antiterrorism), the past (a retrieval of proper speech), or the complicity within the present (the copresence of our speech with the tradition). In each problem of the political we ask ourselves about the depth of political speech. Is this voice truly political, freed from all the cynicism of received ideas, or is it blind terrorism? Is this voice truly human, or is it one more use of the human that elevates a specific race or gender? Is this voice truly an event of style and creation, or is it one more utterance within the literary tradition? Each speech act creates its own question of inside and outside, of belonging and not belonging—its own specific mode of sincerity. It is not just that all speech must repeat the problem of irony and viewpoint or the relation between the already said and what we want to say. Each speech act distributes a field of context that is not just that of height and depth or speaking authentically and merely being correct. The problem of political correctness alerts us to the specific ways in which the division between authenticity and correctness always intersects with divisions that are already given. It is always a determined "other" who is speaking mere rhetoric. When Socrates condemned sophistry he did so in the name of a class of philosophers who could free voice from its worldly economy, and when Rorty appeals to irony he does so in the name of a private speech that does not need the rigors of public policy. The ironic, elevated, or authentic voice always produces a "we" capable of recognizing the irony against a "they" who merely repeat or imitate good speech. "Our" context can only work if we recognize ourselves as more than just another context, more than merely correct. But any critique of the mere "machine" of political correctness will also have its own "machinic contamination," depending upon contexts and stratifications that cannot be fully owned.

What do "we" mean, then, by "politically correct"? As an accusation it refers to a mode of morality: "we" are being made to speak in an imposed or assumed style. (It is "they" who are making us speak in this style, the feminists, the gays, the extremists.) To this extent, political correctness is perilously close to conscience, as well as being conscience's necessary other. In political correctness it seems to be an external or imposed voice that dominates. This is not what we *want to say* so much as what is being said in our place, what we *must say*, regardless of what we mean. This is why political correctness is ripe for humor. We find ourselves speaking in such a way that we no longer mean anything at all. (Deleuze makes much of this in his contrast between humor and irony. Humor is descent, when what we say becomes noise, sound, or inhuman. Irony is elevation, when sense or meaning rises above what we simply say.) The humor directed against political correctness targets an unthinking and absurd automatism in our speech. No one can really speak in this way; the presentation of political correctness in humor gives us an extreme version of the corruption of our language by an anonymous moral code.

Conscience is, like political correctness, also a voice within us that seems to come from on high. But whereas political correctness is reacted against by being accused of being other ("they" are making us speak this way), conscience is silent. Conscience is a higher voice, but it cannot be identified with a they. It is a voice that says nothing, refusing all rules and given dogmas. It is that voice that speaks within us when nothing can tell us what to do. It is the alien voice of conscience that is constitutive of who "we" are. If I do not listen to conscience, if I merely follow others or inclination, then I do not have any being or self. The difference between political correctness and conscience is the difference between humor and irony; it is also the difference between literature and philosophy. Is this voice a merely immanent point of view, a rhetorical device, expressive of sound and style, a repeated and inherited character? Or is this voice an event of speech, an attempt to see beyond the human point of view, a grasp of that difference in general that is not one style among others but the very perception of style? Deciding this difference is also deciding who we are. For each speech act we can ask, Is this an imposed voice that we merely repeat? And who is the imagined "they" that imposes this voice? The "humanity" of conscience that speaks through us all, or the other whose tyranny lies in speaking with the unquestioned authority of the human?

NOTES

Abbreviations

CI	Kierkegaard, *The Concept of Irony*
DR	Deleuze, *Difference and Repetition*
LS	Deleuze, *The Logic of Sense*
P	Joyce, *A Portrait of the Artist as a Young Man*
PR	Kant, *Critique of Practical Reason*
PS	Hegel, *The Phenomenology of Spirit*
RCC	De Man, *Romanticism and Contemporary Criticism*
S	Vlastos, *Socrates*
ST	Roth, *Sabbath's Theater*
TT	Flaubert, *Three Tales*
WL	Hadot, *Philosophy as a Way of Life*

Preface

1 Aristotle, *Metaphysics Books I–IX*, 3.

2 Lactantius, *The Works of Lactantius*, 2:66.

3 Kant, *Critique of Practical Reason*, bk. 2, pt. 2, conclusion, 170.

4 Kant, *Critique of Judgment*, sec. 62, 240.

5 Immanuel Kant, "On the Common Saying: 'This May be True in Theory, but it does not Apply in Practice,'" in Kant, *Kant: Political Writings*, 61–92, 63.

6 Kant, "Religion Within the Boundaries of Mere Reason," 31–191, 80.

7 Freud, "On Narcissism," 65–97; Lacan, "The Mirror Stage," 1–7.

8 "What he projects before him as his ideal is the substitute for the lost narcissism of his childhood in which he was his own ideal" (Freud, "On Narcissism," 88).

9 Freud, "On Narcissism," 90.

10 Freud, "The 'Uncanny,'" 339–76, 357–58.

11 Freud, "On Narcissism," 91.

12 Laplanche, "A Short Treatise," 84–116, 101.

13 Lacan and the Ecole Freudienne, *Feminine Sexuality*, 163.

14 Lacan and the Ecole Freudienne, *Feminine Sexuality*, 155.

15 Hegel, *Aesthetics*, 19.

16 See, for example, Levin, ed., *Modernity*.

17 The classic essay in this respect, drawing on the work of Lacan, is Mulvey's "Visual Pleasure and Narrative Cinema."

18 The idea that looking is a form of interactive engagement with the world is associated with the work of Maurice Merleau-Ponty, who argued for the ways in which the self is produced through its perception rather than preceding perception (*The Primacy of Perception*, 122). But the critique of the detached observer as the primary mode of vision goes back to Edmund Husserl's criticism of the "natural attitude." Before the world is a separate object it is *lived* unselfconsciously, and vision is not yet "theoretical" (Husserl, *Ideas Pertaining to a Pure Phenomenology and to a Phenomenological Philosophy: First Book*).

19 Rorty, *Philosophy*.

20 According to Gregory Vlastos, it is in the Latin writings of Cicero and Quintilian that irony "betokens the height of urbanity, elegance and good taste."

It is in *De Oratore* that Cicero defines irony as urbanity, while Quintilian argues in his *Institutio Oratora* that "ironia may characterize a whole man's life." See *S*, 28–29.

21 Derrida's clearest use and defense of intentionality is in *Limited Inc.*

22 Heidegger, *Being and Time.*

23 Deleuze, *Bergsonism*, 28.

24 Rorty, *Contingency, Irony, and Solidarity.*

25 Jameson, *The Seeds of Time*; Hutcheon, *Irony's Edge*; Lefebvre, *Introduction to Modernity*, 21; Paul de Man, "The Rhetoric of Temporality," in de Man, *Blindness and Insight*, 187–228; Eco, "Postmodernism, Irony, the Enjoyable," 225–28.

26 See Lacoue-Labarthe and Nancy, *The Literary Absolute*; and Bowie, *Aesthetics and Subjectivity.*

1. The Meaning of Irony

1 Richard Rorty, "Philosophy as a Kind of Writing: An Essay on Derrida," in Rorty, *Consequences of Pragmatism*, 92; Rorty, *Contingency, Irony, and Solidarity.*

2 Richard Rorty, "Is There a Problem about Fictional Discourse?" in Rorty, *Consequences of Pragmatism*, 127.

3 Habermas, *Postmetaphysical Thinking*; Hacking, *Why Does Language Matter to Philosophy?*; Dummett, *Origins of Analytical Philosophy.* The material on the "death of the subject" is vast in writing inspired by Continental philosophy—so much so that there have been a number of recent attempts to question this putative "death." See, especially, Cadava, Connor, and Nancy, eds., *Who Comes after the Subject?*

4 Blake's character of "Urizen" is depicted in a number of his works and combines all the features of the dogmatic theology that reason was meant to supplant. Urizen is the very image of a modern and tyrannical reason: constructing immutable laws and calculations, closed to the complexities of experience, and judging the world from on high. See, in particular, William Blake, "The [First] Book of Urizen," in Blake, *The Complete Poetry and Prose*, 70–84. Swift's *Modest Proposal* is one of the classic works of irony and counterenlightenment. The

work presents reason as a rigid procedure of calculation that is blind to the incalculable consequences of its judgments. See Swift, *Jonathan Swift: A Critical Edition of the Major Works*.

5 Hegel, *Aesthetics*, 243.

6 Immanuel Kant, "What Is Enlightenment?" in Kant, *Kant: Political Writings*, 54.

7 Lewis, *The American Adam*.

8 Locke, *Two Treatises of Government*, Second Treatise, sec. 49, 319.

9 Derrida, *Mémoires for Paul de Man*, 18. Derrida goes on to say, " 'America' would be the title of a new novel on the history of deconstruction and the deconstruction of history."

10 This idea has been given a more complex inflection in the New Historicist work of Stephen Greenblatt, whose writings examine and reinforce the history and politics of New World "wonder" (*Marvelous Possessions*).

11 Ralph Waldo Emerson, "Nature," in Emerson, *Selected Essays*, 35–82, 39.

12 Perloff, *The Dance of the Intellect*.

13 "Conceptual treatment of perceptual reality makes it seem paradoxical and incomprehensible; and when radically and consistently carried out, it leads to the opinion that perceptual experience is not reality at all, but an appearance or illusion" (James, *Some Problems of Philosophy*, 80–81).

14 Cavell, *The Claim of Reason*.

15 Alexander Nehamas's work offers a profound investigation into this tradition of the worthiness of the examined life. See, in particular, *The Art of Living*.

16 Rorty, *Contingency, Irony, and Solidarity*, 87.

17 Plato *Republic* 331C–331E, in Plato, *Collected Dialogues*, 580.

18 Plato *Republic* 334B–334C, in Plato, *Collected Dialogues*, 584.

19 Kant had argued that we could have free and unimpeded public use of reason, but private usage—within institutions—ought to be rule-bound. Rorty partly reverses and partly sustains this opposition. Like Kant, Rorty agrees that institutions need to be unquestioning or nonironic in order to function. But whereas Kant saw *public* reason as the proper place for questioning and was therefore committed to a general progression of enlightenment, Rorty places the free use of the questioning attitude within the personality of the ironist (Kant, *What Is Enlightenment?* 55).

20 Rorty, *Contingency, Irony, and Solidarity*, 97.

21 The idea that irony is an attitude or personality has characterized descriptions of Socratic irony from Cicero and Quintilian to German Romanticism and the present. Socrates is not just an interlocutor who uses irony. His existence is ironic. Never claiming to know the truth and questioning those who *do* claim to know, Socrates produces a personality that opens the very possibility of philosophy. The philosopher is not one who merely offers factual statements but is capable of interrogating just what we *mean* when we claim something to be a fact. The Socratic personality employs irony within dialogues but also lives ironically, constantly taking all those concepts we believe to be meaningful and exposing them to the question of just what they really do, or can, mean. The Jena Romantics' account of irony as "transcendental buffoonery" also refers to a position adopted toward meaning and signification (see Schlegel, *Friedrich Schlegel's Lucinde*, 148). The moment we believe we have grasped the meaning of the concept, we have fallen or been duped by the concept's ironic power. It is the very nature of the concept (and meaning) to delimit, select, and systematize our world. Thinking that our concepts are meaningful—that there is some reality that concepts merely label—is to miss the ways in which life necessarily exceeds our conceptual grasp. Paul de Man's description of irony as the "permanent parabasis of tropes" is in line with this tradition, a definition of irony that is also a theory of meaning in general. Tropes such as irony are not local events within meaning—as though our concepts for the most part simply tacked onto an already meaningful world. All language is a trope, a deviation from the real itself. Irony is the exposure of this constitutive gap between meaning and what is meant; this is why the parabasis of tropes, for de Man, is permanent (*Aesthetic Ideology*, 179).

22 Rorty, *Contingency, Irony, and Solidarity*, 80.

23 Most of the linguistic and contemporary philosophical analyses of irony take irony as a figure of speech and begin with an account of irony from a theory of speech acts. Such accounts tend to focus on nonliterary examples of irony and concern the recognition, use, effect, and context of irony. See, for example, Haverkate, "A Speech Act Analysis of Irony," for an account of irony that draws upon John Searle's theory of speech acts. For an analysis of irony in ordinary language use that also relies in part on Searle's theory, see Miller, "Ironic or Not?" In the analyses of irony of this type, including the brief mention of irony made by

Searle, there is an emphasis on the intention and recognition of irony as well as a dependence on a notion of context. There is, however, a *problem* of intention, recognition, and context that, I will argue, is posed by the more complex instances of (usually literary) irony not considered by the speech act tradition.

24 Searle, "Literary Theory and Its Discontents," 646.

25 Searle, "Literary Theory and Its Discontents," 646.

26 Nehamas, *The Art of Living*.

27 According to Nehamas, "Irony, as I have been saying, provides a mask. It does not show what, if anything, is masked. It suggests depth, but it does not guarantee it. Furthermore, I believe, the Socrates of Plato's early dialogues has no depth, no underlying story distinct from what we are given in the texts" (*Virtues of Authenticity*, 72). For Nehamas, what is important about Socrates is not the man or depth that lies *behind* the character. On the contrary, it is the ironic suggestion of depth, without that depth being presented, that enables us to think of Socrates as a character who fashioned and formed himself *as a character.* Not tied to some definitive knowledge of the good man or good life, Socrates could present irony as an existence that created itself through dialogue and speaking (rather than dialogue and irony being tools to convey information).

28 Searle, "Literary Theory and Its Discontents," 641.

29 Searle, "Literary Theory and Its Discontents," 640.

30 Austen, *Pride and Prejudice*, 1.

31 As Nehamas argues, "Often, irony consists in letting your audience know that something is taking place inside you that they simply are not allowed to see. But it also, more radically, leaves open the question whether you are seeing it yourself. . . . Irony often communicates the fact that the audience is not getting the whole picture; but it does not necessarily imply that the speaker has that picture or that, indeed, there is a whole picture to be understood in the first place" (*Virtues of Authenticity*, 103).

32 Plato *Republic* 338C–338D, in Plato, *Collected Dialogues*, 588; Austen, *Pride and Prejudice*, 1; Blake, *The Complete Poetry and Prose*, 10.

33 Husserl, *Ideas Pertaining to a Pure Phenomenology and to a Phenomenological Philosophy: Second Book*, 5.

34 Joyce, *The Essential James Joyce*, 122–27.

35 Heidegger, *The Metaphysical Foundations of Logic*, 23.

36 Davidson, *Inquiries into Truth*.

37 Searle, "Literary Theory and Its Discontents," 646.

38 Fowler, *A Dictionary of Modern English Usage*, 253.

39 William Blake, "Holy Thursday," in Blake, *The Complete Poetry and Prose*, 13.

40 William Blake, "The Little Black Boy," in Blake, *The Complete Poetry and Prose*, 9.

41 William Blake, *Milton*, in Blake, *The Complete Poetry and Prose*, 95.

42 Bloom, *Blake's Apocalypse*.

43 This is how Alasdair MacIntyre characterizes modernity; we speak morally, but such putatively ethical statements have lost all coherence (*After Virtue*).

44 Searle, "Literary Theory and Its Discontents," 638.

45 Derrida, *Limited Inc.*, 117.

46 Derrida, *Writing and Difference*, 43.

47 Flaubert, *Madame Bovary*, 257.

48 LaCapra, *Madame Bovary on Trial*.

49 Carver, *The Stories of Raymond Carver*.

50 Carver, *The Stories of Raymond Carver*, 17.

2. Modern Irony

1 I am leaving the question of just what I mean by "modern" here deliberately vague: vague in the sense of chronology but narrow in the sense of function. Irony is "modern" when it abandons the sense of a higher ironic context of truth that might adjudicate ironized and limited statements. One of the ways in which modernity is defined in the history of ideas is by referring to some historical moment when the foundation of the world on a transcendent value was disrupted (see Dumont, *Essays on Individualism*). Descartes founds truth on the self-evidence of the subject and not given or received knowledge; Hobbes begins his political philosophy without assuming some preordained order; Kant's philosophy is inaugurated by an insistence that human beings could not know or experience anything beyond their finitude. Modernity in art and literature is also no less broad and no less difficult to date; modernity is perhaps the emergence of the "aesthetic" attitude itself, where art becomes autonomous and no longer subordinated to the ends of religion or morality. In both the history of ideas and the history of art, "modernity" is usually defined and dated around some recogni-

tion of the absence of external justifications. Modern irony would also, therefore, have to be an equally shifting periodizing gesture. It would always be possible to read doubt and loss of faith back into earlier texts from some later ironizing point of modern recognition. The problem of dating just when and how irony becomes truly modern should become clearer in the course of this chapter. So while I leave the concept of modern deliberately vague, I also accept that this vagueness is troubling.

2 Kant, *Critique of Practical Reason,* preface, 6.

3 Plato *Phaedo* 69B–69C, in Plato, *Collected Dialogues,* 52.

4 Plato *Phaedo* 82D–83B, in Plato, *Collected Dialogues,* 66.

5 Flaubert, *The Letters,* 173. Compare Flaubert's artist to Nietzsche's aesthetic man, whose elevation is also *immanent:* "Only aesthetic man can look thus at the world, a man who has experienced in artists and in the birth of art objects how the struggle of the many can yet carry rules and laws inherent in itself, how the artist stands contemplatively above and at the same time actively within his work, how necessity and random play, oppositional tension and harmony, must pair to create a work of art" (*Philosophy in the Tragic Age,* 62).

6 Michel Foucault, "Theatrum Philosophicum," in Foucault, *Language Counter-Memory Practice,* 189.

7 Foucault, "Theatrum Philosophicum," 188–89.

8 Foucault, "Theatrum Philosophicum," 189.

9 Spinoza, *On the Improvement of the Understanding,* 86.

10 "A quantum of force is equivalent to a quantum of drive, will, effect— more, it is nothing other than precisely this very driving, willing, effecting, and only owing to the seduction of language (and of the fundamental errors of reason that are petrified in it) which conceives and misconceives all effects as conditioned by something that causes effects, by a 'subject,' can it appear otherwise. For just as the popular mind separates the lightning from its flash and takes the latter for an *action,* for the operation of a subject called lightning, so popular morality also separates strength from expressions of strength, as if there were a neutral substratum behind the strong man, which was *free* to express strength or not to do so. But there is no such substratum; there is no 'being' behind doing, effecting, becoming; 'the doer' is merely a fiction added to the deed—the deed is everything" (Nietzsche, *The Genealogy of Morals,* 45).

11 Friedrich Nietzsche, "On Truth and Lies in a Nonmoral Sense," in Nietzsche, *Philosophy and Truth*, 79–97, 83.

12 Flaubert, *Madame Bovary*, 324–25.

13 Jorge Luis Borges, "Pierre Menard, Author of Don Quixote," in Borges, *Fictions*, 51.

14 Flaubert, *Madame Bovary*, 301.

15 Dummett, *Frege*, 298.

16 Davidson, *Inquiries into Truth*, 274, 270.

17 Flaubert, *Madame Bovary*, 203.

18 Searle, *Speech Acts*, 196.

19 Searle, *Speech Acts*, 196.

20 James Joyce, "The Dead," in Joyce, *The Essential James Joyce*, 138.

21 The opening of "The Boarding House," although not in quotation marks, uses the voice of cliché and hackneyed phrases: "She had married her father's foreman, and opened a butcher's shop near Spring Gardens. But as soon as his father-in-law was dead Mr Mooney began to go to the devil. He drank, plundered the till, ran headlong into debt" (in Joyce, *The Essential James Joyce*, 57–58). Consider the first lines of "A Painful Case," which begins in the voice of uptight bourgeois moralism: "Mr James Duffy lived in Chapelizod because he wished to live as far as possible from the city of which he was a citizen and because he found all the other suburbs of Dublin mean, modern and pretentious" (in Joyce, *The Essential James Joyce*, 89).

22 Joyce, "The Dead," 166.

23 Joyce, "The Dead," 171.

24 Joyce, "The Dead," 173.

25 Searle, *Speech Acts*, 198.

26 Agamben, *Homo Sacer*, 21.

27 Searle, "Literary Theory and Its Discontents," 639.

28 Searle, "Literary Theory and Its Discontents," 639.

3. Socrates and the Soul of Philosophy

1 Plato *Republic* 339D–339E, 331C–331E, 340C, in Plato, *Collected Dialogues*, 588, 580, 590.

2 Plato *Symposium* 175D–175E, in Plato, *Collected Dialogues*, 530.

3 In the *Symposium* Socrates proclaims his inability to invent a proper eulogy. When he had offered to fulfil the task, he claims, he had not realized that it was rhetoric rather than truth that constituted a good speech. "I'm sorry," he seems to be saying, "I thought it was *truth* that was important!":

> And then I saw what a fool I'd been to agree to take part in this eulogy of yours, and, what was worse, to claim a special knowledge of the subject, when, as it turned out, I had not the least idea how this or any other eulogy should be conducted. I had imagined in my innocence that one began by stating the facts about the matter in hand, and then proceeded to pick out the most attractive points and display them to the best advantage. . . .
>
> Now, Phaedrus, it's for you to say. Have you any use for a speaker who only cares whether his matter is correct and leaves his manner to take care of itself?
>
> Whereupon Phaedrus and the others told him to go ahead and make whatever kind of speech he liked. (198**c**–199**c**, 98**d**–98**e**, in Plato, *Collected Dialogues*, 550–51)

4 See, for example, *Lysis* 218B–218D, *Euthyphro* 9A–9D, *Lesser Hippias* 372B–372E, *Protagoras* 334–35, *Meno* 71A, and this from the *Gorgias*:

> Socrates: If my soul were wrought of gold, Callicles, do you not think I should be delighted to find one of those stones wherewith they test gold—the best of them—which I could apply to it, and if it established that my soul had been well nurtured, I should be assured that I was in good condition and in need of no further test?
> Callicles: What is your point in asking me this, Socrates?
> Socrates: I will tell you. I consider that in meeting you I have encountered such a godsend.
> Callicles: Why?
> Socrates: I am convinced that if you agree with the opinions held by my soul, then at last we have attained the actual truth. For I observe that anyone who is to test adequately a human soul for good or evil living must possess three qualifications, all of which you possess, namely knowledge, good will, and frankness. (486**d**–486**e**, in Plato, *Collected Dialogues*, 269)

5 See, for example, *Protagoras* 361, *Lesser Hippias* 376B–376C: "Nor can I agree with myself, Hippias, and yet that seems to be the conclusion which, as far as we can see at present, must follow from our argument. As I was saying before,

I am all abroad, and being in perplexity am always changing my opinion. Now, that I or any ordinary man should wander in perplexity is not surprising, but if you wise men also wander, and we cannot come to you and rest from our wandering, the matter begins to be serious both to us and to you."

6 Plato *Euthydemus* 273D–273E, in Plato, *Collected Dialogues*, 388.

7 Searle explicitly excludes this possibility. There can be nothing about sentence meaning that yields irony, for irony is the feature of a speech act and not *meaning* ("Literary Theory and Its Discontents," 651).

8 Socratic irony is not, I would argue, a question of *what we really mean*. That is, it is not an attempt to find a more coherent rule for the way in which we use our terms; it is a demonstration that none of our uses or definitions captures what we feel our most treasured terms *ought to mean*.

9 Plato *Republic* 331E–334C, in Plato, *Collected Dialogues*, 580–81.

10 Compare also: "Is it not in the course of reflection, if at all, that the soul gets a clear view of the facts?" (Plato *Phaedo* 65C, in Plato, *Collected Dialogues*, 48).

11 Plato *Phaedo* 76D–76E, in Plato, *Collected Dialogues*, 60.

12 "To what extent the Socratic disposition is a phenomenon of decadence: to what extent, however, a robust health and strength is still exhibited in the whole *habitus*, in the dialectics, efficiency, and self-discipline of the scientific man (—the health of the plebeian; his wickedness, *esprit fondeur*; his cunning, his *canaille au fond* are held in check by shrewdness; 'ugly')" (Nietzsche, *The Will to Power*, 432).

13 For Michael Smith, *the* moral problem lies in the objectivity and practicality of moral judgments. When I say, "This is good," I am not just saying that I approve. The very fact that we can dispute whether this *is* good indicates that we are committed to some claim to objectivity. And I am also rationally committed to acting to achieve this good. We would question whether someone really were saying that something was good, if they then failed to act to achieve it (Smith, *The Moral Problem*).

14 Deleuze, *The Fold*, 23.

15 Plato *Socrates' Defense (Apology)* 17A–17B, 20D–20E, in Plato, *Collected Dialogues*, 4, 7.

16 Plato *Phaedo* 80D–80E, in Plato, *Collected Dialogues*, 63.

17 Plato *Meno* 86A, in Plato, *Collected Dialogues*, 371.

4. From Kant to Romanticism

1 Kant writes of the categories: "For if we place them in the pure understanding, it is only by this deduction that we are prevented from holding them, with Plato, to be inborn and from erecting on them transcendent presumptions and theories of the supersensible, the end of which we cannot see, making theology merely a magic lantern of phantoms" (*PR*, bk. 2, chap. 2, sec. 7, 148).

2 "Only the concept of freedom enables us to find the unconditioned for the conditioned and the intelligible for the sensible without going outside ourselves. For it is our reason itself which through the supreme and unconditioned practical law recognizes itself, and the being which knows this law (our own person) as belonging to the pure world of the understanding and indeed defines the way in which it can be active as such a being. Thus it can be seen why in the entire faculty of reason only the practical can lift us above the world of sense and furnish cognitions of a supersensible order and connection, though these cognitions can be extended only as far as is needed for pure practical purposes" (*PR*, bk. 1, chap. 3, 111).

3 Hume, *Enquiries*, 232.

4 Kant, *Immanuel Kant's Critique of Pure Reason*, A141/B181, 183.

5 Herman, *The Practice of Moral Judgment*, 1–22.

6 Kant talks about "the mysterious and wonderful, but frequent, regard which human judgment does have for the moral law" (*PR*, bk. 1, chap. 3, 185).

7 Korsgaard, *Creating the Kingdom of Ends*.

8 O'Neill, *Constructions of Reason*.

9 On the necessarily relational character of knowledge in Kant, see Langton, *Kantian Humility*.

10 Kant, *Prolegomena*, sec. 6, 28.

11 Lacoue-Labarthe and Nancy, *The Literary Absolute*.

12 Although Friedrich Schlegel's *Fragments* (which originally appeared in the *Athenaeum*) define philosophy as the "homeland of irony," it is only *Socratic* philosophy that is seen as ironic. In modernity, Schlegel argued, irony has departed from its philosophical home and has relocated to poetry. Poetry is now seen as the site of the "sublime urbanity of the Socratic muse." Accordingly, "Novels are the Socratic dialogues of our time" (Schlegel, *Friedrich Schlegel's Lucinde*, 148, 145). Hegel, not surprisingly, told a contrasting story: art and po-

etry might once have been adequate vehicles for the truth, but modernity must demand the end of art and the victory of reason (*Aesthetics*, 10–11).

13 Irony is defined in the *Fragments* as "the mood that surveys everything and rises infinitely above all limitations" (Schlegel, *Friedrich Schlegel's Lucinde*, 148).

14 Within English Romanticism, S. T. Coleridge's distinction between Shakespeare and Milton is typical in this regard. Coleridge describes Shakespeare through the Spinozist distinction between *natura naturans* (nature as the power of creation) and *natura naturata* (nature viewed as created object):

> Shakespeare shaped his characters out of the nature within; but we cannot safely say, out of *his own* nature, as an *individual person*. No! this latter is itself but a *natura naturata*, an effect, a product, not a *power*. It was Shakespeare's prerogative to have the *universal* which is potentially in each *particular*, opened out to him in the *homo generalis*, not as an abstraction of observation from a variety of men, but as the substance capable of endless modifications, of which his own personal existence was but one, and to use *this one* as the eye that beheld the other, and as the tongue that could convey the discovery. . . . Shakespeare in composing had no *I* but *I* the representative. (Lecture 7, 1818, in Coleridge, *Coleridge on Shakespeare*)

15 Goethe, *Essays*, 165. The exemplarity of Shakespeare and the distinction between philosophy and literature is expressed in Goethe's tribute to Shakespeare in 1771, which also invokes a number of classic themes in Romantic irony—the invisibility of the authorial position, free will, the intimation of totality and universality, and a *feeling* of truth. As Goethe was later to emphasize, with Shakespeare, "We experience the truth of life and we do not know how" (*Essays*, 167 [1815]).

16 According to Lacoue-Labarthe and Nancy, this difference between literature and the *system* of philosophy explains the peculiar importance of the fragment in German Romanticism. In the fragment the "will to system" is manifest. It is in the singularity of the fragment that the "putting into work" of the system is given. The system is not a completed, present, or given unity but an act *toward* completion or unification (Lacoue-Labarthe and Nancy, *The Literary Absolute*).

17 Schlegel, *Friedrich Schlegel's Lucinde*, 148.

18 Schlegel, *Friedrich Schlegel's Lucinde*, 147.

19 Handwerk, *Irony and Ethics.*

20 Hegel, *Aesthetics*, 65.

21 Hegel, *Aesthetics*, 66.

22 Hegel, *Aesthetics*, 102.

23 Hegel, *Aesthetics*, 11.

24 Hegel, *Aesthetics*, 51.

5. Post-Romanticism and the Ironic Point of View

1 Hegel, *Lectures on the History of Philosophy*, 13.

2 Heidegger, *Kant*, 83.

3 O'Neill, *Constructions of Reason.*

4 To a certain extent, Lacoue-Labarthe and Nancy present their reading of Romanticism as an ironic fulfillment of what the Romantics themselves could not say; they place themselves within Romanticism at the same time as they see Romanticism itself as unable to "grasp its own essence and aim." Romanticism's "own essence" is precisely, for Lacoue-Labarthe and Nancy, the problematic of the subject permanently rejecting subjectivism: "Our own image comes back to us from the mirror of the literary absolute. And the massive truth flung back at us is that we have not left the era of the Subject" (*The Literary Absolute*, 7, 16).

5 Flaubert, *Bouvard and Pécuchet*, 88.

6 Flaubert, *Bouvard and Pécuchet*, 85.

7 Flaubert, *Bouvard and Pécuchet*, 41.

8 Barthes, *Mythologies*, 136; *DR*, 153; Foucault, *Language Counter-Memory Practice*, 190.

9 Barthes, *Mythologies*, 122.

10 Barthes, *Mythologies*, 135.

11 Foucault, *The Order of Things*, 336.

12 Foucault, *Discipline and Punish*, 16.

13 Michel Foucault, "Maurice Blanchot: The Thought from Outside," in Foucault and Blanchot, *Foucault/Blanchot*, 15–16.

14 Foucault, *The Archaeology of Knowledge*, 218.

15 Foucault, *The Order of Things*, 341.

16 Flaubert, *Bouvard and Pécuchet*, 96.

17 Foucault, *The Order of Things*, 28.

18 Foucault, *The Order of Things*, 340.

19 Foucault, *Archaeology*, 209, emphasis added.

20 Foucault, *The Order of Things*, 342.

21 Foucault, "Maurice Blanchot," 12–13.

22 De Man, *Aesthetic Ideology*, 179.

23 De Man, *Aesthetic Ideology*, 179.

24 De Man, *Aesthetic Ideology*, 163.

25 De Man, *Aesthetic Ideology*, 18.

26 Foucault, *The Order of Things*, xxi.

27 Foucault, *The Order of Things*, xxi.

28 Foucault, *The Order of Things*, xxiv.

29 Butler, *The Psychic Life of Power*; Taylor, "Foucault on Freedom and Truth," 69–102; Deleuze, *Foucault*, 94; Fraser, *Unruly Practices*.

30 Foucault, *The History of Sexuality*, 3.

31 Foucault, *The Order of Things*, 339.

32 Deleuze, *Foucault*, 94.

33 Deleuze and Guattari, *A Thousand Plateaus*, 531.

34 Deleuze and Guattari, *A Thousand Plateaus*, 40, 499.

35 Deleuze and Guattari, *Anti-Oedipus*, 39.

36 Deleuze and Guattari, *A Thousand Plateaus*, 4.

37 Habermas, *The Philosophical Discourse of Modernity*; Taylor, "Foucault on Freedom and Truth," 69–102; Macdonell, *Theories of Discourse*.

6. Inhuman Irony

1 Deleuze and Guattari, *What Is Philosophy?* 197.

2 Deleuze, *Foucault*, 94.

3 Deleuze and Guattari, *What Is Philosophy?* 24.

4 Deleuze and Guattari, *A Thousand Plateaus*, 51.

5 Deleuze and Guattari, *What Is Philosophy?* 211.

6 Deleuze and Guattari, *A Thousand Plateaus*, 84.

7 Deleuze and Guattari, *A Thousand Plateaus*, 170.

8 Deleuze and Guattari, *What Is Philosophy?* 218.

9 Deleuze and Guattari, *A Thousand Plateaus*, 164.

10 Deleuze and Guattari, *A Thousand Plateaus*, 492–93.

11 Deleuze and Guattari, *Kafka*.

12 Bergson, *Le Rire*.

13 Deleuze, *The Fold*.

14 Nietzsche, *The Birth of Tragedy*.

15 Friedrich Nietzsche, "On Truth and Lies in a Nonmoral Sense," in Nietzsche, *Philosophy and Truth*, 83.

16 Nehamas, *Nietzsche*.

17 Deleuze and Guattari, *What Is Philosophy?* 59.

18 Husserl, *The Paris Lectures*, 5.

19 Hutcheon, *Irony's Edge*.

20 Pynchon, *The Crying of Lot 49*.

21 Linda Hutcheon refers to this as "historiographic meta-fiction" in *A Poetics of Postmodernism*.

22 Pynchon, *Mason & Dixon*, 5.

23 Jameson, *The Cultural Turn*, 123, 90, 99.

24 Habermas, "Modernity," 3–15.

25 "It is frequently said that philosophy throughout its history has changed its center of perspective, substituting the point of view of the finite self for that of the infinite divine substance. Kant would stand at the turning point. Is this change, however, as important as it is claimed to be? As long as we maintain the formal identity of the self, doesn't the self remain subject to a divine order and to a unique God who is its foundation?" (*LS*, 294).

26 Other examples of the chiasmus in Hegel's *Phenomenology* include "Notion corresponds to object and object to Notion" (*PS*, sec. 80, 51) and " 'I' that is 'We' and 'We' that is 'I' " (*PS*, sec. 177, 110).

27 For a discussion of viewing apparatuses, see Deleuze, *Cinema 1* and *Cinema 2*.

28 Bergson, *Matter and Memory*.

29 Derrida, "How to Avoid Speaking," 3–61.

30 Trollope, *The Warden*, 13.

31 MacCabe, *James Joyce*.

32 Swift, *A Modest Proposal*, 492.

33 Swift, *A Modest Proposal*, 494.

34 Swift, *A Modest Proposal*, 494.

35 Deleuze and Guattari, *A Thousand Plateaus*, 84.

36 Deleuze, *Essays*, 113.

37 Plato *Republic* 338C–338D, in Plato, *Collected Dialogues*, 588.

38 Milton, *Paradise Lost*, 196.

39 Deleuze and Guattari, *Kafka*, 17.

40 Kafka, "The Metamorphosis," 101.

41 Kafka, "The Metamorphosis," 139.

42 Deleuze and Guattari, *Kafka*, 7.

43 Foucault, *The Archaeology of Knowledge*, 218, 227.

44 Foucault, *The Archaeology of Knowledge*, 231.

45 Jameson, *Postmodernism*.

46 James Joyce, *Ulysses*, in Joyce, *The Essential James Joyce*, 484.

47 Ellis, *Glamorama*, 39.

48 Ellis, *Glamorama*, 62.

49 Hutcheon, *Irony's Edge*.

50 Norris, *What's Wrong with Postmodernism*.

Conclusion

1 Searle, "Literary Theory and Its Discontents."

2 Regarding the unnamable, see Derrida:

Here there is a kind of question, let us still call it historical, whose *conception, formation, gestation* and *labor* we are only catching a glimpse of today. I employ these words, I admit, with a glance towards the operations of childbearing—but also with a glance towards those who, in a society from which I do not exclude myself, turn their eyes away when faced by the as yet unnamable which is proclaiming itself and which can do so, as is necessary whenever a birth is in the offing, only under the species of the nonspecies, in the formless, mute, infant and terrifying form of monstrosity. (*Writing and Difference*, 293)

3 "This reduction to intraworldliness is the origin and very meaning of what is called violence" (Derrida, *Writing and Difference*, 57).

4 Derrida, *Writing and Difference*, 57.

5 The force of the Kantian question of the concept's sense "in general" is explored in Harvey, *Derrida*.

6 Derrida, *Writing and Difference*, 152.

7 "The breakthrough toward radical otherness (with respect to the philosophical concept—of the concept) always takes, *within philosophy*, the *form* of an a posteriority or an empiricism" (Derrida, *Dissemination*, 33).

8 Speaking of *différance*, Derrida writes:

> It is literally neither a word nor a concept, as we shall see. I insist on the word "assemblage" here for two reasons: on the one hand, it is not a matter of describing a history, of recounting the steps, text by text, context by context, each time showing which scheme has been able to impose this graphic disorder, although this could have been done as well; rather, we are concerned with the *general system of all these schemata*. On the other hand, the word "assemblage" seems more apt for suggesting that the kind of bringing-together proposed here has the structure of an interlacing, a weaving, or a web, which would allow the different threads and different lines of sense and force to separate again, as well as being ready to bind together. (*Speech and Phenomena*, 131–32)

9 On the metaphorical elevation of the mouth and eye, see Derrida, "Economimesis," and *LS*.

10 Deleuze and Guattari, *A Thousand Plateaus*, 20.

11 Derrida, *Limited Inc.*, 147.

12 Derrida, *Of Spirit*, 134.

13 "The subjectile always has the function of an hypothesis, it exasperates and keeps you in suspense, it makes you give out of breath by always being *posed beneath*. The hypothesis has the form here of a conjecture, with *two* contradictory motifs in one. Thrown throwing, the subjectile is nothing, however, nothing but a solidified interval *between* above and below, visible and invisible, before and behind, this side and that" (Derrida and Thévenin, *The Secret Art*, 78).

14 Derrida and Thévenin, *The Secret Art*, 65.

15 Derrida and Thévenin, *The Secret Art*, 65.

16 Bergson, *Creative Evolution*.

17 Deleuze and Guattari, *What Is Philosophy?* xx.

18 Deleuze and Guattari, *Kafka*, 70.

19 Derrida, *Margins of Philosophy*, 217.

20 Düttmann, *Between Cultures*, 65–102.

21 Ellis, *Glamorama*, 318.

22 Ellis, *Glamorama*, 298.

23 Ellis, *Glamorama*, 301.

Agamben, Giorgio. *Homo Sacer: Sovereign Power and Bare Life*. Trans. Daniel Heller-Roazen. Stanford: Stanford University Press, 1998.

Aristotle. *Metaphysics Books I–IX*. Trans. Hugh Tredennick. Cambridge: Harvard University Press, 1933.

Austen, Jane. *Pride and Prejudice*. Ed. James Kinsley. Oxford: Oxford University Press, 1990.

Barthes, Roland. *Mythologies*. Trans. Annette Lavers. New York: Hill and Wang, 1985.

Bergson, Henri. *Creative Evolution*. Trans. Arthur Mitchell. New York: Dover, 1998.

———. *Matter and Memory*. Trans. Nancy Margaret Paul and W. Scott Palmer. London: Swan Sonnenschein, 1911.

———. *Le Rire: Essai sur la signification du comique*. Reprinted from the *Revue de Paris*. Paris, 1900.

Blake, William. *The Complete Poetry and Prose of William Blake*. Ed. David V. Erdman. New York: Anchor, 1988.

Bloom, Harold. *Blake's Apocalypse: A Study in Poetic Argument*. London: Victor Gollancz, 1963.

Borges, Jorge Luis. *Fictions*. Ed. Anthony Kerrigan. London: Calder, 1965.

Bowie, Andrew. *Aesthetics and Subjectivity from Kant to Nietzsche*. Manchester: Manchester University Press, 1990.

Butler, Judith. *The Psychic Life of Power: Theories in Subjection*. Stanford: Stanford University Press, 1997.

Cadava, Eduardo, Peter Connor, and Jean-Luc Nancy, eds. *Who Comes after the Subject?* London: Routledge, 1991.

Carver, Raymond. *The Stories of Raymond Carver*. London: Picador, 1985.

Cavell, Stanley. *The Claim of Reason: Wittgenstein, Skepticism, Morality and Tragedy*. Oxford: Clarendon Press, 1979.

Coleridge, Samuel Taylor. *Coleridge on Shakespeare: A Selection of the Essays, Notes and Lectures of Samuel Taylor Coleridge on the Poems and Plays of Shakespeare*. Ed. Terence Hawkes. Harmondsworth: Penguin, 1969.

Davidson, Donald. *Inquiries into Truth and Interpretation*. Oxford: Clarendon, 1984.

Deleuze, Gilles. *Bergsonism*. Trans. Constantin Boundas. New York: Zone Books, 1988.

———. *Cinema 1: The Movement-Image*. Trans. Hugh Tomlinson and Barbara Habberjam. Minneapolis: University of Minnesota Press, 1986.

———. *Cinema 2: The Time-Image*. Trans. Hugh Tomlinson and Robert Galeta. Minneapolis: University of Minnesota Press, 1989.

———. *Difference and Repetition*. Trans. Paul Patton. New York: Columbia, 1994.

———. *Essays: Critical and Clinical*. Trans. Daniel W. Smith and Michael A. Greco. Minneapolis: University of Minnesota Press, 1997.

———. *The Fold: Leibniz and the Baroque*. Trans. Tom Conley. London: Athlone, 1993.

———. *Foucault*. Trans. Paul Bové. Minneapolis: University of Minnesota Press, 1988.

———. *The Logic of Sense*. Trans. Mark Lester. Ed. Constantin V. Boundas. New York: Columbia University Press, 1990.

Deleuze, Gilles, and Félix Guattari. *Anti-Oedipus: Capitalism and Schizophre-nia*. Trans. Robert Hurley, Mark Seem, and Helen R. Lane. London: Ath-lone, 1984.

———. *Kafka: Toward a Minor Literature*. Trans. Dana Polan. Minneapolis: University of Minnesota Press, 1986.

———. *A Thousand Plateaus: Capitalism and Schizophrenia*. Trans. Brian Mas-sumi. Minneapolis: University of Minnesota Press, 1987.

———. *What Is Philosophy?* Trans. Graham Burchill and Hugh Tomlinson. London: Verso, 1994.

De Man, Paul. *Aesthetic Ideology*. Ed. Andrzej Warminski. Minneapolis: Uni-versity of Minnesota Press, 1996.

———. *Blindness and Insight: Essays in the Rhetoric of Contemporary Criti-cism*. London: Methuen, 1983.

———. *Romanticism and Contemporary Criticism: The Gauss Seminar and Other Papers*. Ed. E. S. Burt, Kevin Newmark, and Andrzej Warminski. Balti-more: Johns Hopkins University Press, 1993.

Derrida, Jacques. *Dissemination*. Trans. Barbara Johnson. Chicago: University of Chicago Press, 1981.

———. "Economimesis." Trans. R. Klein. *Diacritics* 11.2 (summer 1981): 3–25.

———. "How to Avoid Speaking: Denials." Trans. Ken Frieden. In *Languages of the Unsayable: The Play of Negativity in Literature and Literary Theory*. Ed. Sanford Budick and Wolfgang Iser. New York: Columbia University Press, 1989.

———. *Limited Inc*. Trans. Samuel Weber and Jeffrey Mehlman. Ed. Gerald Graff. Evanston IL: Northwestern University Press, 1988.

———. *Margins of Philosophy*. Trans. Alan Bass. Sussex: Harvester, 1982.

———. *Mémoires for Paul de Man*. Trans. Cecile Lindsay, Jonathan Culler, and Eduardo Cadava. Ed. Avital Ronell and Eduardo Cadava. New York: Colum-bia University Press, 1986.

———. *Of Spirit: Heidegger and the Question*. Trans. Geoffrey Bennington and Rachel Bowlby. Chicago: University of Chicago Press, 1989.

———. *Speech and Phenomena and Other Essays on Husserl's Theory of Signs*. Trans. David B. Allison. Evanston IL: Northwestern University Press, 1973.

———. *Writing and Difference*. Trans. Alan Bass. London: Routledge and Kegan Paul, 1978.

Derrida, Jacques, and Paule Thévenin. *The Secret Art of Antonin Artaud.* Trans. Mary Ann Caws. Cambridge: MIT Press, 1998.

Dummett, Michael. *Frege: Philosophy of Language.* 2nd ed. London: Duckworth, 1981.

———. *Origins of Analytical Philosophy.* London: Duckworth, 1993.

Dumont, Louis. *Essays on Individualism: Modern Ideology in Anthropological Perspective.* Chicago: University of Chicago Press, 1986.

Düttmann, Alexander García. *Between Cultures: Tensions in the Struggle for Recognition.* Trans. Kenneth B. Woodgate. London: Verso, 2000.

Eco, Umberto. "Postmodernism, Irony, the Enjoyable." In *Modernism/Postmodernism.* Ed. Peter Brooker. London: Longman, 1992. 225–28.

Ellis, Bret Easton. *Glamorama.* New York: Alfred A. Knopf, 1999.

Emerson, Ralph Waldo. *Selected Essays.* Ed. Larzer Ziff. Harmondsworth: Penguin, 1982.

Flaubert, Gustave. *Bouvard and Pécuchet.* Trans. A. J. Krailsheimer. Harmondsworth: Penguin, 1976.

———. *The Letters of Gustave Flaubert: 1830–1857.* Ed. and trans. Francis Steegmuller. Cambridge: Harvard University Press, 1981.

———. *Madame Bovary.* Trans. Alan Russell. Harmondsworth: Penguin, 1950.

———. *Three Tales.* Trans. Robert Baldick. Harmondsworth: Penguin, 1961.

Foucault, Michel. *The Archaeology of Knowledge.* Trans. A. M. Sheridan Smith. London: Tavistock Publications, 1972.

———. *Discipline and Punish: The Birth of the Prison.* Trans. Alan Sheridan. Harmondsworth: Penguin, 1977.

———. *The History of Sexuality, Volume One: An Introduction.* Trans. Robert Hurley. Harmondsworth: Penguin, 1984.

———. *Language Counter-Memory Practice.* Trans. Donald Bouchard and Sherry Simon. Ithaca NY: Cornell University Press, 1977.

———. *The Order of Things: An Archaeology of the Human Sciences.* London: Tavistock, 1970.

Foucault, Michel, and Maurice Blanchot. *Foucault/Blanchot.* Trans. Jeffrey Mehlman and Brian Massumi. New York: Zone Books, 1987.

Fowler, H. W. *A Dictionary of Modern English Usage.* 2nd ed. Rev. Ernest Gowers. Oxford: Clarendon Press, 1965.

Fraser, Nancy. *Unruly Practices: Power, Discourse and Gender in Contemporary Social Theory.* Oxford: Polity, 1989.

Freud, Sigmund. "On Narcissism: An Introduction." In *On Metapsychology: The Theory of Psychoanalysis.* Trans. James Strachey. Ed. Angela Richards. Harmondsworth: Penguin, 1984. 65–97.

———. "The 'Uncanny.'" In *Art and Literature.* Trans. James Strachey. Ed. Albert Dickson. Harmondsworth: Penguin, 1985. 339–76.

Goethe, Johann Wolfgang von. *Essays on Art and Literature.* Ed. John Gearey. Trans. Ellen von Nardroff and Ernest H. von Nardroff. New York: Suhrkamp, 1986.

Greenblatt, Stephen. *Marvelous Possessions: The Wonder of the New World.* Oxford: Clarendon Press, 1991.

Habermas, Jürgen. "Modernity—An Incomplete Project." Trans. Seyla Benhabib. In *Postmodern Culture.* Ed. Hal Foster. London: Pluto Press, 1985. 3–15.

———. *The Philosophical Discourse of Modernity: Twelve Lectures.* Trans. Frederick Lawrence. Cambridge: Cambridge University Press, 1987.

———. *Postmetaphysical Thinking.* Trans. William Mark Hohengarten. Cambridge: MIT Press, 1992.

Hacking, Ian, *Why Does Language Matter to Philosophy?* Cambridge: Cambridge University Press, 1975.

Hadot, Pierre. *Philosophy as a Way of Life: Spiritual Exercises from Socrates to Foucault.* Trans. Michael Chase. Ed. Arnold I. Davidson. Oxford: Blackwell, 1995.

Handwerk, Gary J. *Irony and Ethics in Narrative from Schlegel to Lacan.* New Haven CT: Yale University Press, 1985.

Harvey, Irene. *Derrida and the Economy of Différance.* Bloomington: Indiana University Press, 1986.

Haverkate, Henk. "A Speech Act Analysis of Irony." *Journal of Pragmatics* 14 (1990): 77–109.

Hegel, Georg Wilhelm Friedrich. *Aesthetics: Lectures on Fine Art.* Vol. 1. Trans. T. M. Knox. Oxford: Clarendon Press, 1975.

———. *Lectures on the History of Philosophy, Volume Two: Plato and the Platonists.* Trans. E. S. Haldane and Frances H. Simpson. Lincoln: University of Nebraska Press, 1995.

————. *The Phenomenology of Spirit.* Trans. A. V. Miller. Oxford: Oxford University Press, 1977.

Heidegger, Martin. *Being and Time.* Trans. John MacQuarrie and Edward Robinson. Oxford: Blackwell, 1962.

————. *Kant and the Problem of Metaphysics.* 4th ed. Trans. Richard Taft. Bloomington: Indiana University Press, 1990.

————. *The Metaphysical Foundations of Logic.* Trans. Michael Heim. Bloomington: Indiana University Press, 1992.

Herman, Barbara. *The Practice of Moral Judgment.* Cambridge: Harvard University Press, 1993.

Hume, David. *Enquiries Concerning Human Understanding and Concerning the Principles of Morals.* Ed. L. A. Selby-Bigge. 3rd ed. Rev. P. H. Nidditch. Oxford: Clarendon Press, 1975.

Husserl, Edmund. *Ideas Pertaining to a Pure Phenomenology and to a Phenomenological Philosophy: First Book.* Trans. F. Kersten. Dordrecht: Kluwer, 1982.

————. *Ideas Pertaining to a Pure Phenomenology and to a Phenomenological Philosophy: Second Book, Studies in the Phenomenology of Constitution.* Trans. R. Rojcewicz and A. Schuwer. Dordrecht: Kluwer, 1989.

————. *The Paris Lectures.* Trans. Peter Koestenbaum. The Hague: Martinus Nijhoff, 1975.

Hutcheon, Linda. *Irony's Edge: The Theory and Politics of Irony.* London: Routledge, 1994.

————. *A Poetics of Postmodernism: History, Theory, Fiction.* New York: Routledge, 1988.

James, William. *Some Problems of Philosophy: A Beginning of an Introduction to Philosophy.* Lincoln: University of Nebraska Press, 1996.

Jameson, Fredric. *The Cultural Turn: Selected Writings on the Postmodern: 1983–1998.* London: Verso, 1998.

————. *Postmodernism, or, The Cultural Logic of Late Capitalism.* London: Verso, 1991.

————. *The Seeds of Time.* New York: Columbia University Press, 1994.

Joyce, James. *The Essential James Joyce.* Ed. Harry Levin. London: Granada, 1977.

Kafka, Franz. "The Metamorphosis." Trans. Willa and Edwin Muir. In *The

Complete Short Stories of Franz Kafka. Ed. Nahum N. Glatzer. London: Vintage, 1999.

Kant, Immanuel. *Critique of Judgment.* Trans. Werner S. Pluhar. Indianapolis: Hackett Publishing, 1987.

————. *Critique of Practical Reason.* Trans. Lewis White Beck. 3rd ed. New York: Macmillan, 1993.

————. *Immanuel Kant's Critique of Pure Reason.* Trans. Norman Kemp Smith. London: Macmillan, 1933.

————. *Kant: Political Writings.* 2nd ed. Ed. Hans Reiss. Trans. H. B. Nisbet. Cambridge: Cambridge University Press, 1991.

————. *Prolegomena to Any Future Metaphysics.* Trans. Carus. Ed. and rev. Lewis White Beck. Indianapolis: Library of Liberal Arts, 1950.

————. "Religion within the Boundaries of Mere Reason." In *Religion within the Boundaries of Mere Reason and Other Writings.* Trans. and ed. Allen Wood and George di Giovanni. Cambridge: Cambridge University Press, 1998. 31–191.

Kierkegaard, Søren. *The Concept of Irony with Continual Reference to Socrates and Notes of Schelling's Berlin Lectures.* Ed. and trans. Howard V. Hong and Edna H. Hong. Princeton NJ: Princeton University Press, 1989.

Korsgaard, Christine. *Creating the Kingdom of Ends.* Cambridge: Cambridge University Press, 1996.

Lacan, Jacques. "The Mirror Stage as Formative of the Function of the I as Revealed in Psychoanalytic Experience." In *Écrits: A Selection.* Trans. Alan Sheridan. New York: W. W. Norton, 1977.

Lacan, Jacques, and the Ecole Freudienne. *Feminine Sexuality.* Ed. Juliet Mitchell and Jacqueline Rose. Trans. Jacqueline Rose. London: Macmillan, 1982.

LaCapra, Dominick. *Madame Bovary on Trial.* Ithaca NY: Cornell University Press, 1982.

Lacoue-Labarthe, Philippe, and Jean-Luc Nancy. *The Literary Absolute: The Theory of Literature in German Romanticism.* Trans. Philip Barnard and Cheryl Lester. New York: State University of New York Press, 1988.

Lactantius, Lucius Coelius Firmianus. *The Works of Lactantius.* Vol. 2. Trans. William Fletcher. Edinburgh: T&T Clark, 1871.

Langton, Rae. *Kantian Humility: Our Ignorance of Things in Themselves.* Oxford: Clarendon Press, 1998.

Laplanche, Jean. "A Short Treatise on the Unconscious." Trans. Luke Thurston. In *Essays on Otherness.* London: Routledge, 1999. 84–116.

Levin, David Michael, ed. *Modernity and the Hegemony of Vision.* Berkeley: University of California Press, 1993.

Lewis, R. W. B. *The American Adam: Innocence, Tragedy and Tradition in the Nineteenth Century.* Chicago: University of Chicago Press, 1955.

Locke, John. *Two Treatises of Government.* Ed. Peter Laslett. Cambridge: Cambridge University Press, 1960.

MacCabe, Colin. *James Joyce and the Revolution of the Word.* London: Macmillan, 1979.

Macdonell, Diane. *Theories of Discourse: An Introduction.* Oxford: Blackwell, 1986.

MacIntyre, Alasdair. *After Virtue: A Study in Moral Theory.* London: Duckworth, 1981.

Merleau-Ponty, Maurice. *The Primacy of Perception.* Trans. James M. Edie. Evanston IL: Northwestern University Press, 1964.

Miller, Clyde Lee. "Ironic or Not?" *American Philosophical Quarterly* 13.4 (October 1976): 309–13.

Milton, John. *Paradise Lost.* Ed. Alastair Fowler. London: Longman, 1971.

Mulvey, Laura. "Visual Pleasure and Narrative Cinema." *Screen* (autumn 1975).

Nehamas, Alexander. *The Art of Living: Socratic Reflections from Plato to Foucault.* Berkeley: University of California Press, 1998.

———. *Nietzsche: Life as Literature.* Cambridge: Harvard University Press, 1985.

———. *Virtues of Authenticity: Essays on Plato and Socrates.* Princeton NJ: Princeton University Press, 1999.

Nietzsche, Friedrich. *The Birth of Tragedy.* Trans. Douglas Smith. Oxford: Oxford University Press, 2000.

———. *The Genealogy of Morals and Ecce Homo.* Trans. Walter Kaufmann and R. J. Hollingdale. Ed. Walter Kaufmann. New York: Vintage, 1967.

———. *Philosophy and Truth: Selections from Nietzsche's Notebooks of the*

Early 1870's. Trans. and ed. Daniel Breazeale. Atlantic Highlands NJ: Humanities Press; Hassocks: Harvester Press, 1979.

——. *Philosophy in the Tragic Age of the Greeks.* Trans. Marianne Cowan. Chicago: Gateway, 1962.

——. *The Will to Power.* Trans. Walter Kaufmann and R. J. Hollingdale. New York: Vintage, 1968.

Norris, Christopher. *What's Wrong with Postmodernism: Critical Theory and the Ends of Philosophy.* Baltimore: Johns Hopkins University Press, 1990.

O'Neill, Onora. *Constructions of Reason: Explorations of Kant's Practical Philosophy.* Cambridge: Cambridge University Press, 1989.

Perloff, Marjorie. *The Dance of the Intellect: Studies in the Poetry of the Pound Tradition.* Cambridge: Cambridge University Press, 1985.

Plato. *Collected Dialogues.* Ed. Edith Hamilton and Huntington Cairns. Princeton NJ: Princeton University Press, 1961.

Pynchon, Thomas. *The Crying of Lot 49.* London: Cape, 1967.

——. *Mason & Dixon.* London: Jonathan Cape, 1997.

Rorty, Richard. *Consequences of Pragmatism: Essays: 1972–1980.* Minneapolis: University of Minnesota Press, 1982.

——. *Contingency, Irony, and Solidarity.* Cambridge: Cambridge University Press, 1989.

——. *Philosophy and the Mirror of Nature.* Princeton NJ: Princeton University Press, 1980; repr. Oxford: Blackwell, 1980.

Roth, Philip. *Sabbath's Theater.* London: Cape, 1995.

Schlegel, Friedrich. *Friedrich Schlegel's Lucinde; and, The Fragments.* Trans. Peter Firchow. Minneapolis: University of Minnesota Press; London: Oxford University Press, 1971.

Searle, John. "Literary Theory and Its Discontents." *New Literary History* 25.3 (summer 1994): 637–67.

——. *Speech Acts: An Essay in the Philosophy of Language.* Cambridge: Cambridge University Press, 1969.

Smith, Michael. *The Moral Problem.* Oxford: Blackwell, 1994.

Spinoza, Benedict de. *On the Improvement of the Understanding, The Ethics, Correspondence.* Trans. R. H. M. Elwes. New York: Dover, 1955.

Swift, Jonathan. *Jonathan Swift: A Critical Edition of the Major Works*. Ed. Angus Ross and David Woolley. Oxford: Oxford University Press, 1984.

Taylor, Charles. "Foucault on Freedom and Truth." In *Foucault: A Critical Reader*. Ed. David Couzens Hoy. Oxford: Basil Blackwell, 1986. 69–102.

Trollope, Anthony. *The Warden*. Oxford: Oxford University Press, 1928.

Vlastos, Gregory. *Socrates: Ironist and Moral Philosopher*. Cambridge: Cambridge University Press, 1991.

INDEX

absence, 129

absolute: coherence between subjects and, 133–34; as concept formed by reason, 145; Hegel on philosopher as vehicle for revelation of, 166–67; posited from the concept, 135–36

actions: Deleuze's static genesis and, 219; Kant on moral duty/meaning and, 119–21; moral simpliciter, 125; moral will leading to, 115–18; pure, 128

allegory: literal meaning at level of, 193–94; as relying on word/world difference, 156–57

amor fati ethics, 248, 251, 254

anthropological detachment, 77–81

anti-empiricism of philosophy, 262–63

Anti-Oedipus (Deleuze and Guattari), 204

The Archaeology of Knowledge (Foucault), 188

Aristophanes' Socrates, 161

art, 142, 144

"as if" sentence, 111–12, 132

irony by, 109–13; comparing idealism of Hegel and, 134–35, 261–62;
comparing moral concepts of
Hume vs., 114–16; comparing
Romantic idea of the subject and,
127–28; on concepts inferred from
synthesis of experience, 126–27;
"Copernican turn" by, 11; on freedom from speculation, 108; ironic
position taken by, 45–46; on meaning of concepts as evidence, 45–46;
on moral concepts, 114–21; on public reason, 290 n.19; on "vacant
space" of pure concept in experience, 182

Kierkegaard, Søren: analysis of Socratic irony by, 161–66; existentialism
philosophy and irony of, 175–79;
Hegel's irony by, 160–61; on height
of irony and negativity, 169–75; on
ironic existence as risk of irony,
259; on ironist as "above" ordinary
life, 171–72; on irony as freedom
from conceptual truth, 84–85; on
irony as infinite negativity, 160–
61, 168–69, 170–72; on poetry/
poetic standpoint, 173–74; transcendentalism of, 182–83. See also
German Romantics

knowledge: critique of mirror metaphor for, 6–7; Kant on empirical
concepts of, 110–11; soul and
revealed limitation of, 107–8; soul
as active capacity derived from,
111–13. See also moral knowledge

language: difficulty in expressing
meaning using, 143–44; Flaubert's
irony and stylistic use of, 67–70;
implications of complex irony
for, 40–41; intentionality and,
33–34; intertwining of vision
and, 7–8; irony and gap between
world and, 16–17; irony as freeing
vision from inherited, 6–7; irony
as recognition of workings of, 30;
local irony as trope within game
of, 3–4; as meaningful through
event of language, 158–59;
mythification of, 180–82; postmodern, 227–31; speech as
outcome vs. foundation of, 8;
structuralist solution to vertigo
ownership of, 154–55. See also
speech

language games: new concepts used
to shake up, 3–4; role of irony
within, 10

life: affirmative philosophy expressing, 203–4; concepts/events
allowing confrontation of, 216;
Deleuze's on power of difference
and, 208, 210; desire as intensity
of, 202–4; differentiation of, 208,
210, 214, 215; point of view as extension of, 211–12; as structured by
nonlife, 272–73

linguistic (irony as speech act) irony,
16–17

"Literary Theory and Its Discontents" (Searle), 83

Printed in the United States
88113LV00004BB/4/A